Health Psycholog

This accessible primer on health psychology covers the key theories and models of the discipline. Through the use of real-life case studies and examples, it covers a broad range of topics related to the field of health psychology including: health promotion, risky health behaviour and health in healthcare settings. It explains how health psychology serves to not only promote positive health and reduce maladaptive health behaviours, but also support those who are chronically ill.

Unlike medicine, health psychology takes a more holistic approach through the interaction of psychological, social and biological factors to improve health. This book outlines the inter-relationship between how we think and feel, our biological systems and the social contexts in which we live. It discusses how belief and attitude can shape behaviour, the pivotal role of stress and how we can adjust to chronic illness. Drawing from experience, the authors answer important and common questions like *how can we stop people from smoking? Does stress really make us ill? Why don't people take their medication as prescribed?* And *how can we support people to adjust to a chronic health condition?* It also provides a unique focus on children and adolescent health, which considers how developmental changes impact health behaviours and subsequent health.

It is an essential introductory text suitable for students, professionals and general readers interested in this important and emerging topic area. It also provides useful information for those interested in working in the field by providing an overview of what health psychologists do, where they work and the pathways available to become a registered health psychologist.

Dr Erica Cook is a Chartered Psychologist with the British Psychological Society and a Registered Health Psychologist with the UK Health and Care Professions Council (HCPC). She is a senior lecturer and the course director for the Stage 1 Health Psychology programme at the University of Bedfordshire, UK. Her research interests are focused on the intersection of public health and health psychology with a particular interest in improving health outcomes for marginalised and disadvantaged groups.

Dr Lynne Wood is a Chartered Psychologist with the British Psychological Society. She is a senior lecturer and the course director of BSc Health Psychology at the University of Bedfordshire, UK. Her research interests centre around preventing adolescent risk behaviours and improving wellbeing in chronic illness.

The Basics

The Basics is a highly successful series of accessible guidebooks which provide an overview of the fundamental principles of a subject area in a jargon-free and undaunting format.

Intended for students approaching a subject for the first time, the books both introduce the essentials of a subject and provide an ideal springboard for further study. With over 50 titles spanning subjects from artificial intelligence (AI) to women's studies, *The Basics* are an ideal starting point for students seeking to understand a subject area.

Each text comes with recommendations for further study and gradually introduces the complexities and nuances within a subject.

Health Psychology
Erica Cook and Lynne Wood

Women's Studies (second edition)
Bonnie G. Smith

Sigmund Freud
Janet Sayers

Sustainability (second edition)
Peter Jacques

For a full list of titles in this series, please visit www.routledge.com/The-Basics/book-series/B

Health Psychology
The Basics

Erica Cook and Lynne Wood

Routledge
Taylor & Francis Group

LONDON AND NEW YORK

First published 2021
by Routledge
2 Park Square, Milton Park, Abingdon, Oxon OX14 4RN

and by Routledge
52 Vanderbilt Avenue, New York, NY 10017

Routledge is an imprint of the Taylor & Francis Group, an informa business

© 2021 Erica Cook and Lynne Wood

British Library Cataloguing-in-Publication Data
A catalogue record for this book is available from the British Library

Library of Congress Cataloging-in-Publication Data
Names: Cook, Erica, author. | Wood, Lynne, 1969– author.
Title: Health psychology : the basics / Erica Cook, Lynne Wood.
Description: Abingdon, Oxon ; New York, NY Routledge, 2021. |
Includes bibliographical references and index. |
Identifiers: LCCN 2020033952 (print) | LCCN 2020033953 (ebook) |
ISBN 9781138213685 (hardback) | ISBN 9781138213692 (paperback) |
ISBN 9781315447766 (ebook)
Subjects: LCSH: Medicine and psychology.
Classification: LCC R726.5 .C674 2021 (print) |
LCC R726.5 (ebook) | DDC 610.1/9–dc23
LC record available at https://lccn.loc.gov/2020033952
LC ebook record available at https://lccn.loc.gov/2020033953

ISBN: 978-1-138-21368-5 (hbk)
ISBN: 978-1-138-21369-2 (pbk)
ISBN: 978-1-315-44776-6 (ebk)

Typeset in Bembo
by Newgen Publishing UK

Contents

1 The development of health psychology

Contents

Introduction

This chapter focuses on establishing the context of health psychology by explaining the changing patterns of disease and describing the role of health psychology in understanding these needs.

The chapter begins by setting the context of health psychology. Going through a journey in time, we will explore historical views of health and illness from the adoption of the more traditional biomedical model, where the mind and body are viewed as separate entities, to the more modern perspective of the biopsychosocial perspective, which considers a more holistic approach to understanding health and illness.

We will be exploring public health trends and consider how health psychology has evolved to meet the changing needs of health and how this links to current health policy and to the health of the nation. This chapter will explain current health issues and how through policy and practice health psychology can have a positive impact on population health.

Alongside uncovering the aims of health psychology this chapter will end by answering common questions relating to becoming a health psychologist 'What do they do?', 'Where do they work?' and 'how can I become a health psychologist?'.

Historical approaches to health: a biomedical model of health and illness

Introduction to the biomedical model

The history of medicine has shown us how society shapes both our approach and understanding of health, illness and disease. To do this we have to take a step back in history to understand how our thinking of health and illness has changed over the years.

During the Greek classical period an ancient Greek physician, called Hippocrates (460–377 BC) discovered humoral medicine. This idea was then later disseminated by Roman Galen (129–216 AD), labelled as Galen's Theory of Humours, which continued to dominate western medicine up until the nineteenth century [1].

Based upon ancient medical works, the view was that we all have four 'humours' (also referred to as principal fluids): black bile, yellow bile, phlegm and blood, which were produced by various organs in the body. It was proposed that humours existed in cycles according to the seasons; i.e. an illness that occurred in summer was associated with yellow bile, spring with blood, autumn with black bile and winter with phlegm. Treatments were therefore used to counteract the coldness or warmth, for example warm illnesses i.e. those that occurred during the summer were said to affect the yellow bile so cold treatments were used. There was also said to be a strong association with the natural elements: water, earth, fire and air and these with the seasons provided us a useful understanding of how to preserve balance within the body [2].

The idea, and a fundamental premise of this theory was that our characteristics and our disposition defined our health. This idea suggested that our wellbeing was defined by our personality, which in turn was associated with the four elements and their relationship with the four 'humours'. So, being able to diagnose individuals was largely based on observing individuals on their personalities in a bid to gain clues on what might be wrong with them. An individual, for example who was bad tempered and angry was believed to have an imbalanced yellow bile, the humour associated with the summer season.

Treatment focused on balance and restoration. Treatments were achieved by healing, either through physical (diet, medicine, herbal remedies) or spiritual therapeutics (e.g. bloodletting using leeches, clean bedding, prayer, music, relics of saint) [3].

People were beginning to challenge the idea the mind and body were not separate; however, this was controversially challenged by Galen, who argued that the organs were responsible for health. Without any strong evidence to challenge Galen he was able to instill this viewpoint for many centuries [4]. In the seventeenth century René Descartes (1596–1650) sustained this philosophy, postulating the mind (non-material)–body (material also referred to as a machine) dualism. The mind and body were viewed as separate entities and illness was viewed as a malfunction of our machine not the non-material. It was not until the rise of the

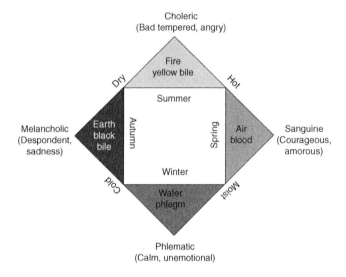

Figure 1.1 Diagram of The Four 'Humours'

twentieth century in response to Freud's psychodynamic theory that this belief was finally challenged.

Challenging the biomedical view of health

Sigmund Freud (1856–1939), a renowned neurologist was met with numerous patients who were presented with 'hysteria paralysis', a condition where an individual suffers paralysis, which after numerous medical tests were told there was nothing physically wrong. Freud proposed that our unconscious psychological conflict could directly impact on physical disturbance or symptoms via the voluntary nervous system. For example, if a patient has a memory of trauma, which they fail to confront this can be converted into physical symptoms. This was later supported by Dunbar (1930s) and Alexander (1940s) who argued that internal conflicts unconsciously produce anxiety and take a physiological toll via the autonomic nervous system. This shift in thinking therefore advocated that there was indeed a link between our body and mind and that they were not separate entities as once believed.

The emergence of the field of behavioural medicine also challenged traditional beliefs that the mind and body are separate entities and work independently. Behavioural medicine represented an interdisciplinary field drawing on elements from psychology, sociology and health education. Defined as 'the field concerned with the development of behavioural science knowledge and techniques relevant to the understanding of physical health and illness and the application of this knowledge and these techniques to prevention, diagnosis, treatment and rehabilitation' [5]. The careful addition of 'behavioural' was not just about semantics, but arguably demonstrated an important shift in thinking about how we understand health and illness. A movement from thinking about our physical and our mental health as separate, this definition argued for a more integrated holistic perspective, one which considered the biological and behavioural factors of health and illness.

As you can see the views of health were rapidly changing. It was at this time that George Engel [6, 7] challenged traditional biomedical thinking and suggested that in addition to the biological aspects (diseases), psychosocial dimensions should be considered. Engel proposed a biopsychosocial model of health, which considered that the cause, manifestation and outcome of health and illness was formed by the interaction of **biological** (our genes and biology), **psychological** (our beliefs, emotions and coping resources) and **social-cultural** factors (where we live, our social support, our cultural background) (see Figure 1.2).

What is health?

Like our understanding of health and illness, how we have defined health has also changed. Historically, health was viewed as the absence of disease, a negative state, in other words you are either healthy or not healthy.

I would like to think that I am healthy. I mean I go swimming two mornings a week and like to go on long walks at the

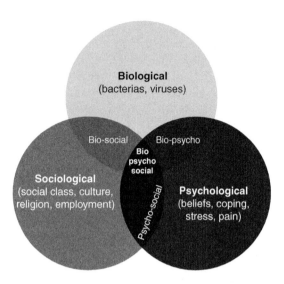

Figure 1.2 The biopsychosocial model showing the interrelationship between the three dimensions adapted from Engel [6, 7]

weekend. Although, I am probably carrying a bit too much weight, certainly my trousers are feeling a bit tighter than they once did. I eat mostly well, but I can't resist the tempting puddings when we are eating out on a Saturday. I probably stop at the drive thru café a bit too often, for my regular Chai Latte and a chocolate brownie. Note to self, I should stick to eating more fruit. My alcohol consumption is maybe a bit higher than it should be, a few too many Pinot Grigio's at the weekend, but it is my down time, that is what I like to say anyway.

(John aged 67)

John states that he feels healthy, but if he were to adopt this definition, he would be classified as 'diseased', but is this a fair reflection? It is argued that there is more to health than just our physical state. It is claimed that our psychological and social

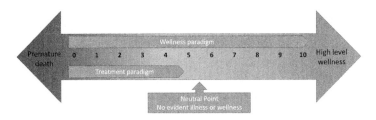

Figure 1.3 Health continuum according to Dr John Travis [10]

health, *in other words the* importance of being able to fulfil our potential and obligations, manage our life and participate in social activities including work are equally important [8]. As put by Smith 'health is the capacity to love and work' [9].

The Illness–Wellness Continuum, proposed by Dr John Travis in 1972, supports the importance of both physical and emotional health [10]. This also moved us away from thinking of ourselves as either healthy or not healthy, but rather we are on a spectrum from the lowest 0, which indicates **premature death** (on multiple medications, poor quality of life, limited function) to the highest 10, which represents **optimal health** characterised by 100 per cent function, activity participation and wellness lifestyle. Travis argued that as Maslow argued for self actualisation optimal health should be something that we can strive to achieve [10].

A more contemporary view of health was proposed by the World Health Organization in 1948 '*Health is a state of complete physical, mental and social well-being and not merely the absence of disease or infirmity*'. This definition, profound in its time, has stayed with us for many years and continues to be the most widely cited definition of health [11]. However, this idea of health has not withstood criticism. Some have argued that this idea of 'complete health' is an illusion, unachievable; can anyone ever really truly say that they are physically, emotionally and socially healthy all of the time? It is argued that the idea of striving for completeness has unintendedly led to the medicalisation of society.

As an aging population with an increasing burden of chronic disease, it minimises the role of our ability to cope with the challenges that we face or how we function in spite of a chronic disease or disability [11]. More recently academics have proposed a new definition which accounts for these factors and overcomes these limitations 'health is the ability to adapt and self-manage in the face of social, physical, and emotional challenges' [12].

What is health psychology?

The movement from thinking about our mind and body as separate to viewing health and illness from a biopsychosocial perspective has been the catalyst for health psychology. Our understanding of how the environment and our behaviour impact on our health, the more holistic approach to conceptualising health along with recent public health trends have made health psychology one of the fastest growing disciplines of psychology in the UK.

Health psychology is described by Matarazzo as

> the aggregate of the specific educational, scientific, and professional contributions of the discipline of psychology to the promotion and maintenance of health, the prevention and treatment of illness, and the identification of etiologic and diagnostic correlates of health, illness, and related dysfunction [13].
>
> (p. 815)

The aim of health psychology is to understand the psychological processes which underpin health and illness and use this knowledge to promote and maintain health, prevent illness and disability and enhance outcomes for those who are ill [14].

Health psychologists therefore may ask the following questions:

- **What is the role of behaviour in the aetiology of illness?** So, what lifestyle factors impact on disease progress, for example smoking and coronary heart disease.
- **How can we predict health behaviours?** To be able to intervene in health behaviour we have to understand why we

behave the way we do. Ultimately how can we make somebody eat more healthily and do more physical activity. We discuss this in more detail in Chapter 3.

- **What is the interaction between psychology and physiology?** How do our levels of stress affect our ability to resist infections? What is the mechanism behind how these processes work?
- **What is the role of psychology in the experience of illness?** Can psychology be used to alleviate symptoms such as pain, nausea and vomiting.
- **What is the role of psychology in the treatment of illness?** How can psychology be used to assist treatment and rehabilitation and be used to improve health outcomes, for example being more physically active to improve symptoms and quality of life.

Why do we need health psychology?

Health in the twenty-first century: the role of lifestyle on population health

If you were born at the beginning of the twentieth century, you would not be expected to live past your 48th birthday. However, born today you could expect to add around 30 years to your life, with the average survival age for males and females being 79 and 83 years respectively [15]. Moreover, it is not only how long we can expect to live that has changed but how we die. For example, between 1901 and 1971 infectious diseases accounted for two thirds of all deaths [15]. Infectious diseases included airborne infections (e.g. respiratory tuberculosis, bronchitis, pneumonia and influenza, measles, Scarlett Fever and whooping cough), water and food borne infections (e.g. cholera, non-respiratory tuberculosis and typhoid) among many others. However, over the past century infectious diseases have fallen dramatically, said to be the result improved nutrition, improved safety of water and better sanitation, as well as changes in our personal behaviour [16].

Fast forward to today, the biggest killers around us include preventable diseases such as cancer and heart disease. Together these

Table 1.1 Leading causes of deaths in males and females in England and
Wales in 2015 [19].

Males	%	Females	%
Heart disease	14.2	**Dementia & Alzheimer's disease**	15.3
Dementia & Alzheimer's disease	8	**Heart disease**	8.8
Lung cancer	6.5	**Stroke**	7.5
Chronic lower respiratory disease	6.2	**Influenza & pneumonia**	6
Stroke	5.6	**Chronic lower respiratory diseases**	6
Influenza & pneumonia	5.1	**Lung cancer**	5.1
Prostate cancer	4.2	**Breast cancer**	3.7
Colorectal and anal cancer	3	**Colorectal cancer**	2.4
Leukaemia and lymphomas	2.6	**Kidney disease**	1.9
Cirrhosis and other liver diseases	1.9	**Leukaemia and lymphomas**	1.9

account for two thirds of all deaths. Put another way two out of
three people can expect to die from a heart related condition or
cancer. Well, you might arguably say, 'we have to die from something don't we?' and yes perhaps you are right, but the problem
we have is that many of the reasons people are dying in modern
Britain isn't because they do not have access to medicines and
good healthcare or are subject to poor sanitation, but rather they
are caused by our risky lifestyle behaviours (see Table 1.1). In
fact recent data suggests that approximately one quarter of all
deaths in the UK are considered avoidable [17]. We have therefore moved from the communicable diseases of the twentieth
century to diseases of lifestyle from the twenty-first century. As
put by the Director of the World Health Organization (WHO)

> in many ways, the world is a safer place today. Safer from
> what were once deadly or incurable diseases. Safer from
> daily hazards of waterborne and food-related illnesses. Safer
> from dangerous consumer goods, from accidents at home, at

work, or in hospitals. But in many other ways the world is becoming more dangerous. Too many of us are living dangerously – whether we are aware of that or not.

(World Health report, 2002, p3) [18]

Health policy: the role of government action for lifestyle change

The question is what should we do about it? We know that this is not a medical problem, not caused by lack of medicine or poor medical care. Instead it is behavioural, it is the individual's health behaviour which is having a negative impact on their health. In that case, should we then just explain this as 'individual choices'? The answer is yes and no. Whilst we need to encourage, motivate and support individuals to engage in a healthy lifestyle we also need policies and interventions that address the social and economic environment that help shape our behaviour.

To help address this problem the UK government have launched a series of health policy papers (see Figure 1.4). Health policy provides us with a strategic framework, think of it as a road map helping us to get to the final destination, heathy living. This 'map' enables us to set our priorities, provides us a vision for what we want to work towards and then establishes short- and medium-term targets to help us obtain that vision.

The first white paper '*The Health of the Nation*' was published in 1992 [20]. This report was the first of its kind focused on reducing alcohol consumption and smoking, two risky health behaviours which were slowly taking force. The message was clear: the reduction of these high-risk behaviours would provide wider national benefit for all. Despite this, public support remained low with scepticism appearing from all sides. Some argued that the government were interfering in their own personal choices, the movement towards a 'nanny state'. On the other side, others argued that this policy was victim blaming. There was limited focus on health prevention or how to support people to change, but rather about curing those who were ill.

In response to this the 'Our Healthier Nation' white paper was launched. This policy moved away from victim blaming 'good health is no longer about blame, but about opportunity

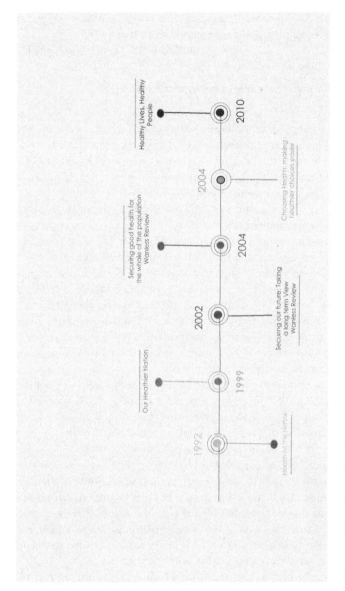

Figure 1.4 Timeline of health policy in the UK

and responsibility' [21] and instead focused on the importance of creating healthy environments.

This policy along with two influential independent reviews [22, 23] shifted the focus from cure to an emphasis on prevention, 're-activating a dormant duty of NHS-to promote good health, not just treat people when they fall sick' [21]. More recent health policy 'Health Lives, Healthy People' has been focused on 'empowering' not only individuals but the communities where they reside, providing the public tools to address their own particular needs and address change where needed [24].

Health psychology today, where are we now?

There have been major public health achievements over the recent decades. People can expect to live longer, healthier and lead more productive lives than ever before. The most notable achievements have centred on improvements in vaccine preventable with fewer infectious diseases. We have also seen improved levels of physical activity, and large reductions in alcohol and drug use. There have been strong attempts to tackle food manufactures with improving nutrition for the wider population. There has also been a notable reduction of smokers year on year, supported through the implementation of smoke free legislation banning smoking in all enclosed workplaces and public spaces [25]. Health policy has also gone some way in reducing health incqualities [26].

Health psychologists are well placed in contributing to health policy and practice in the UK. At a theoretical level there is an increased attempt to understand the modifiable determinants of health and illness and how we can design interventions to change health behaviours at an individual, group and community level (see Chapter 3). Health psychology has also contributed to policy development, providing the evidence base on what approaches appear to have the most potential in public health contexts. On a practice level health psychology can present evidence-based strategies to support healthcare professionals who can supporting populations in many different healthcare contexts [27].

Research methods in health psychology

Our choice of what methods to use often comes from prior questions such as what is my research question? What is my epistemology? Or rather what is my theoretical assumptions to what I am interested in? We can then start working out what methods may be the most suitable (Figure 1.5). In health psychology we use a range of both qualitative and quantitative methods. It is important to note that there is no one perfect research method, they each have advantages and disadvantages. Therefore, you have to make an informed decision, choosing the best method available to meet your desired objectives.

Qualitative studies

Qualitative methods are particularly useful for understanding subjective meanings and experiences surrounding health and illnesses. We can use a range of methods such as interviews and

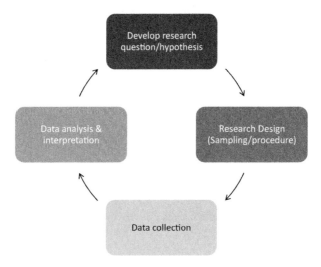

Figure 1.5 The research process

focus groups to collect qualitative data from participants. Focus groups are particularly useful when you want to see if there are any common group similarities in their attitudes and how they feel about something. Qualitative data is then subjective to data analysis procedures with common approaches such as thematic analysis, narrative analysis and interpretative phenomenological analysis (IPA). There are certainly a number of advantages to using qualitative methods. They can allow for a valuable insight into the participant's world, letting them say how they feel in a non-directive way. This of course can provide us with rich and valuable data, which would not be possible from quantitative methods. However, there are some limitations which we would need to consider. Interviews and focus groups can be very time consuming, once you factor in the time it takes to recruit participants and interview them we also have the time taken to transcribe the data, which, dependent on the length of the interview or focus group can be particularly time consuming.

The interviewer is a crucial part of this process; they need to be experienced and be skilled in facilitating interviews and focus groups. Further, the interviewers' influence and social position in relation to the participants cannot be ignored.

Quantitative studies

Quantitative studies involve the collection of numerical data through a range of methods most commonly, including: questionnaires, experiments and cohort studies.

Questionnaires are a self-report research instrument where participants are asked to respond to a series of questions or statements. Questionnaires that seek to obtain quantitative data will use closed questions, i.e. the participant can only respond to using a pre-determined answer. The responses can be placed into categories, called nominal data, which can be dichotomous, for example 'yes' or 'no', or can include more options. Questions can also provide ordinal (or ranked) data, which often using Likert rating scales to measure the strength of something, for example I enjoy going to the gym (1) 'strongly agree', (2) 'slightly agree', (3) 'neither agree or disagree', (4) 'disagree' and (5) 'strongly disagree'. Questionnaires have been successfully used to measure many things including psychological theories, levels of stress, intelligence and personality and many more. The other advantage is that they are cheap and quick to administer and a useful method particularly if you want to obtain information from a large population. The questionnaires are also standardised, so all participants are asked the same question in the same order and so we can be confident that the results are consistent. However, they also come with some limitations. Have you ever answered a questionnaire to something and wanted to give more detail? Whilst they ask for a fixed answer, they do not allow us to provide a justification or reason to why we picked the answer we did. We also do find that response rates can be low, we refer to this as the ***non-response bias***. Imagine we wanted to assess stress levels in the general population, so we sample people from all social classes, genders and ethnicities. It may well be that only the wealthier White British respond and suggest that stress levels are generally low. However, when we have a low response rate (viewed as 60% or lower) it may be that the data we hold is not representative of the wider sample we wanted to recruit from. Another common issue we have to consider in using questionnaires is the impact of ***social desirability bias***. This is where people respond in a way that makes them look better than they really are. So, if we asked someone how much alcohol they consume, they may put less than they actually do.

A cohort study is a type of longitudinal study which samples a cohort (a group of people who share a defining characteristic) over a period of time. They are particularly useful in the field of medicine and epidemiology and can establish risk of disease over an extended period of time. One of the most famous cohort studies was that of Doll and Hill in 1951, who sent out a questionnaire about smoking habits to all the doctors who were registered on the British Medical Register [28]. They collected 34,440 questionnaires from male doctors born before 1900–1919 and then followed them up to observe mortality. Even by the time of the first set of preliminary results were analysed in 1954, there was evidence to link smoking with lung cancer and increased mortality. This breakthrough evidence was enough to challenge existing beliefs that smoking was not harmful and subsequently has influenced health policy and governmental action regarding the advertising of nicotine products.

Experiments are particularly useful when we are trying to support or refute a hypothesis, and can provide insight into cause and effect, for example does playing classical music *cause* a reduction in pain. They typically include sophisticated designs and controls which can minimise the effects of variables outside of the independent variable. Experiments and trials play a particularly important role in determining the effectiveness of behaviour change interventions. However, we should be aware of some criticisms related to experiments. Sometimes we can see positive results but then when we do the same intervention (or experiment) to another population we find the results are not positive. The reason for this is the transportation problem, i.e. what works in one situation might not work in another. Another issue, particularly in relation to testing the effectiveness of behaviour change interventions is the issue of *dose* and *fidelity*. Behaviour change interventions are complex, it is not as simple as giving one paracetamol to a patient who has a headache to see if it helps reduce the symptoms. Let's say we wanted to see if patients who received behaviour change counselling were more likely to lose weight compared to those who did not. Many factors may influence this; how many times the counsellor saw the patient, how many different counsellors there were, if counsellors followed the same approach, counsellor effects (gender, age, ethnicity, experience etc.), and so forth. Controlling for these factors is not easy and so often we need additional methods to help us determine this.

Systematic reviews and meta-analysis

We should also not underestimate the importance of **systematic reviews** and **meta-analysis** in synthesising evidence. If you have a research question the chances are that someone has tried to answer it. Let's imagine you wanted to see if telling young children the risks of smoking would reduce their chances of smoking in the future. You could design an experimental study; in one secondary school you could attend classes of all students and tell them of the dangers of smoking and in another you do nothing, and this would be your control. You could then compare students' smoking rates before the study, after the study and then follow them up every year thereafter. In principle this sounds like a great idea, except that we have forgotten to see if anyone else has done this, but more importantly if this intervention worked. Research is very expensive and let's not forget the children's (and school's) time we are taking up. It would be a shame if we did this unnecessarily.

So, let's say we look at the literature and after a quick look at Google we find a similar study conducted in the North of England that found that this intervention didn't work. So, feeling disheartened you look to change your intervention. However, what about if this study did not work, not because of the intervention, but because it was poor quality. For example, perhaps they did not have a control group, so we do not know if the intervention reduced smoking initiation when compared to those who did not receive the intervention. Or perhaps they only included a small number of children, too small to detect a meaningful difference. This is where systematic reviews come in. They are a type of literature review that uses systematic methods to collect secondary data, critically appraise research studies, and synthesise findings qualitatively or quantitatively. They help us to the answer the research question 'will providing children the risks of smoking reduce the uptake of smoking?' using a comprehensive and complete summary of all the current evidence available. Meta-analysis is a way of synthesising evidence using statistical procedures to combine the data derived from a systematic review. So, using our example, we could do a systematic review combining all the numerical data from multiple randomised controlled trials, which used the intervention we are interested in to see how effective this intervention is.

Careers in health psychology

What do health psychologists do and where do they work?

Health psychologists use their knowledge to promote general well-being and understand illness. They are specially trained to help people deal with the psychological and emotional aspects of health and illness alongside supporting those who are chronically ill.

Health psychologists promote healthier lifestyles and try to find ways to encourage people to improve their health. With expertise in behaviour change they have extensive knowledge of how to design, implement and evaluate evidence-based interventions to change health behaviour, which can be used to target individuals, social groups or communities. Health psychologists can also add value in the improvement of healthcare delivery, from training healthcare professionals to communicate more effectively with their patients through to changing patient behaviour in healthcare settings (e.g. improving hand hygiene in hospitals).

Health psychologists work in a variety of settings including hospitals, universities and public health agencies. See below for

Government
• Advise on policy making
• Developing effective population interventions
• Proposing national advertising strategies.

Universities: Teaching and Research
• Teaching health psychology and related fields to undergraduate and postgraduate students
• Supervising and supporting students through their health psychology training
• Conducting health psychology research

Healthcare settings
• Working in local hospitals: involvement in multidisciplinary treatment of long-term health conditions such as coronary heart disease and pain management
• Working in primary care: supporting patients to manage long-term health conditions, supporting lifestyle changes and stress management

• **Community and local authorities**
• Supporting community initiatives to promote healthy living in local populations (e.g. smoking, diet, physical activity, drugs and alcohol services)
• Improve uptake to public health screening programmes (e.g. NHS Health Checks)
• Design and deliver targeted interventions to improve health outcomes in the community

• **Private and third sector agencies**
• Providing expertise to support voluntary and community groups to improve health outcomes of those they support

Figure 1.6 Examples of health psychology roles

some examples of where a health psychologist might work and the roles ofr which they could be responsible.

Health psychologists normally choose to work in either an applied or in an academic setting. To help you understand how their roles may differ two example job roles are provided. Job advert 1 is looking for a health psychologist to work in an NHS setting and join a pain management multi-disciplinary team. They are seeking help and support to develop interventions to support patients and families with chronic pain management. In academic settings, commonly universities, health psychologists are employed in lecturing, supervision and research roles related to their field. Job advert 2 is looking for a health psychologist to work in a university to join the academic team to support the curriculum in health psychology. Universities will often ask for a PhD, although being a Registered Health Psychologist and Chartered member of the BPS will often suffice.

It would be difficult for us to give you an example of every health psychology job role. As you have learnt, these roles are diverse, taking place in many different organisations working with numerous population groups. However, we can provide an insight of a practicing health psychologist, Dr Sabrina Robinson, who shares how she became a health psychologist and what a typical day for her may look like.

A day in the life of a health psychologist
Dr Sabrina Robinson

I am a Chartered Psychologist registered with the British Psychological Society (BPS) and a health psychologist registered with the UK Health and Care Professions Council (HCPC). I became a registered health psychologist in 2016 having completed my BSc Human Psychology at De Montfort University Leicester, MSc Health Psychology at the University of Bedfordshire and finally my Professional Doctorate in Health Psychology at London Metropolitan University.

I am passionate about using psychological approaches to develop sustainable health and wellbeing in the workplace and have supported a wide range of organisations over the years to explore ways they can support the wellbeing of their workforce.

Box 1.1 Job advert 1: Health psychologist practitioner

We are pleased to be able to offer this exciting opportunity to work with one of the world leaders in innovative pain management services. We are a multidisciplinary team (consultants, clinical nurse specialists, physiotherapists and administrators) who are developing the worldwide research and clinical benchmarking protocols in pain management interventions. The team are dedicated to developing services which deliver first class care and support to clients experiencing chronic pain and their families and highly value the role of psychology in this care pathway.

We are looking for a dedicated, innovative and skilled HCPC registered health psychologist who wants to expand their knowledge of developing clinical services to support those who experience chronic pain. The post holder would be working as part of the multi-disciplinary team to support clients and families by taking a lead on the pain management programme, developing outpatient psychology clinics and pathways and providing direct clinical and research support to the pain management programme. The post holder will be skilled in a range of therapeutic approaches relevant to health psychology which can be applied to direct and indirect working.

In particular I am interested in the impact that workplace practices (both organisational and individual) can have on employee health status, work-life balance and performance with their role. My belief is that in order for organisations to thrive they must first support their greatest asset – their employees. In doing so a central element of this is the health and wellbeing of employees. Whereby there should be a focus on creating positive workplace environments, preventing excessive work-based stress, building individual and team resilience and supporting people to flourish and reach their full potential.

Box 1.2 Job advert 2: Academic health psychologist

An exciting opportunity has arisen in the School of Psychology to recruit a highly motivated academic to support the research strength and teaching capacity in the area of health psychology.

The successful candidate will have a PhD in health psychology or a related field and/or be a HCPC Registered Health Psychologist and full chartered member of the British Psychological Society. The candidate should have an established research profile, and experience of supervising research students, tutorials and practicals.

The role will encompass involvement and/or responsibility for developing the health psychology methods curriculum on both our undergraduate and postgraduate programmes, alongside our education academics, depending on experience and seniority.

I am currently Wellbeing Lead at Essex County Council, working within their Organisation Development and People & Service Transformation function driving the wellbeing agenda for their 7,500 employees. The purpose of my role as Wellbeing Lead is to build our employee wellbeing strategy, action plan and infrastructure, focusing on four keys pillars of wellbeing: mental, physical, social and financial wellbeing.

Utilising psychological principles and with a focus on health behaviour change the purpose of this strategy is to ensure that the health and wellbeing of our people is woven through everything that the council does. The focus is on evaluating practices around policies and procedures, day-to-day operations, performance and productivity, absence and presenteeism rates, leadership and management styles, employee morale and recruitment and retention rates. Based on this evaluation developing a workforce wellbeing strategy that: improves employee sense of health and wellbeing; increases employee engagement and motivation;

improves performance, development and productivity; fosters better employee relationships and ultimately puts the council in a stronger position to reach its ambitions.

The day to day in my role can really vary and that is probably what I enjoy most. A core focus for me at present is on strategy development and creating a corporate approach to workforce wellbeing. This involves consultation and stakeholder engagement – gaining views from across the workforce on how the strategy should be shaped and what the desired outcomes are for the organisation. A significant proportion of my role therefore is focused on collaboration and building professional relationships across teams and functions. As wellbeing affects all within the organisation it is about agreeing a corporate approach in which benefits can be seen by individuals, teams, functions and the wider community. At present I am working on a range of multidisciplinary projects for which day-to-day tasks can include conducting brief literature reviews, virtual team meetings, meetings with providers, presenting findings and recommendations to leadership and presenting across the workforce around wellbeing and the current offer. Other regular tasks include: administrative activities, management meetings, training design and delivery including taking part in live events and also working on my own professional development including taking advantage of both formal and informal learning opportunities (webinars have been very useful of late!).

I am proud to be representing the rapidly developing field of health psychology and to be utilising the knowledge and skills I have gained over the years in both my academic and professional life to encourage individuals in a work environment to improve their health.

How to become a health psychologist

To practice as a health psychologist in the UK you must be registered with the Health Care Professions Council (HCPC). The HCPC is a regulator of all health and care professions in the UK including all practitioner psychologists.

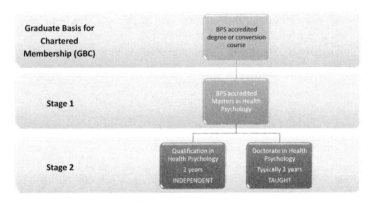

Figure 1.7 Flow chart demonstrating the different stages on how to become a health psychologist

To begin with you will need to gain Graduate Basis for Chartered Membership (GBC), which is achieved through completing a psychology degree accredited by the British Psychological Society (BPS) or through the successful completion of a BPS accredited conversion course. The BPS provide a full list of all GBC courses available.

Once you have achieved GBC status you then need to complete postgraduate training. This is broken down into two stages.

Stage one

Stage one involves the completion of a BPS accredited master's degree in health psychology. This stage is focused on developing the theoretical and academic aspects of the discipline. You will cover a wide range of topics as part of this course, some of which will include: health behaviour change, biological mechanisms of health and disease, stress, chronic health and illness, applications of health psychology and research methods.

This course will take one year to complete (two years part time). There are many institutions that offer this course, and the

BPS provide a full list of all accredited courses available in the UK. Entry requirements can vary among universities, however, a 2:1 degree classification or above is often desirable, sometimes essential.

Stage two

This stage is focused on gaining work experience and practitioner skills. You will be required to take part in at least two years of structured supervision practice and build upon the academic components of your Masters. You will need to demonstrate skills related to the delivery of professional practice, psychological interventions, research, consultancy and teaching and training. Importantly, the completion of Stage two will enable you to become a Chartered Psychologist. This allows you to use the designated and highly regarded title 'CPsychol'. This title reflects the highest standard of psychological knowledge and expertise.

There are multiple routes to completing Stage two, which are outlined below:

- **Option 1:** Completion of a Society accredited Doctorate in Health Psychology at an accredited university. This route is often referred to as the 'taught' route and may be selected by those who would prefer to attend and complete their Stage two at a university setting.
- **Option 2:** Completion of the Society's Qualification in Health Psychology (QHP), which involves a minimum of two years of structured supervised practice. This is often referred to as the 'independent route' and is most suitable for those who choose not to, or are unable to attend, a university based Society-accredited Stage two training programme.
- **Option 3:** Another option, and not uncommon, is for PhD students to complete the option 2 'independent route' alongside their PhD. The reason being is that many of the skills they have to demonstrate overlap, for example, conducting research, delivering interventions as examples.

What can you expect to earn as a health psychologist?

In the NHS, a newly qualified health psychologist enters the NHS at band 7 with progression to band 8a a few years after qualification. Progression through the NHS grades is typically achieved through applying for new roles. Grade 8b/c/d roles are for a Consultant Health Psychologist role, with typically six or more years of practice experience. Posts do go up to band 9 in the NHS for Heads of Psychology Services. Details of the most recent salary scales can be found on the NHS Careers website www.healthcareers.nhs.uk/working-health/working-nhs/nhs-pay-and-benefits/agenda-change-pay-rates.

In a university, a newly qualified lecturer (via PhD, doctorate) will normally be appointed as lecturer dependent on experience. Universities differ in how the job progression works and the job titles used. In some universities, you will progress from lecturer, to senior lecturer to reader, to professor. However, if you have a teaching background there is also a teaching progression route. Some universities refer to roles such as associate professor roles, these are similar to the senior lecturer/reader role. Progression is attained through either evidencing a strong research profile (research publications, attracting grant income) or demonstrating a strong contribution to the teaching learning and administration within the department.

Interested in health psychology, now what?

If you are interested in health psychology and want more infor mation then please visit the British Psychological Society careers page https://careers.bps.org.uk/area/health. There is also a range of useful organisations and networks that you should consider joining for added benefits, provided below.

The **British Psychological Society (BPS)** www.bps.org. uk is a registered charity, which acts as the representative body for psychology and psychologists in the UK. It is made up of members from all walks of life whose primary interest is in the development and application of psychology for the greater public good. The Society comprises several divisions, each dedicated to a specialty, and is responsible for the promotion of excellence and ethical practice in the science, education and practical applications of psychology.

You can join the BPS as a student member, this is open to everyone studying on a BPS accredited undergraduate degree or conversion course. You will get a host of benefits from joining, including access to *The Psychologist* and *PsychTalk*, membership to your local branch, providing you with networking opportunities and valuable information for your studies, access to the BPS Student online community where you can engage, interact and network with other psychology students as well as learn from industry professionals, exclusive discounts on books, events, e-learning and not to mention free online access to the Society's archive of academic journals. Once you graduate you can become a graduate member of the BPS, which is a prerequisite for many of the accredited post-graduate and Doctoral programmes.

The British Psychological Society also has a **Division of Health Psychology,** which promotes the professional interests of health psychologists and assists its members with the development of their professional skills in research, consultancy, teaching and training. They offer lots of useful resources including: advertising relevant events, provide careers advice and support and you will also receive a regular edition of the *Health Psychology Update*, a publication edited by the Division of Health Psychology. Join to become a student member by visiting www.bps.org.uk/member-microsites/division-health-psychology.

There are also local health psychology networks that you may find useful:

Midlands Health Psychology Network www.mhpn.co.uk/, which operates as a professional forum for health psychology enthusiasts across the East and West Midlands to share clinical and research experiences and information. They host numerous events for all members throughout the year including: an annual conference, CPD workshops, training and networking events. All members will also receive a quarterly newsletter where members are kept up to date with local health psychology events, job and training opportunities.

The **Behavioural Science and Public Health Network** www.bsphn.org.uk/ is also a useful organisation, which aims to bring together professionals (and students) with an interest in behavioural and social science and public health. Benefits include: discounted fees for events, workshops and CPD sessions, annual conference, publications and dissemination from events and regular updates.

Final overview and summary

- Health has been recently defined as 'the ability to adapt and self-manage in the face of social, physical, and emotional challenges' [12]. Whilst there has been debate on how health should be conceptualised it remains clear that there is increased focus on the importance of our social and emotional health.

- Across time there has been a shift from the more traditional biomedical view, where the mind and body were viewed as separate entities, to the more contemporary viewpoint, where the mind-body are entwined and suggests that behavioural factors can influence our health and illness. This biopsychosocial approach proposes that biological, psychological and social factors act together to determine an individual's health or vulnerability to disease.

- Health psychology aims to understand the psychological processes that underpin health and illness and use this knowledge to promote and maintain health, prevent illness and disability and enhance outcomes for those who are ill[14].

- Whilst in recent decades we have seen major public health achievements, one death in every four still could be prevented. Health psychologists are well placed to address this through their knowledge of the modifiable determinants of health and illness, and development and evaluation of interventions to change health behaviours at an individual, group and community level. Understanding health behaviour will also serve to reduce the ever-increasing health inequalities that exist in our society.

References

[1] Jouanna, J. (2012). The legacy of the Hippocratic Treatise *The Nature of Man: The Theory of the Four Humours*. In: *Greek Medicine from Hippocrates to Galen*. edn.: BRILL, 335–359.

[2] Javier, H. (2014). The Four Humours Theory. *ESSAI, 12*(1), 21.

[3] Nutton, V. (2005). The fatal embrace: Galen and the history of ancient medicine. *Science in Context, 18*(1), 111–121.

[4] Lloyd, G. (2007). Pneuma between body and soul. *Journal of the Royal Anthropological Institute, 13*, S135–S146.

[5] Schwartz, G. E., Weiss, S. M. (1978). Behavioral medicine revisited: An amended definition. *Journal of Behavioral Medicine, 1*(3), 249–251.

[6] Engel, G. L. (1977). The need for a new medical model: A challenge for biomedicine. *Science, 196*, 129–135.

[7] Engel, G. L. (1980). The clinical application of the biopsychosocial model. *American Journal of Psychiatry, 137*, 535–544.

[8] World Health Organisation (1948). *Constitution of the World Health Organisation*. Geneva, Switzerland: WHO Basic Documents.

[9] Richard Smith (2008). The end of disease and the beginning of health [https://blogs.bmj.com/bmj/2008/07/08/richard-smith-the-end-of-disease-and-the-beginning-of-health/]

[10] Travis, J. W. (1984). The relationship of wellness education and holistic health. *Mind, Body and Health*, 188–198.

[11] Godlee, F. (2011). What is health? *BMJ, 343*, d4817.

[12] Huber, M., Knottnerus, J.A., Green, L., Horst, Hvd., Jadad, A. R., Kromhout, D., Leonard, B., Lorig, K., Loureiro, M. I., Meer, J. W. Mvd. et al. (2011). How should we define health? *BMJ, 343*:d4163.

[13] Matarazzo, J. D. (1984). Behavioural health: A 1990 challenge for the health sciences professions. In: *Behavioural Health: A Handbook of Health Enhancement and Disease Prevention*. edn. Edited by Matarazzo, J. D., Miller, N. E., Weiss, S. M., Herd, J. A., Weiss, S. M. New York: Wiley.

[14] Division of Health Psychology [www.bps.org.uk/member-microsites/division-health-psychology]

[15] Bailie, L., Hawe, E. (2012). *Causes of Death: A Study of a Century of Change in England and Wales*. London, UK: Office of Health Economics.

[16] McKeown, T., Brown, R. G., Record, R. G. (1972). An interpretation of the modern rise of population in Europe. *Population Studies, 26*(3), 345–382.

[17]   Office for National Statistics (2019). *Avoidable mortality in the UK: 2017*. ONS.

[18]   World Health Organisation (2002). *The World Health Report: Reducing Risks, Promoting Healthy Life*. Geneva, Switzerland: WHO.

[19]   Mortality statistics – underlying cause, sex and age [www.nomisweb.co.uk/query/construct/summary.asp?mode=construct&version=0&dataset=161]

[20]   Department of Health (1992). *The Health of the Nation – A Strategy for Health in England*. HMSO.

[21]   Department of Health (1999). *Saving Lives: Our Healthier Nation*. London, UK: HMSO.

[22]   Wanless, D. (2002). *Securing Our Future: Taking a Long-term View – the Wanless Report*. Edited by Department of Health: Department of Health.

[23]   Wanless, D. (2004). *Securing Good Health for the Whole Population*. Norwich, UK: HMSO.

[24]   Department of Health (2010). *Healthy Lives, Healthy People: Our Strategy for Public Health in England*. London: The Stationery Office.

[25]   Adult smoking habits in the UK (2017). www.ons.gov.uk/peoplepopulationandcommunity/healthandsocialcare/healthandlifeexpectancies/bulletins/adultsmokinghabitsingreatbritain/

[26]   Thomson, K., Hillier-Brown, F., Todd, A., McNamara, C., Huijits, T., Bambra, C. (2017). The effects of public health policies on health inequalities: a review of reviews. *The Lancet*, 390:S12.

[27]   Contributing to public health policy and practice [https://thepsychologist.bps.org.uk/volume-18/edition-11/contributing-public-health-policy-and-practice]

[28]   Doll, R., Peto, R., Boreham, J., Sutherland, I. (2004). Mortality in relation to smoking: 50 years' observations on male British doctors. *BMJ*, *328*(7455):1519.

2 A bio/psycho/social approach to health and wellbeing

Contents

Chapter overview

A biopsychosocial approach to health and wellbeing

In the first chapter we explored the context of health psychology and considered the changing patterns of health. This chapter will link to the previous chapter and explore the holistic approach to healthcare. The chapter will consider the biopsychosocial approach and draw together the interrelationships between how people think and feel, their social environments and biological systems and mechanisms. We will focus on these relationships to form an appreciation of the holistic nature of health and wellbeing and consider the role of health psychology within the multi-disciplinary team. In order to do this we will focus on some of the key physiological systems such as the central nervous system, the endocrine system, the immune system and digestive system and consider the interrelationships between these systems and psychosocial factors such as social networks, the environment, mood and behaviour. To illustrate this we will focus on examples of pain, diabetes, autoimmune diseases and obesity.

The biopsychosocial approach

In the previous chapter you were introduced to the concept of the biopsychosocial approach. In order to consider health in the modern age it is important to move away from the notion that people are passive recipients of illness and instead consider that people are active agents in health and wellbeing. There has been a shift in the pattern of disease from communicable diseases to those that are attributed to lifestyle factors such as diet, exercise and the social and physical environments in which we live.

Pain

Pain could be considered to be an evolutionary adaptive mechanism to alert the body to harm or injury.

But, is pain purely a physiological phenomenon?

Early researchers would say that it was. These early theorists considered pain to be a response to a painful stimulus. How much pain an individual experienced was therefore viewed in terms of the extent of tissue damage, with a direct link between pain stimulus and experience.

Challenges to this view came from examples of pain that occurred in the absence of any organic tissue injury such as phantom limb pain. This is where an individual feels pain in a limb that has been amputated and is no longer there, and therefore cannot be explained in terms of stimulus and response. Also, during the Second World War it was noted that individuals with the same degree of tissue damage often differed in how they reported pain, with 80 per cent of civilians requesting pain relief compared to 25 per cent. This was interpreted as a difference in meaning of pain, for the soldiers the war was over [1]. Therefore, pain is not purely a monolithic entity [2], but is multidimensional and includes both sensory and affective aspects, the location, how intense it is, how long it lasts, memories and meaning.

Let us go on to consider pain within the biopsychosocial framework.

Biological factors

The central nervous system

In acute pain, it is thought that there are four basic processes [3] involved in the physiology of pain: transduction, transmission, perception and modulation.

Transduction

The free nerve endings (nociceptors) of primary nerves that are situated in body structures such as the skin, gastrointestinal tract, liver, muscles and bones, carry signals to the central nervous system. These nociceptors respond to harmful stimuli such as tissue damage and inflammation (which puts pressure on the nerve endings). Harmful stimuli could come from such things as injury, trauma and surgery. Depending on which of these free endings are stimulated, the individual will describe different experiences, for example C fibres are small in diameter and are unmyelinated (insulated) and so they conduct impulses more slowly and so individuals may use words such as dull, burning or aching and it may be spread across an area. A-delta fibres are large in diameter and do have a protective sheath and so they are fast conducting and the pain seems to be localised, sharp, stinging or pricking.

Transmission

Transmission describes how the signal travels from the site of transduction to the brain. It is considered to have three stages.

> Stage 1 – from site of transduction to the spine (dorsal horn)
> Stage 2 – spinal cord to brain stem (thalamus)
> Stage 3 – from thalamus to other areas of the brain to be processed

Multiple areas are involved in processing the information received, for example how bad is it? The somatosensory cortex, for example is involved in the perception and interpretation of the information (intensity, type, location) and also related to past experiences and memory. The limbic system is associated with the emotional and behavioural response to the information such as attention, mood, motivation, and also in processing the pain and past experiences.

Modulation

Modulation refers to changing or inhibiting transmission of pain through endogenous opioids. Similarly, pain can be modulated by pharmacological agents such as analgesia (pain relief medication).

However, this explanation cannot always explain the pain experience, already we can see that the perception and interpretation of the pain signal can involve past experience, memory, emotions and behaviour, even when considering acute pain. Therefore, we can begin to see that pain cannot be explained entirely by physiology alone.

Further challenges to the purely biological explanation come from chronic pain. This is defined as pain that can last longer than six months. It may not have a discernible organic cause [4], but despite this studies that have used scans to look at the activation of the brain have found that there remains extensive activation [5]. We subsequently need to look to other theories to explain the pain experience.

Psychological factors

The Gate Control Theory (GCT)

The gate control theory of pain [6] is based upon physiological mechanisms of pain but also attempts to integrate psychology. Within this theory is the concept that the nervous system is always active and so any new information can either amplify or diminish neural signals. It is also proposed that there is a gate in the dorsal horn. When the gate is open there is increased activity and more pain is perceived and when the gate is closed this decreases activity and less pain is perceived (see Table 2.1).

This theory was significant as it included psychological factors that could affect the pain experience such as emotional and behavioural factors. However, the theory was criticised over the gate, which remined hypothetical. Later with the development of technology the theory was extended to describe a neuromatrix, that can be seen on scans, such as functional magnetic resonance imaging, instead of a gate [7], which described a system that was widespread and that could be determined genetically, but be shaped by nerve inputs and experiences and impressed within the neuromatrix. This theory suggests that even when a limb has been amputated because the body, and associated experiences, normally feel the limb, it is possible to feel it in the absence of any input. This then indicates

Table 2.1 The Gate Control Theory – factors that open and close the gate

Open	Close
PHYSICAL FACTORS e.g. transduction, transmission	PHYSICAL FACTORS e.g. medication, stimulation of small fibres
EMOTIONAL FACTORS e.g. anxiety, depression	EMOTIONAL FACTORS e.g. happiness, relaxation
BEHAVIOURAL FACTORS e.g. focusing on the pain, boredom	BEHAVIOURAL FACTORS e.g. concentration, distraction

that psychosocial factors interact with physiological factors and affect the overall pain experience.

Let's consider some examples of evidence:

Anxiety

Anxiety seems to increase pain perception, for example in a study on children with migraines and people with backpain and pelvic pain, high anxiety was linked with increased pain [8]. In chronic pain, people may get stuck in an anxiety pain cycle where their pain prevents them from moving for fear of exacerbating pain, which can then lead to muscle tension and increased perception of pain.

Learning

The way that pain tolerance, behaviours and how pain is communicated can be influenced by culture via social learning, for example a ritual of celebration in Southern India involved being suspended by hooks inserted into the back, and yet these people did not display signs of pain. In a more traditional sense of learning and conditioning, associations can be made with particular places and pain, for example the dentist. There may also be an association between how parents respond to pain and their children. In one study it was found that there was a correlation between pain catastrophising in parents and their adult children [9], which may have been due to a learned coping style.

Cognition

The way people think about their pain could also affect the pain experience, for example attention. Pain can demand attention and increased attention to pain has been related to expressing greater amounts of pain. The flip side is that distraction can decrease the amount of pain expressed [10]. Also, patterns of dysfunctional thinking such as catastrophising ('it's hopeless', 'it will never get better', 'it's unbearable', 'how will I cope?') can affect how an individual copes with pain and the overall pain experience [11]. Some researchers have found that catastrophising increases attention towards the pain [12]. Females tend to catastrophise more, and express higher levels of pain and higher levels of disability [13; 14]. Some researchers have suggested that individuals that catastrophise pain have a special pain schema (memory store) that consists of distorted thinking and negative beliefs about pain, pain experiences and their actual ability to cope with pain [15]. This type of behaviour may elicit support from others and reinforce the behaviour (through conditioning), which may then affect their ongoing ability to cope [15].

A person's belief in their ability to be able to control their pain also has an impact on their pain experience and levels of functioning. Early work found that if people have control of the on/off switch for a painful stimulus then they could endure more pain [16]. Indeed, other studies have found that if people perceive that they are able to have some control over their pain then this can improve overall wellbeing [17].

So, therefore, it seems that our experience of pain is affected by the way we interpret the experience of pain and this can be affected by our genetics [18] as some pain syndromes seem to run in families; our mood; beliefs about pain and expectations, such as whether someone believes that they have a high pain threshold. Therefore, pain is a multi-faceted experience with many factors that can influence the experience, which fit within a biopsychosocial framework (see Figure 2.1).

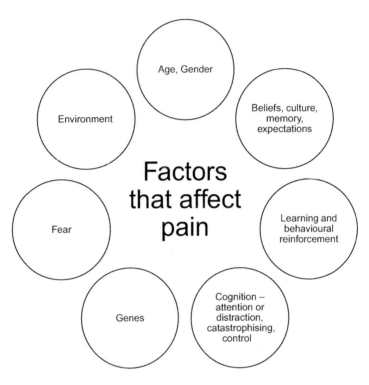

Figure 2.1 Factors that affect pain

Treatment for pain (see Table 2.2)

Whilst pharmacological agents (pain killers) may be successful in treating acute pain, they may become less effective when used for the treatment in chronic pain.

Why does pain relief stop working as well?

This may be due to disease progression and deterioration, but could also be explained by the process of neuroadaptation. This is the process of the body adjusting to the chemicals within the pharmacological agent, and changes occur in the neuronal circuits by which the person needs more of the drug to have any effect. Pharmacological agents such as opiates (morphine) also carry the risk of addiction. This will mean that the drugs will seem less effective and so a biomedical approach alone is not enough to help people cope with their chronic pain.

What can health psychologists do to improve pain?

Understanding that pain is a complex phenomenon that is affected by an interaction between physiological, psychological and social factors, health psychologists can work as part of a multi-disciplinary team to help people manage chronic pain. Interventions that target dysfunctional cognition, such as catastrophising or that aim to increase functionality have demonstrated some success in increasing quality of life, physical and emotional functioning [19].

Cognitive behaviour therapy has been demonstrated to be useful in a number of studies for reducing chronic pain by targeting unhelpful behaviours, physical sensations and dysfunctional thinking [20; 21]. However, it is not useful for everybody and recently there has been an emphasis on **acceptance and commitment therapy**, which is based on acceptance of both positive and negative experiences and action towards future life goals [22]. One study compared the two treatments and found that both those that received CBT and ACT had improved physical functioning and mood and there was no significant difference between groups [23].

What about alternative therapies?

Alternative therapies, such as the use of sound, have found some mixed results, for example music therapy is considered to alter neural pathways that are associated with the perception of pain [24]. A Cochrane review of 52 studies with 1867 participants and 1796 controls found that listening to music reduced perceived pain and decreased the need for opioids [25] and may be useful for some people.

Table 2.2 A summary of some of the types of treatment

Type of Treatment	Actions
Pharmacological agents	Analgesia (pain killers), such as opioids (e.g morphine), non-steroidal anti-inflammatories (e.g. Ibuprofen) that interfere with the pain messages and suppressing pain-induced activity in the brain
Pain management	Multi-disciplinary team (Anaesthetists, specialist nurses and Doctors, physiotherapists, occupational therapist and psychologists) providing analgesia, nerve blocks, physiological therapy, psychological therapies
Cognitive Behaviour Therapy	Psychological Therapy that works on modifying thinking
Acceptance Commitment Therapy	Psychological Therapy that works on acceptance and pursuit of life goals

Brief summary of pain

Overall, pain is complex and many factors can affect the pain experience including physiological factors (such as nociception, adaption), psychological factors (such as dysfunctional thinking, attention, control), social factors (such as reinforcement) and the effects of the interaction between these factors, such as experiences and memory imprinting on pain mechanisms.

We have now considered pain, but what about other prevalent chronic health conditions? Can we apply the biopsychosocial approach in understanding these? Take Type 2 diabetes, for example in 2019 1 in 10 people had been diagnosed with Type 2 diabetes according to Diabetes UK, with many more maybe going undiagnosed.

Diabetes

What is diabetes?

Diabetes Mellitus is a complex disorder. Diabetes has traditionally been thought of as an endocrine disorder, with the focus placed on the function of cells in the pancreas and the regulation of sugar levels in the blood.

The endocrine system

The endocrine system itself is more complex and consists of glands that secrete hormones directly into the blood stream and link to a specific cell. They also link to the central nervous system.

The pancreas itself is a complex organ. Why is this? Because as well as producing hormones, it also produces digestive enzymes. The endocrine part of the pancreas consists of the islets of Langerhans, which house cells that are implicated in glucose control. The different types of cells and their function are included in the Table 2.3.

Table 2.3 Cells of the pancreas and their function

Cell	Purpose	Function
Alpha Cells	Acts when sugar levels are low.	Produce glucagon. Action of glucagon is to stop beta cells producing insulin and raise blood sugar by triggering muscles to break down muscle and the liver to release stored glycogen for energy.
Beta cells	Acts when sugar levels are high	Stop alpha cells producing glucagon. Produce insulin which triggers uptake of glucose into cells to be used as energy. Activates liver to store glucose as glycogen. Excess glucose is stored as fat.

If we were to consider Diabetes Mellitus (DM) from a bio-medical or simply biological perspective then we might consider it to be a collection of disorders that are unified by a diminished insulin action. The two most common types of DM are Type 1, which is considered to be caused by an autoimmune destruction of the beta cells in the pancreas, and Type 2, considered to be a decrease in production of insulin or insulin resistance. DM is a chronic disorder that interferes with the way that carbohydrate, protein and fact are metabolised [26], and is considered to be related to lifestyle (see Table 2.4 for a summary of the differences in Type 1 and Type 2).

Irrespective as to the cause, DM is characterised by high amounts of sugar in the blood. Because of the increased amount of sugar in the blood, the symptoms tend to be increased thirst, the increased need to urinate (especially at night) and increased hunger (as glucose cannot be taken into the cells to be used as energy).

Type 1 Diabetes requires management with insulin as the pancreas is not producing any. This means that those with Type 1 will need to adhere to their insulin regime, to prevent hyperglycaemia and hypoglycaemia. There is a role for health psychologists in

Table 2.4

Type 1	Type 2
Autoimmune destruction of the beta cells (no insulin produced) which results in high blood sugar (hyperglycaemia)	Beta cells are producing insulin, but not enough/cells resistant to insulin which results in high blood sugar
Onset usually prior to 40	Onset often after 40
Cannot be prevented	Can be prevented/delayed (change to diet and exercise, weight loss)
Symptoms:	
Great thirst	Symptoms: Feeling thirsty
Fatigue	Frequent urination (especially at night)
Frequent urination	
Weight Loss	Weight loss and loss of muscle bulk
Skin Infections	Can have symptoms for years and not realise.
Itchy genitalia	

supporting patients to manage Type 1, but for the purpose of this chapter we will be focusing on Type 2.

Let us now focus on Type 2 and consider why this is related to lifestyle factors and why there is a need for the biopsychosocial approach in understanding both the cause and management.

It is a disease of lifestyle!

Type 2 DM is considered to be a lifestyle disease because the most common modifiable risk factor is obesity, and in particular when fat accumulates around the middle which is called central adiposity (see figure for other risk factors). Although obesity may increase the risk of developing Type 2 DM, it should be noted that those of normal weight can also develop Type 2 DM [27].

The main complications of Type 2 DM can arise from having a high blood sugar. The onset may be gradual and may go unnoticed and therefore complications may arise before the individual is aware that they have Type 2 DM. If a person is producing less insulin or there is insulin resistance, then there will be a build-up of circulating glucose in the blood. This results in the body trying to get rid of this excess through urinating more, which then also results in an excessive thirst. As cells are unable to utilise the sugar for energy, the body will break down muscle and fat as an alternative energy source and so the person may lose weight.

The aetiology of Type 2 is linked with a number of risk factors (see Table 2.5).

What is the role of the health psychologist in understanding Type 2 diabetes?

The role of the health psychologist is to understand the factors that predict Type 2 so that they can target prevention strategies to prevent or delay onset. We have already seen that Type 2 diabetes is no longer considered to be a disease of the pancreas but is actually a disease of lifestyle.

Table 2.5

Type 2 Risk Factors
Being over 40
Being from a minority ethnic group and over 25 and having 1 or more of the following:
Family history of Type 2 DM (parent, brother, sister)
Waist over 31.5 inches or 37 inches in men (35 in Asian men)
High Blood Pressure or coronary vascular disease
Polycystic ovary disease
Impaired glucose tolerance test (GTT)
Impaired fasting glucose
Gestational Diabetes
Metabolic syndrome (central obesity, high blood pressure, high tryglycerides, low HDL, Insulin resistance)

Using a biopsychosocial approach in understanding the aetiology of Type 2 DM

Examples of biological factors

It's in the genes. Some people are more pre-disposed to developing Type 2 if they have one or more parents with Type 2 diabetes. However, genes cannot be considered purely on their own as the genetic propensity of contracting Type 2 also interacts with other factors, such as the way people live their lives and the environment in which they live, which can influence onset [28]. The genetic component is in itself also complex, as over 120 different variants have been identified [28].

   It's about fat. In terms of the impact of environment and life-style, one of the biggest risks to developing Type 2 diabetes seems to be obesity. Those particularly at risk seems to be those with central adiposity (fat distribution around the tummy, often referred to as an apple shape). The biological mechanisms of the link between fat and insulin resistance associated with Type 2 diabetes are complex. As an overview, there seems to be a link in the way that the excess intake of food is stored as fat in the body, and how this is linked with the release of inflammatory substances (adipokines) [29], which interrupt the action of insulin [30]. The implication is that cells can then become resistant to insulin and/or the beta cells that produce insulin can be affected and produce less insulin. **This then is a clear example of the interaction between behaviour (intake of food), and how this can affect physiology.**

Examples of psychological factors

It's about behaviour. We have already started to consider behavioural lifestyle factors such as diet. There are five key behavioural factors that health psychologists focus on and these are diet, exercise, alcohol use, smoking and drug use.

The link between diet and Type 2. Diet and sedentary behaviours are considered to be the main lifestyle factors that contribute to Type 2 diabetes [31]. However, the literature around diet and the link to Type 2 is somewhat varied. First, there is some evidence that there may be a relationship between the higher consumption of processed meats and sugar sweetened drinks and low consumption of coffee and wholegrains [32] and risk of Type 2 diabetes.

Evidence

Some research has demonstrated that those people who consumed wholegrain foods were less likely to develop Type 2 diabetes. Therefore, could we conclude that the consumption of wholegrain foods reduces the risk of Type 2 (Aune et al., 2009)?

Why might wholegrains be beneficial?

The protective factor of wholegrain products may be due to the high concentration of fibres that lead to a delay in how quickly they pass through the stomach and therefore slowing the release of glucose into the blood stream. It has been suggested that this improves insulin sensitivity due to a reduced required insulin response after food (Aune et al., 2009).

Is it just about eating wholegrains?

This is a simplistic view and it is much more complex than this. Eating behaviours may be indicative of other lifestyle factors, for example research has found that higher intake of sugary drinks and processed foods may also be linked with higher rates of obesity, sedentary behaviour, smoking and poorer eating habits generally [33; 34]. On the other hand, those who eat more wholegrains may have healthier lifestyle behaviours in general and this then demonstrates the complexity of the interaction between lots of different factors that may predict the development of Type 2 diabetes. It is not one aspect of a person's life, but a combination of factors.

What about exercise?

Exercise is an important factor. Being physically active can improve insulin sensitivity and the metabolism of insulin. This is because exercise creates a need for glucose in the muscles, therefore decreasing the amounts of glucose in the blood. It can also decrease the amount of fat in the body [35], which demonstrates both short term and longer-term benefits. Physical inactivity, or sedentary behaviour as it is commonly known, can lead to obesity, such as spending a lot of time sitting in front of the TV [32]. It may also encourage snacking.

Can personality influence onset?

There is some evidence that personality may influence health behaviours and therefore pre-dispose individuals to develop Type 2 diabetes. Let us consider the personality trait of conscientiousness as an example.

What is conscientiousness?

Conscientiousness is considered to be associated with being responsible, hardworking, reliable, goal-directed and compliant to rules and norms. An early link was found between those who demonstrated higher levels of conscientiousness and life expectancy [36]. A more recent study found that those who are high in the personality trait of conscientiousness tend to have reduced risk of disease [37].

*What is the relationship between conscientiousness
and Type 2 diabetes?*

There has been some research that has found that low levels of
conscientiousness seem to be related to Type 2 DM. This may be
because those who are lower in conscientiousness also tend to do
less exercise [38]. On the flip side, conscientious persons may be
more likely to be careful about what they eat [37]. Again, here we
can see the complexity of a number of factors that can predict the
onset of Type 2, personality traits may influence our behaviours,
that may lead to obesity and inflammation, which may inhibit
the production of insulin and the uptake of glucose into cells to
be used as energy. However, lifestyle is also complicated by the
environment in which we live.

Social and environmental factors

So far we have considered that a number of factors can influence the development of Type 2 and we started by saying that
genes did not alone predict the onset of Type 2 diabetes but in
fact interacted with the environment, but what does this mean?
In simple terms we exist in an environment that is shaped by us
and in turn shapes us. This was termed as reciprocal determinism
by the psychologist Bandura [39]. If we can consider that genes
may pre-dispose an individual to a particular disease, but it is their
environment that can affect onset. Let us consider obesity as an
example of this interaction.

The obesogenic environment

Some people consider that we are living in an obesogenic environment, or in other words an environment that contributes to
individuals becoming obese. Of course, this is not a one-way
relationship, as it is society that shapes the environment. It is a
well-known fact that there has been an increase in sedentary
behaviour, such as sitting more, having labour-saving devices
in the home and work that is desk-based [40]. There is also
increasing availability of varied and highly palatable foods that are
calorie dense that promote and enable people to be obese [41].

There is some evidence that there is a pattern of lower socio-economic status being linked to greater amounts of obesity [42] and that this group is generally more prone to unhealthy life-style patterns. This could be explained by the stress of living in poorer environments and having less income. There is evidence that stress encourages the consumption of foods that are highly palatable and calorie dense, which is popularly known as comfort eating [43; 44]. In one laboratory study that looked at comparing women in higher socio-economic groups and those in in lower socio-economic groups it was found that women in the lower socio-economic bracket ate more food overall and particularly those foods that were high in fat and sugar.

What about culture?

There is evidence that there are differences in the propensity to develop Type 2 diabetes across different cultures. Let us consider the example of those of Southeast Asian descent who seem to be particularly at risk [45]. This higher risk is despite lower rates of obesity, as Asian populations tend to have lower BMIs than other cultural groups. The key seems to be contained within the rate of visceral fat, which is fat that accumulates around the organs. People of Southeast Asian descent tend to have higher rates of visceral fat [46]. Therefore it may be that this visceral fat, coupled with the genetic propensity (alleles that are linked with insulin secretion) [47], explains the higher risk of Type 2 diabetes in this population. Evidence from other cultural groups has suggested that non-fat individuals may benefit from weight loss because individuals may have a personal fat threshold and once this is exceeded, then Type 2 will occur [27].

Type 2 diabetes can therefore be considered a complex disorder that involves the interrelationship of biological, psychological and social factors.

The digestive system and obesity

The digestive system

The digestive system (alimentary canal) is approximately 8.4 metres long (adults) [48] and stretches from the mouth to the anus. It consists of a number of different organs – mouth, pharynx, oesophagus, stomach, small intestine, large intestine, rectum and anal canal. There are also some subsidary organs such as the teeth, salivary glands, liver, pancreas and gall bladder [49].

The alimentary canal has four main layers that protect it and assist in the movement along it – the mucosa, submucosa, muscularis and serosa. Of note is the link between the muscularis and the autonomic nervous system (which might explain the gastrointestinal symptoms we feel when stressed).

Digestion of food takes place in stages, see Table 2.6.

Table 2.6

It begins in the mouth! (cephalic stage)	The sight and smells of food activate saliva and digestive juices in anticipation. The taste buds stimulate saliva and the stomach and gall bladder and pancreas. Teeth break down the food through grinding, shredding, tearing and chewing and the tongue shapes it into a bolus. Saliva contains salivary amylase that begins to break down starch and lysosome (antibacterial enzyme) that acts as a lubricant.
Mouth to stomach	It takes approximately 6 seconds for food to pass from the mouth, down the oesophagus and into the stomach
Stomach (gastric phase)	Is a muscle sack that is shaped like a J. It has a volume of 50 mls when empty and stretched to 1.5. litres after a meal.
	There are a number of cells that produce a number of substances within the stomach, ghrelin which stimulates hunger, goblet cells that produce mucous to protect it against the acid, parietal cells that release hydrochloric acid (kills bugs) and intrinsic factor (aids absorption of B12), G cells that secrete gastrin to control acid and chief cells that produce pepsinogen which is converted to pepsin by the acid.
	When the bolus arrives the stomach muscles churn and mix food with acid and pepsin (breaks down protein). The solids are broken down into a substance known as chyme and this is passed into the small intestine.

(continued)

Table 2.6 Cont.

Intestinal Phase	Stops the production of gastric juices and slows chyme exit. The acid is neutralised and fats and proteins stimulate the release of cholecystokinin which stimulates the pancreas to release pancreatic juice which makes the gall bladder contract and slows down the stomach emptying which makes us feel full and satiated (Tortora and Derrickson, 2009).
Small intestine	It is here that fats, proteins and carbohydrates are digested. The gall bladder secretes bile which breaks down fat. Pancreatic amylase breaks down polysaccharides (complex suagrs) into monosaccharides (simple sugars). These sugars are either absorbed or excess is stored as glycogen in the liver or muscles. When these cells are saturated it is converted to fat and stored as fat. Pancreatic trypsin and intestinal juice also convert proteins to amino acids. Lipids (fats) are emulsified with bile salts from the liver and then pancreatic lipase turns them into fatty acids and monoglycrides.
Large intestine	It is here that water and salts are absorbed leaving just waste. There are over 500 different bacteria here. They case the release of gas by fermenting unabsorbed nutrients (especially carbs).
Liver	Has a role in breaking down protein into new proteins or urea to be excreted. Has a role in maintaining glucose levels – stores glycogen and converts back to glucose. Also stores fat and converts it into energy and triglycerides.

So why do we need to eat?

We need to eat to provide energy to maintain bodily functions such as thinking, breathing and moving. We also need nutrients to enable us to grow, to repair and to defend against invaders.

So what is the right amount of food?

The right amount of food is the amount that is needed to carry out these vital bodily functions.

Figure 2.2

What is a calorie?

A calorie is equal to the amount of heat that is needed to raise the temperature of a gram of water to 1 degree Celsius and the basal metabolic rate is the minimum calories that are needed to maintain all of the bodily functions when we are at rest. This is likely to be different in each individual depending on their age, activity levels, medications, hormones and therefore it may be difficult for individuals trying to maintain control over their weight to know how much they should be eating. Eating more calories than the body uses can lead to weight gain.

Obesity

It may be difficult to conceive that obesity is a chronic illness, but there is currently an obesity epidemic with 64 per cent of the adult population falling into the overweight or obese category [50] and 70 per cent in the USA [51]. Obesity is defined as an excess of body fat and occurs when more calories are consumed than are used, causing excess energy to be stored as fat around the organs in the abdominal cavity (visceral) or under the skin. Individual differences in the way that the body stores fat have health implications with greater health risk being associated with abdominal obesity (visceral fat) [52].

Obesity is associated with a number of different health conditions. We have already considered the link between obesity and Type 2 diabetes, but it is also associated with other chronic illnesses such as hypertension (high blood pressure), high cholesterol levels, coronary heart disease and stroke, and premature mortality [53].

So why do people become obese?

The biological model of obesity suggests that obesity occurs when the calories in are greater than the calories expended leading to storage of excess nutrients as visceral fat or subcutaneous fat. If we were to consider this from a physiological theoretical stance then we would assume that once we had consumed the right amount of calories then satiety would occur.

Is eating driven purely by satiety? Or do we eat even when we are not hungry? Let us consider these questions with an example from research in Box 2.1.

Box 2.1

Eating in the absence of hunger: an example from research (Fisher & Birch).

Background: Being exposed to calorie dense highly palatable foods in the absence of hunger is considered to contribute to obesity.

Aim: The aim of the study was to examine whether eating in the absence of hunger was stable in young girls over a two-year period and was associated with a greater risk of being overweight.

Method

Design: The design was a repeated measures experimental design. The independent variable was the palatable snack food and the dependent variable was the amount of snack food consumed.

Participants: 196 Caucasian girls from the Pennsylvania area. The participants were studied at age 5 and at 7.

Materials: The materials consisted of a packed-lunch type lunch (rolls, sandwich meat, carrots, cheese, apple-sauce, cookies and milk) and portions of 10 pre-weighed snack foods e.g. popcorn, chocolate chip cookies, crisps (potato chips), ice-cream.

The girls' height and weight were also measured, and parents were asked to complete the parental restriction section of the Child Feeding Questionnaire (Birch et al. 2001).

Procedure: The girls were invited to the laboratory on two occasions, once before they started kindergarten and once before second grade. The children were weighed and their height was recorded, they were then given generous portions of lunch. When they had eaten they were asked to rate their level of fullness. They were then shown some toys and containers of snack food and were told they could play with the toys and eat whatever they liked.

Results: Eating in the absence of hunger was stable across time for most girls. Those who ate more snack foods in the absence of hunger at age 5 were also likely to eat higher amounts of snack foods in the absence of hunger at age 7. Girls who were overweight tended to eat more snacks in the absence of hunger at age 5 and age 7. Those children whose parents reported more restriction were also more likely to eat in the absence of hunger.

Conclusion: This study demonstrates that an environment where there is a variety of readily available calorie-dense palatable foods may contribute to obesity and eating in the absence of hunger in some children. There were individual differences in responses, and these were stable across time. Restrictive feeding practices by parents were not necessarily successful, and they also concluded that children should be encouraged to respond to feelings of fullness.

From this example we can see that there were individual differences in the way that the children responded to eating, and the number of palatable snacks that were consumed. Understanding why these differences may occur can help in the understanding of obesity both in childhood and later into adulthood and help in the design of effective interventions.

Biological factors

Let us start with considering some of the biological factors that might explain differences in the propensity to becoming obese.

One of the pre-disposing factors may be individual differences in genes, and there is one school of thought that considers obesity to be a heritable trait. Evidence for this comes from studies on twins that have been adopted and have shown that their weight was more closely linked with their biological parents than their adoptive ones [54]. However, it may or may not be just one gene, but the contribution of a number of genes (polygenic) that are present and the effects of which are then amplified by the environment [55].

So what other biological factors affect eating behaviour?

A physiological approach may assume that homeostatic mechanisms that are associated with hunger (the need for energy) and satiety (feeling full) may regulate eating behaviour. In this hypothesis, obesity would be the cause of a reduced sensitivity to satiety cues [56].

There are a number of hormones that can affect eating behaviour: ghrelin, leptin and neuropeptide-y. The amount of these hormones that are found in the body is dependent on body weight and on the composition of the meal [57].

Leptin

This hormone is secreted by adipocytes (fat cells) and fluctuates according to changes in the number of calories that are ingested. In evolutionary terms, it's main function is to defend against any loss of body fat, which may affect the ability to survive or reproduce [58]. So leptin would seem to be essential for maintaining normal levels of energy in a simple stimulus–response model in that–you eat when you are hungry and stop when you are not.

So why then, if there is this internal regulation of fat stores and energy does obesity occur?

Research[59] has found that giving animals leptin subsequently reduced the amount of food they consumed, however, over long periods of time, food intake actually returned to normal when fat stores have been depleted. We might assume then that giving obese people leptin would make them lose fat, but this is not the case (except in conditions where there is a leptin deficiency), which seems to indicate that just like insulin resistance obesity may cause a resistance to leptin [58].It is suggested that as well as genes having an effect on leptin, environment may well also play a role with the ever increasing availability of highly palatable, calorie dense foods that drive over eating [58].

Ghrelin

Ghrelin is a hormone that is secreted in the stomach and along with leptin has the short term effect of stimulating food intake by increasing peristalsis. Therefore, prior to a meal there is an increase in ghrelin and post-meal there is a decrease [60]. It is considered to interact with leptin to provide a hunger signal. Research has indicated that the amount of leptin and ghrelin that is produced depends on the body weight of the individual and on the composition of the meal itself [61]. One study found that greater feelings of satiety may be found with higher carbohydrate meals in those of normal weight and lower carbohydrate meals in obese/overweight men [57]. Lower carbohydrate meals may therefore be beneficial to weight loss by increasing satiety in obese individuals.

Neuropetide Y

Neuropeptide Y is involved in many different processes that are involved in homeostasis. In terms of obesity, the functions are not fully understood, but there is some evidence that it may affect weight gain. Some research has suggested that it stimulates appetite and the production of new fat stores, particularly in the abdominal region, and particularly when stressed [62]. Diets that are high in sugar and carbohydrate can also stimulate the release of neuropeptide-y and further increase appetite.

The problem with looking at obesity and eating behaviour purely from a physiological perspective is that physiological theories assume that hunger and satiety are influenced by gastrointestinal hormones and brain transmitters. Whilst these are contributory factors in obesity this fails to consider the more hedonic system and the pleasurable and positively reinforcing effects of food, the attractiveness of food. It also fails to consider the availability of food and also learned preferences – what we like to eat [58]. How much is our food intake driven by an evolutionary need for fuel for the body? and how much is it driven by the more hedonistic properties of pleasure, conditioning, individual differences and the impact of the social environment?

We have already considered that physiological hormones are affected by other factors such as stress and the environment. Also remember that relationships are not just one way, and just as these hormones can affect intake of calories, so too can the environment and changes in nutritional status, such as over eating, affect the action of the hormones, and the hormones may adapt and change one's appetite [63]. We have already discussed how hormones can affect the formation of further fat cells, which can then subsequently affect appetite, demonstrating the interaction between biological processes and behaviour. It is also apparent that there is an interaction between biological processes, behaviour and the environment in which we live.

Let us consider some of the psychological factors that can affect eating behaviour.

Psychological factors

Eating behaviour and appetite are important factors to consider in trying to explain obesity. Eating is driven by both bodily needs and desires. An early theory of obesity was the externality theory [64; 65]. This theory proposed that people who are obese are more driven by external cues to eat than responding to internal cues of satiety, which could lead to over-eating. Visual food cues have been found to activate the reward centres of the brain. In a study where participants were shown high calorie foods and low calories foods, greater activation in the reward system was found in response to high calorie foods [66]. There also seems to be a difference between those participants who are obese and those who are of normal weight when looking at the brain's response to food cues. In one study they found that obese people who were hungry demonstrated activation in areas that have been linked with addiction in response to high calorie food cues [67]. So is this indicative of a learned response? Let's consider how eating may be a conditioned response to food cues.

Conditioning

There is evidence that cues that are associated with food such as how we are feeling or thinking can be conditioned and produce a physiological response (Boulton, 2011). We have talked before about the obesogenic environment and there are cues to eat everywhere. Take for example the smell of cooking, freshly baked bread or cake, it is cues like this from the environment or internal cues of how we feel, or what we are doing that may stimulate appetite [68]. Exposure to food cues creates a desire to eat [69], but also a physiological response such as salivation and also cognitive responses such as activation in areas of the brain and attention [68]. This is explained using the example of the classical conditioning paradigm (see Figure 2.3).

Let us consider this in an alternative example.

Research has found that these types of associations occur with a number of different types of stimuli in laboratory experiments such as virtual environments [70], objects and emotions [71]. What this means is that we can associate cues with eating, and this then may have an effect on individual desires to eat food. But not everyone is overweight, so it may be that some people are more susceptible than others, i.e. there are individual differences in susceptibility.

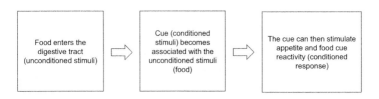

Figure 2.3 Let us consider this in an alternative example

Bryony repeatedly eats chocolate whilst watching
entertainment on her favourite streaming app. In this scenario,
watching entertainment may then become associated with
eating chocolate, and subsequently just opening the app may
induce a craving for chocolate

Figure 2.4 A case study example

The behavioural susceptibility theory suggests that there is an interaction between those individuals that have a genetic predisposition to be more highly responsive to food cues, are more likely to overeat in an environment where there are many cues to eat. Also, that those that are genetically predetermined to having weaker satiety signals are more likely to eat more. So individual differences in susceptibility can also affect the way that individuals behave. Let us go on to consider how individual differences may also affect eating behaviour when under stress.

Stress and eating behaviour

Eating behaviour can be influenced by emotions especially as a coping mechanism in times of stress, which is commonly be termed comfort eating. Studies have indicated that there are individual differences in food consumption under stress with the majority of around 70 per cent being prone to over-eating [72; 73]. In a metanalytical review of the literature consisting of 33 studies and 2,491 participants researchers concluded that negative affect is associated with higher food consumption, especially in those that are binger eaters or restrained eaters [74]. Other studies have found that negative mood and daily hassles are also associated with eating snacks that are high in fat and sugar [75; 76; 77].

The link between overeating and emotions may in part be due to physiology and the neurotransmitter serotonin. Serotonin is mood elevating and seems to be linked to appetite. When our mood drops, we tend to crave sweet food, and eating sweet food (carbohydrates) seems to increase serotonin and mood. This could then become a conditioned response with mood affecting food intake as previously described. However, obesity cannot just be explained by what energy we take in, but also by how much energy we expend.

Activity

There have been a number of studies that have linked a lack of physical activity and obesity [78; 79]. However, sedentary lifestyles are not simply a lack of physical activity, but a multifaceted disease of the modern age. Typically, sedentary behaviour is considered to be where the dominant behaviour is sitting down or lying down and the overall energy expenditure is very low. Lack of activity or sedentary behaviour involves prolonged amounts of time spent TV watching, sitting at a computer or laying down. Some research conducted on 42, 612 participants in a Canadian study [80], aged 20–64 years, in 2008, found that a quarter of those that watched TV for 21 hours or more a week were obese. Frequent computer users of 11 hours or more per week were also more at risk of obesity than those that used computers for less than 5 hours a week. Of the different types of sedentary behaviour TV watching seems to be the behaviour consistently associated with obesity, even when accounting for palatable foods that might be consumed while watching [81].

Social factors

As previously stated, the Western diet of highly palatable food is considered to form a culture and environment that is obesogenic [41]. The availability of food, palatability of food such as calorie dense foods and the portion sizes are also contributory factors. Deprivation, socioeconomic status and the way that society constructs views on obesity can also contribute to obesity. Negative attitudes or stereotyping obese people, contrary to helping them to lose weight has the opposite effect. Weight stigma occurs when people are blamed for their illness as a result of being immoral or lazy and that their weight is within their personal control because they are eating too much and exercising too little [82]. The mantra of eat less and move more is prevalent in popular media, but this may in fact perpetuate obesity in a vicious cycle. Weight stigma may in fact increase weight gain through eating behaviour and, because it may act as a stressor, with the associative physiological changes, and a change in affect that may increase eating behaviour [83].

Summary

Obesity can therefore be seen as a complex disorder that cannot be explained simply by calories in being less than calories out, but is a multifaceted condition that is affected by genes, psychological factors and social factors.

Autoimmune diseases

Inflammation is a primary mechanism of many modern-day health conditions such as obesity, Type 2 diabetes and also depression. Inflammation is a function of the immune system which defends the body against invaders. Autoimmune conditions occur when the immune system treats cells in the body as invaders (or non-self) and attacks them. In this section of the chapter, the biopsychosocial approach will be taken to consider the factors that might contribute to the onset of autoimmune conditions. In understanding the mechanisms and the psychosocial factors that contribute to autoimmune system disorders health psychologists will be able to consider potential interventions to improve quality of life.

The immune system

The immune system is a complex system that is made up of tissues, organs and cells that protect the body from invaders and remove cells that are damaged. The immune system consists of a number of organs and structures that are situated around the body:

- The lymphatic system, which includes lymphatic vessels that carry lymph around the body including the meninges in the brain and clusters of lymph nodes in the neck, armpits, groin and abdomen.
- Thymus gland – triangular shaped gland that sits behind the sternum, which is large in childhood and gets smaller after puberty. Also produces a hormone which is involved in T-cell maturation and differentiation.
- Bone marrow (produces white blood cells).
- Spleen (filters blood and creates new blood cells).

The immune system offers a team approach [84] and consists of two main systems, and simply put these are the innate system and the adaptive system:

- The innate system is non-specific and so it protects against a range of threats.
- The adaptive is specific and is involved in specific immunity and resistance against one specific invader.

Simplified overview of the innate system

Innate or natural immunity consists of the skin, the natural anti-microbial substances that are found in secretions from epithelial membranes that line the respiratory, digestive and genitourinary tracts. It also consists of the surveillance of invaders from white blood cells and the inflammatory response, for example:

Inflammation

- Inflammation occurs at the site of an injury or infection, which is the collection of white blood cells called neutrophils and macrophages. Their job is to release toxins to engulf (phagocytose) any invaders.
- Macrophages also produce cytokines that have a range of effects including fever and inflammation to promote healing.

Simplified overview of the specific system

Lymphocytes make up about 20–30 per cent of the white blood cells. These are natural killer (NK) cells, B – lymphocytes (produced in bone marrow) and produce antibodies that bind to antigens and T-lymphocytes (made in bone marrow and matured by hormones in the Thymus). T-cells are only programmed to recognize one type of antigen and this means that if a t-cell has been manufactured for chicken pox then it will not react to a different infection such as measles. There are also a number of other cells that exist and support these cells:

- Cytotoxic T-cells – kill infected cells.
- Helper T-cells – these are very important as they support cytotoxic T-cells and also macrophages help in the manufacture of B-cells.
- Suppressor T-cells that are the brakes for the T and B cells and that could play a role in prevention of the development of autoimmunity.
- Memory T-cells that survive after the threat and can respond quickly if re-infected.

The first time that there is exposure to an infection there is a delayed rise in antibodies which tends to peak 1–2 weeks' post infection. This is because it takes time to activate the T-cells. Any subsequent exposure is likely to be much more powerful [49].

Immunity can either be acquired actively or artificially. An active immunity is when the body responds to the antigen and produces it's own antibodies. This could come from having the disease or being infected, but without displaying symptoms or through the administration of vaccines that are either dead or live-weakened pathogens, which stimulate immunity but not the disease. Passive, naturally acquired immunity can also pass from mother to child through the umbilical cord and breast milk.

However, sometimes things can go awry and some people can have an inappropriate hypersensitive immune response, which can result in anaphylaxis, such as in an allergy to peanuts or can be cytotoxic, when the body can direct an antibody reaction against the self and destroy tissue, which is what happens in auto-immune conditions.

Autoimmune conditions seem to have increased in recent years and there are now over 80 different identified autoimmune diseases (immunology.org) such as Type 1 diabetes, multiple sclerosis, rheumatoid arthritis, Crohn's disease, Systemic Lupus Erythematosus (SLE), Hashimoto's thyroiditis to name a few.

Previous research has considered that autoimmune diseases are the result of an interaction between multiple genetic factors and environmental factors[47]. This then suggests that there is a need for a biopsychosocial approach to understanding these conditions.

Genes

There is some evidence that some autoimmune conditions may be hereditary and may be explained in some part by genes [85], although the exact mechanism may not yet be fully understood.

Gender

Autoimmune conditions tend to be more common in females. This may be due to the fact that women tend to have greater immune reactivity than men, which protects them against infections. However, this greater reactivity may be influenced by sex hormones (oestrogen) and may also be the reason why they are more prone to autoimmune diseases [86].

Psychological factors

Psychological factors that may affect the onset of autoimmune conditions are health behaviours that people may engage in, for example smoking, which has been associated with multiple scler-osis [87]. Another behavioural factor that has been considered is dietary behaviour. The high fat, high salt, high sugar diets that are associated with western diets are linked with obesity and metainflammation, which has also been associated with autoimmune disease [88]. Sugar has also been found to increase inflammation, particularly free sugar that is added to cereal, tea and coffee and sugar-sweetened beverages [89]. Further evidence can be gained by studies that look at low calorie diets that are rich in fruits, vegetables and fish and have been found to act on proinfmammatory molecules and assist in restoring gut microbiota that can then decrease inflammation [90]. Therefore, a diet which could be considered both a behaviour (psychological) factor and also an environmental (social) factor through availability and societal norms, and may interrelate with genetic factors to increase the risk of developing autoimmune conditions and exacerbate existing conditions.

Social factors

As well as the effects of deprivation on food availability and diets there may be a disproportionate risk from the environments in which we live. Those living in poorer neighbourhoods with high levels of deprivation may be more at risk of developing autoimmune conditions. The amount of air pollution and emissions have also been associated with increased risk of autoimmune rheumatic diseases. In a Canadian urban study, where other risk factors were adjusted for, researchers found that fine particulate pollution increased the risk of systemic autoimmune rheumatic diseases [91]. Other researchers have suggested that the environment may have an effect on the way that genes express themselves and change them through exposure to environmental factors such as smoking, exposure to sunlight and nutrition, which could alter DNA [92], thus demonstrating the complexity of the interactions between biopsychosocial factors.

So what can we conclude?

There are many different types of autoimmune conditions that seem to be linked with the way that we live and the way that we interact with our environments. Therefore, it is generally considered that the development of an autoimmune disease is linked to having a genetic pre-disposition coupled with exposure to environmental factors that affect the immune system [93], such as diet, air pollution, smoking and also individual difference factors such as gender.

Chapter summary

In this chapter we have considered a key model in health psychology, which is the biopsychosocial approach. This approach acknowledges that health is complex and cannot be explained simply by biology alone, but by a complex interrelationship between biological factors such as genes, cells and organs and also psychological factors such as lifestyle (e.g. health behaviours, personality, affect) and the social environments in which we live. We have demonstrated this link by considering the aetiology of some common chronic conditions, pain, Type 2 diabetes, obesity and autoimmune conditions. Why is it important to understand the complexity of the relationships between interacting factors? One of the key factors in health psychology is to gain an understanding of factors that may predict ill health so that we can target interventions to promote health appropriately. It is also important to understand the complexity of conditions and the contribution health psychology can make to the multidisciplinary team in improving patient outcomes.

References

[1] Beecher, H. K. (1946). Pain in men wounded in battle. *Annals of Surgery*, *123*(1), 96–105. PMID: 17858731

[2] Turk, D. C., & Wilson, H. D. (2013). *Chronic pain*. In A. M. Nezu, C. M. Nezu, P. A. Geller, & I. B. Weiner (Eds.), *Handbook of Psychology: Health Psychology* (pp. 292–317). John Wiley & Sons.

[3] McCaffery, M. MS, RN, FAAN & Pasero, C., MS, RN (1999). Teaching patients to use a numerical pain-rating scale, *The American Journal of Nursing*, *99*(12),12–22.

[4] Calvino, B., & Grilo, R. M. (2006). Central pain control. *Joint Bone Spine*, *73*(1),10–16. DOI:10.1016/j.jbspin.2004.11.006

[5] Tracey, I. (2008). Imaging pain. *British Journal of Anaesthesia*, *101*(1), 32–39. DOI: 10.1093/bja/aen102

[6]   Melzack, R., & Wall, P. D. (1965). Pain mechanisms: A new theory. *Science, 150,* 971–979. DOI: 10.1126/science.150.3699.971

[7]   Melzack, R. & Katz, J. (2013). Pain. WIREs *Cognitve Science, 4,* 1–15. DOI:10.1002/wcs.1201

[8]   McGowan, L. P. A., Clark-Carter, D. D., & Pitts, M. K. (1998). Chronic pelvic pain: A meta-analytic review, *Psychology & Health, 13*(5), 937–951. DOI: 10.1080/08870449808407441

[9]   Kraljevic,.S, Banozic, A., Maric, A., Cosic, A., Sapunar, D., & Puljak, L. (2012). Parents' pain catastrophizing is related to pain catastrophizing of their adult children. *International Journal of Behavioral Medicine, 19*(1), 115–119. DOI:10.1007/s12529-011-9151-z

[10]   Chan, S. C. C., Chan, C. C. H., Kwan, A. s. K., Ting K-H, Chui, T-Y. (2012). Orienting attention modulates pain perception: An ERP study, *PLoS One.* 7(6), e40215. 10.1371/journal.pone.0040215

[11]   Leung, L. (2012). Pain catastrophizing: an updated review. *Indian Journal of Psychological Medicine, 34*(30), 204–217. DOI: 10.4103/0253-7176.106012

[12]   Gracely, R. H., Geisser, M. E., Giesecke, T., Grant, M. A. B., Petzke, F., Williams, D. A.. & Clauw, D. J. (2004). Pain catastrophizing and neural responses to pain among persons with fibromyalgia, *Brain, 127*(4), 835–843. DOI:10.1093/brain/awh098

[13]   Jensen, M. P., Turner, J. A., Romano, J. M., & Lawler, B. K. (1994). Relationship of pain-specific beliefs to chronic pain adjustment. *Pain,57*(3),301–309.DOI:10.1016/0304-3959(94)90005-1

[14]   Keefe, F. J., Lefebvre, J. C., Egert, J. R., Affleck, G., Sullivan, M. J., & Caldwell, D. S. (2000). The relationship of gender to pain, pain behavior, and disability in osteoarthritis patients: the role of catastrophizing. *Pain, 87*(3), 325–334. DOI:10.1016/s0304-3959(00)00296-7

[15]   Sullivan, M. J., Thorn, B., Haythonthwaite, J. A., Keefe, F., Martin, M., Bradley, L. A., Lefbvre, J. C. (2001). Theoretical perspectives on the relation between catastrophising and pain, *The Clinical Journal of Pain, 17,* 52–64. DOI:10.1097/00002508-200103000-00008

[16]   Bowers, K. S. (1968). Pain, anxiety, and perceived control. *Journal of Consulting and Clinical Psychology, 32*(5, Pt.1), 596–602. DOI:10.1037/h0026280

[17]   Vallerand, A. H., Crawley, J., Pieper, B., Templin, T. N. The perceived control over pain construct and functional status. *Pain Medicine, 17*(4), 692–703. DOI:10.1111/pme.12924

[18] Lindstedt, F., Berrebi, J., Greayer, E. et al. (2011). Conditioned pain modulation is associated with common polymorphisms in the serotonin transporter gene. *PLoS One, 6*(3), e18252. DOI:10.1371/journal.pone.0018252.

[19] Majeed, M. H., Ali, A. A., Sudak, D. M. (2019). Psychotherapeutic interventions for chronic pain: Evidence, rationale, and advantages. *International Journal of Psychiatry and Medicine, 54*(2), 140–149. DOI:10.1177/0091217418791447

[20] Bailey, K. M., Carelton, R. N., Vlaeyen, J. W., Asmundson, G. J. G. (2010). Treatments addressing pain-related fear and anxiety in patient with chronic musculoskeletal pain: a preliminary review. *Cognitive Behavioural Therapy, 39*, 46–63. DOI:10.1080/16506070902980711

[21] McCraken, L. M., Turk, D.C. (2002). Behavioral and cognitive-behavioral treatment for chronic pain. *Spine, 27*, 2564–2573. DOI:10.1097/00007632-200211150-00033

[22] Hayes, S. C., Strosahl, K., Wilson, K. G. (1999). *Acceptance and Commitment Therapy: An Experiential Approach to Behavior Change.* New York: Guilford.

[23] Wetheree, J. L., Afari, N., Rutledge, T., Sorell, J. T., Stoddard, J. A., Petkus, A. J., Solomon, B. C., Lehman, D. H., Liu, L., Lang, A. J. & Atkinson, J. H. (2011). A randomised controlled trial of acceptance and commitment therapy and cognitive-behavioral therapy for chronic pain. *152*, 2098–2107. DOI:10.1016/j.pain.2011.05.016

[24] Holden, R. & Holden, J. (2013). Music: A better alternative than pain? *British Journal of General Practice, 63*(615), 536. DOI: 10.3399/bjgp13X673748

[25] Cepeda, M. S., Carr, D. B., Lau, J., & Alvarez, H. (2006). Music for pain relief. *Cochrane Database Systematic Review, 2*, CD004843. DOI: 10.1002/14651858.

[26] Al-Goblan, A. S. M., Al-Alfi, M. A. & Khan, M. Z. (2014). Mechanisms linking diabetes mellitus and obesity. *Diabetes, Metabolic Syndrome and Obesity: Targets and Therapy, 7*, 587–591. DOI: 10.2147/DMSO.S67400

[27] Taylor, R. & Holman, R. R. (2015). Normal weight individuals who develop Type 2 diabetes: the personal fat threshold. *Clinical Science, 128*(7), 405–410. DOI:10.1042/CS20140553

[28] Prasad, R. B . & Groop, L. (2015). Genetics of Type 2 Diabetes-Pitfalls and Possibilities, *6*(1), 87–123. DOI: 10.3390/genes6010087

[29] Ellulu, M. S., Patimah, I., Khaza'ai, H., Rahmat, A., & Abed, Y. (2017). Obesity and inflammation: the linking mechanism and

the complications. *Archives of medical science: AMS*, *13*(4), 851–863. DOI: 10.5114/aoms.2016.58928

[30]   Sears, S. &   Perry, M. (2015). The role of fatty acids in insulin resistance. *Lipids in Health and Disease*, *14*, 121. DOI: 10.1186/s12944-015-0123-1

[31]   Paulweber, B., Valensi, P., Lindström, J., et al. (2010). A European evidence-based guideline for the prevention of type 2 diabetes. *Hormone and Metabolic Research*, *42*, Suppl 1, S3-S36. DOI:10.1055/s-0029-1240928

[32]   Bellou, V., Belbasis, L., Tzoulaki, I., Evangelou, E. (2018). Risk factors for type 2 diabetes mellitus: An exposure-wide umbrella review of metaanalyses. *PLoS ONE 13*(3): e0194127. Doi:10.1371/journal.pone.0194127

[33]   Aune, D., Ursin, G.,Veierød, M. B. (2009). Meat consumption and the risk of type 2 diabetes: a systematic review and meta-analysis of cohort studies. *Diabetologia*, *52*, 2277–2287. DOI:10.1007/s00125-009-1481-x PMID: 19662376 24.

[34]   Imamura, F., O'Connor, L., Ye, Z., Mursu, J., Hayashino, Y., Bhupathiraju, S. N. et al. (2015). Consumption of sugar sweetened beverages, artificially sweetened beverages, and fruit juice and incidence of type 2 diabetes: systematic review, meta-analysis, and estimation of population attributable fraction. *BMJ*, *351*, h3576. DOI:10.1136/bmj. h3576 PMID: 26199070 25.

[35]   Mabusela, M. S., Mashinya, F., & Moraba, M. M. (2015). Effect mechanisms of physical activity on the improvement of insulin sensitivity and glucose metabolism in type 2 diabetes – reverse mechanism approach; a review: health and physical activity. *African Journal for Physical Health Education, Recreation and Dance*, *1*(1),15.

[36]   Friedman, H. S., Tucker, J S., Schwartz, J. E. et al. (1995). Childhood conscientiousness and longevity: health behaviors and cause of death. *Journal of Personality and Social Psychology*, *68*(4), 696–703. DOI:10.1037//0022-3514.68.4.696

[37]   Cheng, H., Treglown, L., Montgomery, S., Furnham, A. (2015). Associations between familial factor, trait conscientiousness, gender and the occurrence of Type 2 diabetes in adulthood: Evidence from a British cohort. *PLoS ONE*, *10*(5), e0122701. DOI:10.1371/journal.pone.0122701

[38]   Jokela, M., Elovainio, M., Nyberg, S. T., Tabák, A. G., Hintsa, T., Batty, G. D., et al. (2014). Personality and risk of *diabetes* in adults: Pooled analysis of 5 cohort studies. *Health Psychology*, *33*, 1618–1621. DOI 10.1037/hea0000003 23957901

[39] Bandura, A. (1977). *Social Learning Theory.* Englewood Cliffs, NJ: Prentice Hall.

[40] Henson, J., Dunstan, D. W., Davies, M. J., & Yates, T. (2016). Sedentary behaviour as a new behavioural target in the prevention and treatment of Type 2 diabetes. *Diabetes Metabolism Research and Reviews, 32*(Supp 1), 213–220. DOI: 10.1002/dmrr.2759

[41] Johnson, F., & Wardle, J. (2014). Variety, palatability, and obesity. *Advances in Nutrition (Bethesda, Md.), 5*(6), 851–859. DOI:10.3945/an.114.007120

[42] Ball, K., & Crawford, D. (2005). Socioeconomic status and weight change in adults: a review. *Social Science and Medicine, 60*(9), 1987–2010. DOI:10.1016/j.socscimed.2004.08.056

[43] Adam, T. C. & Epel, E. S. (2007). Stress, eating and the reward system. *Physiology and Behaviour, 91,* 449–458. DOI:10.1016/j.physbeh.2007.04.011

[44] Sominsky, L. & Spencer, S. J. (2014). Eating behaviour and stress: a pathway to obesity. *Frontiers in Psychology, 5,* 434. DOI 10.3389/fpsyg.2014.00434

[45] Chan, J. C., Malik, V., Jia, W. et al. (2009). Diabetes in Asia: epidemiology, risk factors, and pathophysiology. *JAMA, 30*(20), 2129–2140. DOI: 10.1001/jama.2009.726

[46] Rhee, E-J. (2015). Diabetes in Asians. *Endocrinology and Meatbolism, 30*(3), 263–269. DOI: 10.3803/EnM.2015.30.3.263

[47] Cho, Y. S., Chen, C. H., Hu, C., Long, J., Ong, R. T., Sim, X., Takeuchi, F., Wu, Y., Go, M. J., Yamauchi, T., Chang, Y. C., Kwak, S. H., Ma, R. C., Yamamoto, K., Adair, L. S., Aung, T., Cai, Q., Chang, L. C., Chen, Y. T., Gao, Y., et al. (2011). Meta-analysis of genome-wide association studies identifies eight new loci for type 2 diabetes in east Asians. *Nature Genetics, 44*(1), 67–72. DOI:10.1038/ng.1019

[48] Thibodeau, G. A., & Patton, K. T. (2008). *Structure & Function of the Body.* St. Louis, MI: Mosby/Elsevier.

[49] Waugh, A., & Grant, A. (2013). Ross and Wilson: Anatomy and *Physiology in Health and Illness* (12th edition). Churchill Livingstone.

[50] *Health Survey for England 2017* [NS]. National statistics. Publication Date: 4 Dec 2018 https://digital.nhs.uk/data-and-information/publications/statistical/health-survey-for-england/2017 [accessed 4.7.2020)

[51] Sarwer, D. B., & Grilo, C. M. (2020). Obesity: Psychosocial and behavioral aspects of a modern epidemic: Introduction to the

special issue. *American Psychologist*, 75(2), 135–138. DOI:10.1037/amp0000610

[52]   Yusuf, S., Hawken, S., Ounpuu, S., Bautista, L., Franzosi, M. G., Commerford, P., Lang, C. C., Rumboldt, Z., Onen, C. L., Lisheng, L., Tanomsup, S., Wangai, P., Razak, F., Sharma, A. M., & Anand, S. S. (2005). Obesity and the risk of myocardial infarction in 27,000 participants from 52 countries: a case-control study. *Lancet*, 366, 1640–1649. DOI 10.1016/S0140-6736(05)67663–5

[53]   Després, J-P. (2012). Body fat distribution and risk of cardio-vascular disease. An update. *Circulation*, 126(10), 1301–1313. DOI:10.1161/CIRCULATIONAHA.111.067264

[54]   Stunkard, A. J., Sørensen, T. I., Hanis, C., Teasdale, T. W., Chakraborty, R., Schull, W. J., Schulsinger, F. (1986) *An Adoption Study of Human Obesit, New England Journal of Medicine*, 314(4), 193–198. DOI: 10.1056/NEJM198601233140401

[55]   Thaker, V. V. (2017). Genetic and epigenetic causes of obesity, *Adolescent Medicine State of the Art Reviews*, 28(2), 379–405. PMID: 30416642

[56]   Stroebe, W., Papies, E. K., & Aarts, H. (2008). From homeostatic to hedonic theories of eating: Self-regulatory failure in food-rich environments. *Applied Psychology: An International Review*, 57(Suppl 1), 172–193. DOI: 10.1111/j.1464-0597.2008.00360.x

[57]   Adamska-Patruno, E., Ostrowska, L., Goscik, J. *et al.* (2018). The relationship between the leptin/ghrelin ratio and meals with various macronutrient contents in men with different nutritional status: a randomized crossover study. *Nutrition* Journal, 17, 118. DOI:10.1186/s12937-018-0427

[58]   Myers, M. G., Jr, Leibel, R. L., Seeley, R. J., & Schwartz, M. W. (2010). Obesity and leptin resistance: distinguishing cause from effect. *Trends in Endocrinology and Metabolism: TEM*, 21(11), 643–651. DOI:10.1016/j.tem.2010.08.002

[59]   Halaas, J. L., Gajiwala, K. S., Maffei, M., Cohen, S. L., Chait, B. T., Rabinowitz, D., Lallon, R. L., Burley, S. K., Friedman, J. M. (1995) Weight-reducing effects of the plasma protein encoded by the obese gene. *Science*, 269, 543–546. DOI:10.1126/science.7624777

[60]   Klok, M. D., Jakobsdottir, S., & Drent, M. L. (2007). The role of leptin and ghrelin in the regulation of food intake and body weight in humans: a review. *Obesity Review*, 8, 21–34. DOI:10.1111/j.1467-789X.2006.00270.x

[61]   Korek, E., Krauss, H., Gibas-Dorna, M., Kupsz, J., Piarek, M., & Piatek, J. (2013) Fasting and postprandial levels of ghrelin,

leptin and insulin in lean, obese and anorexic subjects. *Prz Gastroenterologiczny, 8,* 383–389.

[62] Kuo, L., Kitlinska, J., Tilan, J. *et al.* (2007). Neuropeptide Y acts directly in the periphery on fat tissue and mediates stress-induced obesity and metabolic syndrome. *Natural Medicine, 13,* 803–811. DOI:10.1038/nm1611

[63] Beck, B. (2006). Neuropeptide Y in normal eating and in genetic and dietary-induced obesity. *Philosophical transactions of the Royal Society of London. Series B, Biological sciences, 361*(1471), 1159–1185. DOI:10.1098/rstb.2006.1855

[64] Schachter, S. (1971). Some extraordinary facts about obese humans and rats, *American Psychologist, 26,* 129–144.

[65] Schachter, S., & Rodin, J. (1974). *Obese Humans and Rats.* Lawrence Erlbaum.

[66] Stoeckel, L. E., Weller, R. E., Cook, E. W. (3rd), Twieg, D. B., Knowlton, R. C. & Cok, J. E. (2008). Widespread reward-system activation in obese women in response to pictures of high-calorie foods. *Neuroimage, 41*(2), 636–647. DOI:10.1016/j.neuroimage.2008.02.031

[67] Dimitroppoulos, A. (2012). Greater corticolimbic activation to high-calorie food cues after eating in obese vs. normal-weight adults. *Appetite, 58*(1), 3030–3312. DOI: 10.1016/j.appet.2011.10.014

[68] Van den Akker, K., Schyns, G., & Jansen, A. (2018). Learned overeating: applying principles of pavlovian conditioning to explain and treat overeating. *Current Addiction Reports, 5,* 223–231. doi:10.1007/s40429-018-0207-x

[69] Bouton, M. E. (2011). Learning and the persistence of appetite: Extinction and the motivation to eat and overeat. *Physiology and Behaviour, 3,* 51–58. DOI:S0031-9384(10)00425-7 [pii]10.1016/j.physbeh.2010.11.025

[70] Astur, R. S., Carew, A. W., Deaton, B. E. (2014). Conditioned place preferences in humans using virtual reality. *Behavioural Brain Research, 267,* 173–177. DOI:10.1016/j.bbr.2014.03.018.

[71] Bongers, P., van den Akker, K., Havermans, R., & Jansen, A. (2015). Emotional eating and Pavlovian learning: does negative mood facilitate appetitive conditioning? *Appetite, 89,* 226–236. DOI: 10.1016/j.appet.2015.02.018

[72] Oliver, G. & Wardle, J. (1999). Perceived effects of stress on food choice. *Physiogy and Behavior, 66,* 511–515. DOI:10.1016/s0031-9384(98)00322-9

[73]   Kandiah, J., Yake, M. & Willett, H. (2008). Effects of stress on eating practices among adults. *Family and Consumer Sciences, 37*, 27–38. DOI: 10.1177/1077727X08322148

[74]   Cardi, V., Leppanen, J. & Treasure, J. (2015). The effects of negative and positive mood induction on eating behaviour: A meta-analysis of laboratory studies in the healthy population and eating and weight disorders. *Neuroscience and Biobehavioral Reviews, 57*, 299–309. DOI: 10.1016/j.neubiorev.2015.08.011

[75]   O'Connor, D. B., Jones, F., Conner, M., McMillan, B., & Ferguson, E. (2008). Effects of daily hassles and eating style on eating behavior. *Health Psychology, 27*(1, Suppl), S20–S31. DOI:10.1037/0278-6133.27.1.S20

[76]   Jones, F., O'Connor, D. B., Conner, M., McMillan, B., & Ferguson, E. (2007). Impact of daily mood, work hours, and iso-strain variables on self-reported health behaviors. *Journal of Applied Psychology, 92*(6), 1731–1740. DOI:10.1037/0021-9010.92.6.1731

[77]   Zenk, S. N., Horoi, I., McDonald, A., Corte, C., Riley, B., Odoms-Young, A. M. (2014). Ecological momentary assessment of environmental and personal factors and snack food intake in African American women. *Appetite, 83*, 333–341. DOI:10.1016/j.appet.2014.09.008

[78]   Telford, R. D. (2007). Low physical activity and obesity: causes of chronic disease or simply predictors? *Medicine and Science in Sports and Exercise, 39*(8), 1233–1240. DOI: 10.1249/mss.0b013e31806215b7.

[79]   Bullock, V. E., Griffiths, P, Sherar, L. B., & Clemes, S. A. (2017). Sitting time and obesity in a sample of adults from Europe and the USA. *Annals of Human Biology, 44*(3), 230–236. DOI: 10.1080/03014460.2016.1232749.

[80]   Shileds, M., & Tremblay, M. S. (2008). Sedentary behaviour and obesity. *Heath Reports, 19*(2), 19–30. PMID: 18642516

[81]   Heinonen, I., Helajärvi, H., Pahkala, K. et al. (2013). Sedentary behaviours and obesity in adults: the Cardiovascular Risk in Young Finns Study. *BMJ Open,* 3:e002901. DOI10.1136/bmjopen-2013- 002901

[82]   DeJong, W. (1993). Obesity as a characterological stigma: the issue of responsibility and judgments of task performance. *Psychologial Reports, 73*(3), Pt 1, 963–970. DOI: 10.2466/pr0.1993.73.3.963.

[83]   Toniyama, A. J. (2014). Weight stigma is stressful. A review of evidence for the Cyclic Obesity/Weight-Based stigma model. *Appetite, 82*, 8–15. DOI: 10.1016/j.appet.2014.06.108

[84] Sompayrac, L. (2019). *How the Immune System Works* (6th Ed.). Hoboken, NJ: Wiley Blackwell.

[85] Leslie, R., & Hawa, M. (1994). Twin studies in auto-immune disease. *Acta Geneticae Medicae Et Gemellogiae: Twin Research, 43*(1–2), 71–81. DOI: 10.1017/S000156600000297X

[86] Zandman-Goddard, G., Peeva, E., & Shoenfield, Y. (2007). Gender and austoimmunity. *Autoimmunity Reviews, 6*(6), 366–372. DOI: 10.1016/j.autrev.2006.10.001

[87] Wingerchuk, D. M. (2012). Smoking: effects on multiple sclerosis susceptibility and disease progression. Therapeutic advances in neurological disorders, 5(1), 13–22. DOI: 10.1177/1756285 611425694

[88] Manzel, A., Muller, D. N., Hafler, D. A., Erdman, S. E., Linker, R. A., & Kleinewietfeld, M. (2014). Role of "Western diet" in inflammatory autoimmune diseases. *Current Allergy and Asthma Reports, 14*(1), 404. DOI: 10.1007/s11882-013-0404-6

[89] O'Connor, L., Imamura, F., Brage, S., Griffin, S. J., Wareham, N. J. & Forotti, N. G. (2018). Intakes and sources of dietary sugars and their association with metabolic and inflammatory markers. *Clinical Nutrition, 37*(4), 1313–1322. DOI: 10.1016/ j.clinu.2017.05.030

[90] DeFillipo, C., RAmazzoth, M., Poulet, J. B., Massart, S., Collini, S., Pieracani, G. & Lionetti, P. (2010). Impact of diet in shaping gut microbiota revealed by a comparative study in children from Europe and rural Africa. *Proceedings of the National Academy of Sciences of the USA, 107*(33), 14691–13696. DOI:10.1073/ pnas.1005963107.

[91] Bernatsky, S., Smargiassi, A., Johnson, M., Kaplan, G. G., Barnabe, C., Svenson, L., Brand, A., Bertazzon, S., Hudson, M., Clarke, A. E., Fortin, P. R., Edworthy, S., Bélisle, P., & Joseph, L. (2015). Fine particulate air pollution, nitrogen dioxide, and systemic autoimmune rheumatic disease in Calgary, Alberta. *Environmental Eesearch, 140*, 474–478. DOI:10.1016/j.envres.2015.05.007

[92] Ngo, S. T., Steyn, F. J., McCombe, P. A. (2014). Gender differences in autoimmune disease. *Frontiers in Neuroendocrinology, 35*(3), 347–369. DOI:10.1016/j.yfrne.2014.04.004

[93] Wang, L., Wang, F. S., Gershwin, M. E. (2015). Human autoimmune disease: a comprehensive update. Journal of Internal Medicine, 278(4), 369–395. DOI: 10.1111/joim.12395

3 Attitudes, beliefs and behaviour

Models of health behaviour change

Contents

Introduction

The ultimate question health psychologists ask is 'How can we get an individual to change their health behaviour?' Yet, before we can change a health behaviour we must first understand the reasons why an individual may choose to engage or not engage in the health behaviour in question. For example, why do some people choose to smoke even though we have known for over 50 years that it is linked to cancer and premature death?

Health psychologists draw on a wide range of evidence-based theoretical models to help us understand psychological predictors that influence a decision to engage or not engage with a health behaviour. These theories enable us to understand individual health beliefs and motivation in relation to a given behaviour and, consequently, enable us to intervene and support individuals to make positive behaviour change. In short, theoretical frameworks outline factors which should be considered when trying to change behaviour. A theory may explain:

- factors influencing a phenomenon (e.g. why some people smoke);
- the relationship between these factors (e.g. whether this decision is related to levels of knowledge and risk perceptions, attitudes, beliefs about smoking, influence of other people (social norms) and so on;
- the conditions in which these relationships occur (e.g. do smoking rates fall when there is high media attention highlighting risk?).

This chapter aims to describe the components of key theoretical models that have been used and developed to explain why people engage in health-risk, health-protective or health-enhancing behaviours. There are two main groups of models which will be considered, commonly referred to as (1) 'social cognition models' and (2) 'stage models'. Social cognition models, refer to a group of similar models which argue that cognitive and affective factors (beliefs and attitudes) are the proximal determinants of behaviour. We will look at some of these theories in detail; Social Cognitive Theory (SCT), Health Belief Model (HBM), Protection Motivation Theory (PMT), Theory of Reasoned Action (TRA) /Planned Behaviour (TPB). Stage models, such as the Transtheoretical Model (TTM) use similar concepts, although these are organised in a different way, namely arguing that behaviour change involves movement through a sequence of stages. Each model will be described, and then applied to a range of health behaviours and then finally, evaluated in light of the evidence of its effectiveness.

This chapter will end with a case study of a health psychologist, who works in a real life setting within smoking cessation, looking at how these theories help guide her practice.

Introduction to social cognition models

Historically, we were viewed as passive agents to illness with treatment solely in the hands of the healthcare professionals. However, health psychology operates under the assumption that the leading causes of mortality and morbidity are attributable to our individual lifestyle behaviour, which is modifiable. So, instead of being passive to illness there is a belief that we as individuals can actively change our own health behaviour through the uptake of health enhancing behaviours (e.g. eating healthily, keeping physically active) and avoiding risky health behaviours (e.g. smoking). If we can accept these assumptions then we are saying that we can change an individual's health behaviour i.e. someone who smokes can quit smoking and in turn we can intervene to help someone quit smoking.

Health behaviour is extremely complex. How we view our health is not a shared concept, influenced by our cultural background, our age, gender and the communities in which we reside [1]. As such there is not one universal way to determine why someone is healthy and someone is not. We therefore need to identify factors that are outside the individual's control which could help us understand the mechanisms of health behaviour change and maintenance. In health psychology, and more specifically the area of health behaviour change, we use a group of theories called Social Cognition Models (SCM) to achieve this. Traditionally it was assumed that the largest predictors of our health behaviour remain dependent on our individual differences (age, gender) and social factors (where someone lives and others around them). However, social cognitive theorists argue that it is the cognitive (attitudes and beliefs) factors which have been shown to act as the most direct influence of behaviour. Thus, SCM incorporate all of these factors and in turn suggest that personal (e.g. age, gender, personality), cognitive (e.g. attitudes, beliefs) and environmental factors act as mutual causes of each other.

Social Cognitive Theory

We do what we see: the historical development of the Social Cognitive Theory

The influence of the social environment on our behaviour can be traced back to the 1930s through the work of Holt and Brown, who argued that animals imitate by watching others within their environment [2]. This work paved the way for theorists to understand the role of the social environment and imitation on human behaviour, a term later coined as 'social learning' [3].

Bandura, well regarded for his work on social learning, advanced this through the completion of a series of ground breaking studies, labelled the Bobo Doll Experiment [4, 5]. In these studies children were exposed to aggressive and non-aggressive role models acting differently towards a 'bobo doll' toy. The aggressive models hit the bobo doll shouting 'Hit him', 'Kick him' whilst children watched as they were waiting in a room purposefully full of toys that they were told they could not play with. The aggressive was ignored (punished) by the experimenter, with the non-aggressive model allowed to play with toys after (rewarded). The children who observed an adult role model acting aggressively to the 'bobo doll' imitated this behaviour (modelling). The findings also revealed that not only does learning take place when we are rewarded and punished, but we also learn from watching others being rewarded and punished, a concept Bandura defined as 'observational learning'. Thus, in Bandura's development of the Social Learning Theory, he argued that we do not learn new behaviours by just failing or succeeding (behavioural), but instead our behavioural action is dependent on observational learning and, consequently, our choice of whether we want to replicate the behaviour modelled [6]. In the 1980s Bandura relabeled Social Learning Theory as Social Cognitive Theory (SCT) [7].

Overview of the Social Cognitive Theory

At the core of SCT are three components: (1) '***Person***', their personality, their genetics and other personal factors that influence how the individual views the behaviour; (2) '***Behaviour***', what the person does and how this behaviour influences the person and environment, and finally; (3) '***Environment***', the social world around us and how this influences our behaviour and the person, for example, our friends and what they do, the places around us, social norms i.e. how we think other people and society would expect us to behave. These three components all interact and influence each other and together are referred to as 'reciprocal determinism' (Figure 3.1).

The SCT assumes that our behaviour (what we do) and what motivates us is governed by forethought, in other words we carefully consider what will be necessary or may happen in the future. With this in mind there are three core processes that influence our specific actions, which include (1) self-efficacy, (2) outcome expectancies and finally, (3) goals and socio-structural factors [7, 8] (see Figure 3.2). We will discuss these in full below.

Core process 1: outcome expectancies

An integral component of the SCT is outcome expectancies. These expectations relate to our estimate that our behaviour will lead to a perceived desirable or undesirable outcome. We are in effect weighing up the pros and cons of a behaviour and then

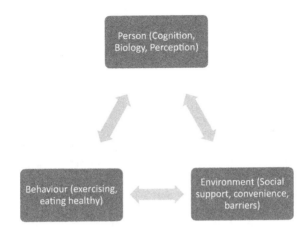

Figure 3.1 Reciprocal determinism in the SCT

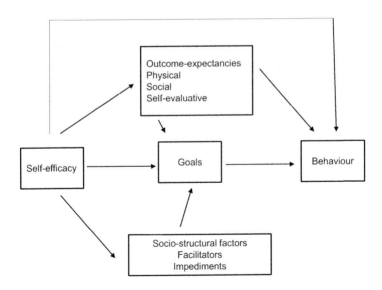

Figure 3.2 Social Cognitive Theory [8]

deciding if the outcome is worth it. If, for example, going for a jog several times a week, is expected to cause an improvement in health and wellbeing, the person will be more likely to go for a jog. If they expect to be too tired or embarrassed they will be less likely to do it.

Self-efficacy 'the belief that we are capable'

Self-efficacy beliefs are self-regulatory beliefs which determine a) whether actions will be initiated; b) how much effort will be expended; and finally, c) how long it will be sustained in the face of obstacles and failures. These beliefs collectively influence our ability to prepare for behavioural action and can enhance (or impede) our levels of motivation. These beliefs are shown to not only influence the challenges that people decide to meet, but also how high they set their goals, for example '*I intend to reduce my smoking*', Vs. '*I intend to quit smoking altogether*'. These are ultimately beliefs focused on success not failure.

Bandura [7] argues that self-efficacy beliefs are derived from four information sources, these include: performance attainments; vicarious experience; verbal persuasion; and our physiological state.

- **Performance accomplishments**
  - Our previous performance accomplishments are shown to be the most influential source of self-efficacy information 'I have done it before and can do it again'.
- **Vicarious experience**
  - We are what we see. According to Bandura [9], watching others (either succeeding or not) shapes our beliefs of our own ability.
- **Verbal persuasion**
  - We draw on others' encouragement and conviction to perform a task.
- **Physiology**
  - Physiological feedback is shown to impact on an individual's level of self-efficacy. For example, if an individual becomes anxious during a task this could

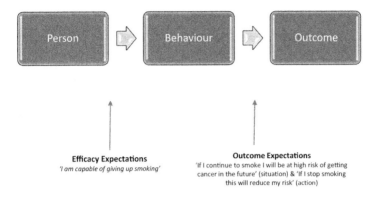

Figure 3.3 Illustration of relationship between expectancies, behaviour and outcome [6]

negatively hinder a person's belief that they can perform or maintain a given behaviour.

According to the SCT the likelihood of behaviour is dependent on both outcome and efficacy expectations. For example, if the behaviour is to give up smoking, the outcome is to have improved health, then we must believe that (1) we are capable of quitting smoking (efficacy expectations) and that (2) quitting smoking will benefit our health (outcome expectancies) (Figure 3.3).

Core process 2: socio-structural factors

These are the environmental factors which can influence our behaviour that may facilitate or impede our behaviour. If we were interested in children's nutrition as an example we might be interested in access to healthy food at schools and at home.

Core process 3: goal setting

Goal setting is also an important factor in performance and behavioural attainment. Those who set goals have been shown to exert more effort when compared to those who do not. The goals that we set are a direct influence of our capability (self-efficacy), socio-structural factors and outcome expectancies (Figure 3.2). Another important aspect is self-regulation, self-generated thoughts, feelings and actions which influence our goal attainment and motivation.

There are three psychological sub functions which are:

- **Self-monitoring**
    - When we deliberately pay attention to our performance, what we are doing and then evaluate the effects they produce on our health we use this information to set realistic goals and then evaluate our progress in achieving them. The more closely we look at our performance the more likely we are to set ourselves more progressive and realistic goals, which enables us to focus all of our efforts on achieving what we set out to do.
- **Self-reactive influences**
    - These are the incentives which influence our motivation to change our own behaviour. We are more likely to pursue an action if it produces positive self-reactions than those that do not. Put simply, 'why should I bother?'
    - The incentive could be health status, physical appearance, approval of others, economic gain, or other consequences [10]. What is more important is that the individual is incentivised. Let's take a final year university student as an example, the student may do lots of revision for their final exam because of their desire to get a high grade. We can see that the student is therefore motivated by their aspiration to achieve a high grade.
- **Judgemental sub function**
    - We observe and evaluate ourselves based on our own personal standards. These standards are not something we are born with, instead they are developed within our social environment, surrounded by those who are important to us, for example our family, friends, neighbours and wider community networks.
    - These standards, gained through a mechanism called 'social modelling', are formed from how important

people around us teach us, how they respond to our behaviour and how we, in turn, judge ourselves based on their reaction and standards [11].

- However, we must remember that others' standards are not always consistent, in other words, whilst some people might be good at telling us how to eat healthily we might know through our observations that they themselves do not eat healthily. Therefore, we try to develop our standards upon our reflections of multiple social influences.

Summary and future directions

The SCT has been applied to understand a wide range of health behaviours including: sexual risk behaviour [13], physical exercise [14], nutrition and weight control [15], addictive behaviour [16] and medication adherence [17]. Several reviews have suggested that interventions based on Social Cognitive Theory (SCT [38] can lead to small to moderate effects with strongest effects seen in physical activity [18; 19]. Consequently the SCT has been viewed as a useful framework for understanding and intervening in health behaviour [20]. Self-efficacy, or an individual's self-belief that they are capable of performing a behaviour, has been consistently shown to directly influence behaviour with self-efficacy viewed as the most important predictor of the SCT in explaining behaviour [21]. It is therefore not surprising that the development of self-efficacy has since gone on to be a core and integral component in many theories developed later.

Despite this, there have been some noteworthy limitations that should be considered. A common problem in evaluating the success of the SCT (although not unique to just the SCT) is assessing if this theory has been measured correctly. A common pitfall is that the questionnaires developed to measure the theory have not been able to measure the theory accurately. This is further complicated by misinterpretations of how the mechanisms of the SCT operate and link. Therefore, we need more clarity on how the variables operate and more consistent and concrete approaches to measurement.

Box 3.1 Case study: applying the SCT to understand exercise behaviour

Jon, is inactive and has high blood pressure. He has recently been told by his healthcare provider that increasing his levels of physical activity (e.g. attending a gym) would benefit his health.

According to the SCT before Jon could attend the gym he would need to:

- Believe that he could attend the gym despite the challenges, failures and obstacles that he may face (self-efficacy);
- Believe that going to the gym would benefit him (outcome expectancies);
- Have access to a gym, and be able to afford the membership to attend the gym (social-structural);
- Be incentivised to go to the gym (improve appearance, improve health and wellbeing), value others around him who attend a gym and pay attention to his behaviour (self-regulation);
- Have realistic goals to enable him to achieve his target behaviour (goals).

If we wanted to intervene using the SCT we might typically teach Jon skills that help start and maintain his level of physical activity (e.g. instruct how to use equipment, teach Jon how to monitor performance and set new goals), whilst also improving Jon's social and physical environment to facilitate rather than hinder the target behaviour (e.g. improving access to gyms, cost effective memberships, more suitable opening and closing times) [12].

Another issue, again not unique to the SCT is that a large number of studies are based on self-report data. There is a large variation between what people self-report when compared to more objective measures. For example, an individual who asked to self-report how many minutes exercise they have performed in the last week is more likely to overestimate their actual level of activity and this consequently overestimates the effect of the intervention. In fact, evidence suggests that studies that have been based on more objective data did not provide any support for the SCT [8]. Therefore, it could be argued that basing our evidence on self-report data alone is not a valid approach and instead we need to utilise more objective measures, so in the example of physical activity we could compare self-report data (e.g. 'how many times did you do 30 minutes of moderate to vigorous activity in the past week') to data received from accelerometers. There are of course some behaviours which are more difficult to objectively measure, for example, condom use, self-examination behaviours, therefore we need to consider these limitations when interpreting the results.

Health Belief Model

The Health Belief Model (HBM), developed in the 1950s is the oldest and most commonly used social cognition model used in public health and health promotion [22]. The HBM, similarly to the SCT, is a value-expectancy theory, based on the idea that our behaviour is the subjective value of the outcome 'Why should I do this?' and subjective expectation of achieving the outcome 'Am I able to do this'. However, unlike the SCT, HBM focuses on individual representations of health and determines that these are key influences in health behaviour.

The HBM suggests that the likelihood of taking behavioural action is dependent on three core beliefs: 1) perceived threat, 2) expectations and 3) cue to action.

Sophie has been invited to attend a cervical smear test, a routine screening test offered to all women aged 25 years and older as a method to detect abnormal cells on the cervix. Let's imagine we wanted to determine the likelihood of Sophie attending a cervical screening test. Presented in Figure 3.4, according to the HBM we would need to determine:

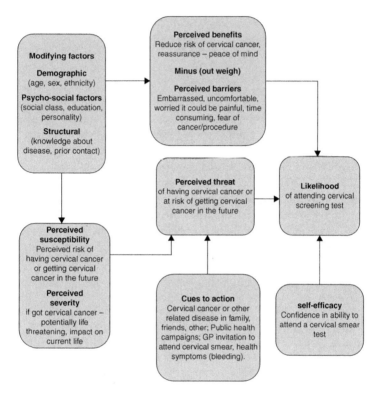

Figure 3.4 Belief Model applied to the likelihood to attend cervical screening [22]

1. **Perceived threat: Is the individual ready to act?**
   - She would need to feel that she is at **perceived threat** (of getting cervical cancer). This threat is based on the belief that she is susceptible (perceived susceptibility) to getting cervical cancer, for example. '*It is possible that I could get cervical cancer in the future*', and that this threat is severe (**perceived severity**), for example '*Getting cervical cancer would be very serious*'.
2. *Expectations: What is the estimation of the costs and benefits of the behaviour?*

- She would also need to believe that following a health recommendation (attending a cervical smear test) would be beneficial (**benefits**) in reducing the perceived threat, and that these benefits would outweigh any obstacles (**barriers**). For example, '*Having a smear test would reduce my risk of getting cervical cancer and give me reassurance, for me this would be more important that any embarrassment or inconvenience that I may feel*'.

3. **Cue to action: Is the individual aware of the potential consequences?**
   - Internal signals that something is wrong (pain, discomfort) or external stimuli such as health campaigns or screening programmes are necessary to set in motion the cognitions above.

Modifying factors are also said to influence the way we think. These include **demographics** (age, gender and ethnicity), **socio-psychological** (personality, social economic status, peer and group pressure) and **structural influences** (knowledge about disease, prior contact with disease) to influence her expectations and perceived threat.

The HBM was later revised in the 1980s [23] with the addition of **self-efficacy**, which was defined as the likelihood of behavioural action being dependent on her belief that she could successfully take a recommended health action (i.e., attend a cervical smear comfortably and with confidence).

If we go back to Sophie, according to the Health Belief Model interventions to encourage her to make and attend a cervical smear test would include:

- Inform Sophie of the **benefits** of attending a cervical smear test and try to reassure her of the **barriers.**
- Support Sophie to feel confident in her ability to attend a cervical smear test **(self-efficacy).**
- Make Sophie aware of her risk of cervical cancer and the severity of having cervical cancer, and inform her that the **perceived threat** would be reduced through attending a cervical smear test.

Summary and future directions

The HBM was first developed to understand the reasons why people attend or don't attend tuberculosis screening [22]. Since then, this model has been used to understand a wide range of health behaviours [22], which have included:

- uptake of healthcare services [24];
- screening attendance and behaviour [25–27];
- safe sex and condom use [28];
- smoking [29];
- patient adherence and self-care behaviours [30].

The HBM, viewed as pioneering in its time, has generated more research than any other theoretical model. However, the use of this model has been variable and frequently has failed to explain a large proportion of health related behaviour [31]. This may be due to the fact that the constructs within the model have not been adequately defined. Consequently, various methods of measurement have been used, which has subsequently led to diverse results. Therefore, it remains unclear if the poor predictive value is an artefact of poor measurement or definition or if this is because the HBM cannot adequately explain health behaviour [31].

In understanding the effectiveness of the HBM there remains a greater argument. That being said, can our behaviour be purely explained by our personal characteristics such as how old we are, and where we live? Can our behaviour be explained simply by the perceived barriers we see? If so, this would suggest that we always do what we should do, we are fully in control and consequently this is governed by our conscious perceptions of the world. However, academics have argued that behaviour cannot be this simply explained. Instead, could our behaviour be more effectively determined by our habits (regular activities in which we take part), emotions (how we feel e.g. fear, denial) and other unconscious and/or otherwise non-rational reactions to the external world. For example many smokers are in denial that smoking is risky for their health, this is an emotional response to external factors that dictate that smoking is unhealthy [31].

Protection Motivation Theory

Fear based appeals such as commercial advertisements that warn us of the effects of smoking, have been a common approach used in health promotion to change public attitudes and behaviour.

According to the Drive-fear Model (the oldest theory of fear appeals) we are motivated to achieve homeostasis, which is a physiological state of equilibrium [32]. These persuasive fear-based messages aim to induce an unpleasant emotional state. We then adopt a 'new' behaviour (e.g. stop smoking) to reduce this fear (e.g. getting lung cancer), this in turn restores homeostasis, which ultimately reinforces our modified behaviour (i.e. smoking cessation).

The Protection Motivation Theory (PMT) [33] was used to understand the impact of these appeals and examine the processes involved to determine the mechanisms of behaviour change. The PMT contains elements from the SCT and HBM. However, unlike the HBM, this model articulates links and relations between the variables.

According to the PMT information that we acquire from **environmental sources (**i.e. fear appeals) and **intrapersonal sources** (i.e. our personalities and prior experiences) two important cognitive factors that influence us:

1) threat appraisal, a function of perceived susceptibility to illness and severity;
2) coping appraisal, a function of response efficacy and self-efficacy beliefs.

The outcome of these appraisals is suggested to influence an intention to change behaviour (protection motivation). The strength that reflects our motivation to protect our health is also thought to directly predict behaviour (Figure 3.5). Therefore, an individual is most likely to change behaviour i.e. give up smoking in response to a fear-arousing health message if they believe:

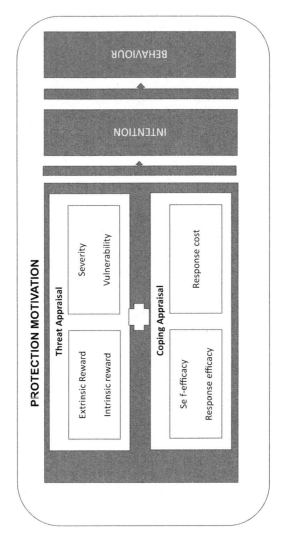

Figure 3.5 Protection Motivation Theory

(a) they are susceptible to disease (vulnerability) 'My chances of getting lung cancer are high';

(b) that the disease will have a severe consequence (severity) 'Lung cancer is a serious illness';

(c) There is a link between the protective behaviour and reduced risk of disease (response effectiveness) 'If I give up smoking I will reduce my chance of getting lung cancer';

(d) They are capable of engaging in protective behaviour (self-efficacy) 'I am confident I can give up smoking'.

Summary and future directions

The PMT has been applied to a range of health promoting and compromising behaviours which have included: physical activity [34]; dietary behaviour [35]; screening behaviour [36]; alcohol consumption [37]; smoking [38] and treatment adherence [39].

- Meta-analyses have found that both threat and coping appraisal components of PMT were useful in predicting health related intentions [40];
- Coping appraisal (i.e. perceived response efficacy, self-efficacy and response costs) has been identified as the most important cognition [41] compared to threat appraisal [40].
- Therefore, the most successful approach to motivating people to change using this theory has been through changing an individual's perception of self-efficacy, for example setting achievable goals, providing feedback on performance, reflecting on past achievements [41].

However, there are some limitations that should be considered.

- The PMT assumes that we are rational thinkers, however, as we mentioned previously this is not always the case. Whilst we may know all the risks linked to a behaviour that we do or do not do, this may not influence our performance of it.
- Some argue that 'emotion' is not effectively explained, for example how do the cognitive processes influence our emotions, and in turn how does this influence our behaviour.

- There is also the risk that scaring somebody does not always lead to positive change, in fact it could lead to a negative outcome. Imagine a smoker who watched an advertisement campaign of a person dying from a smoking related disease (fear arousing stimuli), the fear of this happening to the individual and leaving their family makes them really scared. However, as a coping mechanism this negative arousal may inadvertently make them smoke more, or perhaps adopt another maladaptive behaviour. As such it has been suggested that 'emotional response' should be included within the PMT as a mediating factor for an individual's coping response.

Theory of Reasoned Action and Theory of Planned Behaviour

The Theory of Reasoned Action (TRA) developed by Fishbein [42], is a deliberative processing model which implies that an individual's attitudes are formed after careful consideration of the available information, a sum of the likelihood and evaluation of the potential outcome. The **likelihood** that an action might promote a given outcome, for example 'If I eat more healthily I will improve my health' and **evaluation** of outcomes achieved/avoided and desirable and negative consequences 'being healthy will improve my health'.

This model was developed in response to criticisms of previous models and attempted to address the gap between our attitudes and our behaviour i.e. whilst an individual may have positive attitudes to eating more healthily (attitude) this does not necessarily mean they will eat more healthily (behaviour). The TRA suggested that the gap between our attitudes and behaviour is bridged by our **'intentions'** to perform a given behaviour i.e. our motivation to exert effort into the performance of a behaviour.

The TRA is also centred on the idea that an individual's beliefs about their social world plays a central role in decision making, referred to as **'subjective norms'**. The concept of putting the individual in their social context and acknowledging social influences on an individual contrasted with previous cognitive influences, for example SCT, HBM. **Subjective norms**, similarly to attitudes are the sum of two beliefs:

(1) 'normative beliefs', the behaviours that others may expect of me, for example 'my family and friends think that I should eat healthily'.
(2) the degree to which an individual wants to comply with others, for example 'I want to eat healthily as my family and friends want me to'.

The development of the theory of planned behaviour

The TRA, whilst well received in its time began to suffer from mounting criticism that it lacked explanatory power to adequately predict health behaviour. This model was subsequently succeeded by the theory of planned behaviour, which expanded the TRA model with its design and adaption to take into account Bandura's pioneering work of self-efficacy [43]. This was considerably important as research clearly identified during this period that including a self-efficacy element to the TRA could strengthen the theoretical model through its application to complex health behaviours. The succession of this newer model revolved around the inclusion of '**perceived behavioural control**', the degree to which the behaviour is perceived to be under the control of the individual.

The TPB, like the TRA suggests an individual's intention is the central factor to perform a given behaviour. Motivational factors are central to our intention to perform a behaviour and are key indicators to how hard an individual is willing to try and how much effort they will exert to perform the behaviour [44]. The stronger the intention the stronger the performance. The TPB has three conceptually independent determinants, which in turn predict intentions, these are: attitudes, subjective norms and perceived behavioural control (see Figure 3.6). The TPB stipulates that our behavioural **intentions,** for example 'I am going to start eating healthily', are the main antecedent to behavioural **action** 'Individual starts eating more healthily'. These intentions are based on a combination of three factors: a)

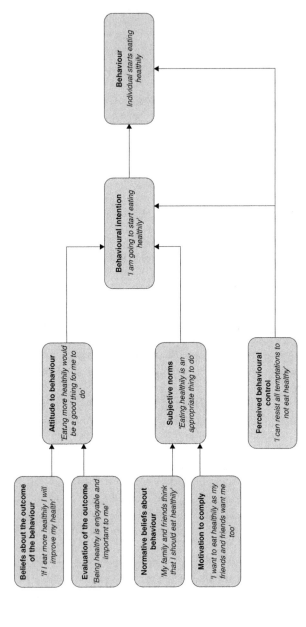

Figure 3.6 Theory of Planned Behaviour applied to healthy eating

attitude to the behaviour 'eating more healthily would be a good thing for me to do', b) **subjective norms** 'eating healthy is an appropriate thing to do' and c) **perceived behavioural control** 'I can resist all temptation to not eat healthily'.

Summary and future directions

The TPB has been used to predict several health behaviours including: healthy eating [45], alcohol consumption [46], drug use [47], physical activity [48], smoking [49], blood donation [50], HIV prevention and condom use [51] amongst many others.

To understand how successful this model has been Armitage and Conner [52] conducted a meta-analytic review, a study which uses statistical methods to pool the results from multiple studies to create a single more precise estimate of the outcome. This study specifically analysed 185 independent studies which applied the TPB to a wide range of health behaviours in a variety of contexts. The findings confirmed that the TPB was more superior in explaining behaviour to that of the TRA and HBM [31]. Research has also shown that:

- intention and perceived behavioural control remain consistent psychological predictors of behaviour [53];
- interventions that have resulted in large changes in intention are likely to also change behaviour [54].

However, the TPB has not withstood criticism. Some limitations have included:

- The role of subjective norms has been challenged as they are consistently found to be the weakest predictor of intentions [52]. However, this may be a consequence of not being measured correctly, or not having considered descriptive norms i.e. what those around actually do rather than what they approve of.
- When behaviour measures have been self-reported (i.e. reported by the individual) there has been an exaggerated increase in reported behaviour [52].

- There is also a large discrepancy between the predictability of intention and behaviour. This is mostly related to 'included abstainers', individuals who form an intention and subsequently fail to act [55].

Stage models of change

The Transtheoretical Model [56] was developed from a study which compared the experience of smokers who quit on their own, against smokers who received professional treatment. Prochaska and DiClemente argued that 'change' is an intentional process that occurs in stages rather than a one-time event. Thus the stages of change were born.

Stages of change 'When you change'

The TTM suggests that there are six sequential stages of change. These stages are:

1. **Precontemplation**
   - The individual is not interested in changing their behaviour in the next six months 'I am not planning to quit smoking in the next 6 months'.
2. **Contemplation**
   - The individual is deciding to change their behaviour in the next six months 'I will decide to quit smoking in the next 6 months'.
3. **Preparation**
   - Individual is preparing to change and take action in the next month, they are developing strategies for change and have a plan of action 'I am ready to quit smoking'.
4. **Action**
   - The individual has changed their behaviour within the last six months 'I have quit smoking'.
5. **Maintenance**
   - The individual has changed their behaviour for more than six months 'I have quit smoking for more than six months'.

6. Termination
- Behaviour change has been permanently adopted and the individual has no temptation to relapse 'I have not smoked for more than 5 years and have no desire to smoke in the future'.

These stages are viewed as a revolving door, where an individual can enter, exit and re-enter at any stage (Figure 3.7). An individual may, for example be sparked into going from stage 1 (precontemplation) to taking action (stage 4) following a recent health scare and consequently go onto successfully quit and terminate the behaviour (stage 6). Relapse is an expected part of this model and is most common in the action stage (Figure 3.7).

The TTM also features (1) processes of change 'How you change, (2) self-efficacy 'Confidence to change' and (3) decisional balance 'Why you change'.

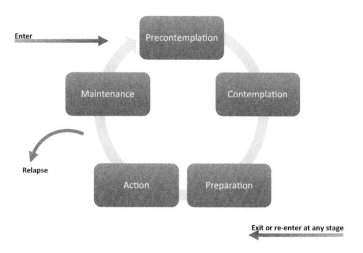

Figure 3.7 The Stages of Change: The revolving-door based on Figure 2, p. 283 [56]

1. Processes of change

There are 10 processes of change (experiential and behavioural), which enable individuals to move and progress between the stages.

Experiential processes are the cognitive and affective processes where we gain relevant information based on our own actions and experiences.

I. **Consciousness Raising [Increasing Awareness]**
    - *Enhancing knowledge and tips to support the behaviour change 'I recall information people had given me on how to stop smoking'.*
II. **Dramatic Relief [Emotional Arousal]**
    - *This relates to the experience of emotions of the health risks of the behaviour 'I react emotionally to warnings about smoking cigarettes'.*
III. **Environmental Re-evaluation [Social Reappraisal]**
    - *Where an individual considers the negative impact of the old behaviour or the positive impact of the behaviour change on the individual's social and physical environment 'I consider the view that smoking can be harmful to the people around me'.*
IV. **Social Liberation [Environmental Opportunities]**
    - *This is where we notice public support, 'I find society changing in ways that make it easier for the nonsmoker'.*
V. **Self-Re-evaluation [Self Re-appraisal]**
    - *Where we create a new self-image, 'My dependency on cigarettes makes me feel disappointed in myself'.*

Behavioural processes are generated through environment events and behaviours including:

VI. **Stimulus Control [Re-Engineering]**
    - How we manage our environment 'I remove things from my home that remind me of smoking'.
VII. **Helping Relationships [Supporting]**
    - Where we obtain support to help us 'I have someone who listens to me when I need to talk about my smoking'.

VIII. Counter Conditioning [Substituting]

- We substitute the unwanted behaviour by replacing it with something more positive 'I find doing other things with my hands is a good substitute for smoking'.

IX.   Reinforcement Management [Rewarding]

- We reward positive behaviour change 'I reward myself when I don't smoke'.

X.   Self-liberation [Committing]

- Where we make a commitment to change 'I make a commitment not to smoke'.

These processes, whilst all important, are influential for progression during different stages of change (Figure 3.8). This is useful to know because it helps us to develop stage based interventions tailored to the individual. For example Joan, 56, who smokes 20–30 cigarettes per day is referred by her GP to see a health psychologist. Following an assessment Joan is found to be in the pre-contemplation stage i.e. she is not planning to quit smoking in the near future. According to the processes of change suitable interventions to encourage her to move to the contemplation stage would be:

- increase Joan's knowledge about the dangers of smoking and provide her tips and advice on how she could quit smoking (consciousness raising);
- invoke an emotional reaction to her health behavior, for example receive pictures of the dangers of smoking, see others who have been negatively impacted by smoking (emotional arousal);
- support Joan to consider the impact of her smoking to others around her (environmental re-evaluation).

You may notice that the process 'social liberation' is not included, this is because it is unclear of its relationship to particular stages.

2. Self-efficacy

An individual's level of self-efficacy and their ability to resist temptation is an important factor in achieving movement across

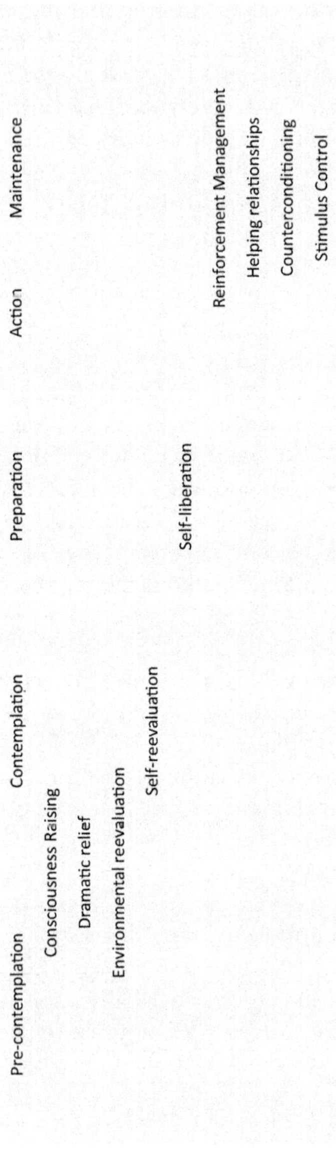

Figure 3.9 Processes which influence progression across the stages of change

the stages. This refers to individuals' confidence that they can manage high risk situations without relapsing and resist the desire to perform the unhealthy behaviour in challenging situations.

3. Decisional balance

This is the process of weighing up the pros and cons of changing the target behaviour. The relative weight people assign to the pros and cons of a behaviour which influences an individual's decision to change their behaviour.

Summary and future directions

Over the past three decades the TTM has been the most popular stage model applied to a wide range of health behaviours, which have included:

- smoking cessation [57];
- physical activity and exercise [58];
- fruit and vegetable intake [59];
- weight management [60];
- condom use [61]);
- sun protection [62].

The appeal of the TTM is that it acknowledges that people are at various stages of behaviour change; which can then be targeted by using stage-matched intervention strategies. However, the extent to which the TTM is a model of behaviour change has been hotly debated. Whilst this model has been popular among clinicians and healthcare professionals, this optimism has not been shared by academics.

Despite some research, which has shown that decisional balance and stages of change are important factors in understanding health behaviour [63], overall effectiveness of the TTM has been weak. A systematic review of 37 RCTs across multiple health interventions including dietary change, physical activity, multiple lifestyle changes and the uptake of unhealthy behaviours such as alcohol use. Findings concluded that there was little evidence to support the effectiveness of transtheoretical interventions [64].

A main criticism has been centred on the 'stages of change'. Stage matching interventions have proven problematic; it is often difficult to clearly identify the stage that the individual is in [65]. Further, the model is not predictive and the stages are not discrete. Researchers have therefore argued that we should focus less on the stage but instead focus on the behaviour change itself. For example just because an individual moves from being in the 'precontemplation stage' to the 'contemplation' state does not mean that they will achieve behaviour change success. In fact the concept of stage based models has been criticised more generally. As Bandura, the founder of the SCT states, 'human functioning is simply too multifaceted and multidetermined to be categorized into a few discrete stages' [6]. Many scholars have argued that the model should be disregarded [66]. However, it is argued that this model has been taken out of the context it was meant for. As Povey et al. [67] explain, stage models such as the TTM were originally designed as descriptive devices to enable clinicians to create appropriate interventions for people with addictive behaviours rather than models or tools to predict and explain behaviour with a certain level of academic rigour.

Box 3.2 Case study: A health psychologist (Jo Meola, Smoking Cessation Advisor)

A trainee health psychologist, smoking cessation lead discusses their role of applying the Transtheoretical Model of Change to an individual in practice.

Richard was in his mid-thirties, a regular smoker of around 20–30 cigarettes per day. He started smoking from around the age of 15 years. Richard had a steady reliable job, was married and a dad to three children (aged 2, 6, 8). His wife and friends all smoked around him). Not once did Richard ever worry about his smoking behaviour or the impact it might have at the time or in the future on his health. Richard had no medical conditions and rarely visited his GP, yet always had 'a cough'; this was linked to his grandmother who also had a lifelong cough but had never smoked in her life, so was put down to a hereditary trait.

This was until one day when Richard's marriage fell apart and his circumstances and lifestyle changed. He became aware of all the unhealthy behaviours in which he was engaging and decided that stopping smoking would protect his future health for him and his children. This can be viewed as a '*social reappraisal*' where an individual considers the negative impact of their behaviour. Richard initially began to think about all the pros and cons (*decisional balance*) linked to smoking and decided that trying to stop would be a good idea (*contemplation*). From this Richard tried to stop smoking alone (*action*). However, he continued to socialise with friends who smoked and soon returned to his initial behaviour (*relapse*).

However, he soon realised the benefits of stopping smoking outweighed the benefit of continuing to smoke (*decisional balance*) so he went to his GP who gave him some brief information about the benefits of stopping together with some medication to help with the nicotine withdrawal (*increasing awareness*) and advised him to go back in a couple of weeks. This enabled Richard to try to quit smoking again (*action*), but unfortunately only for a short time as one week later he starting smoking again (*relapse*).

Finally, and fairly soon afterwards, following one defining moment Richard made the decision that he was going to stop smoking. He announced that he 'did not want to become ill' or 'die early from smoking' (*self-liberation*). A real-life video was released on social media of a similar aged smoker who was dying of cancer who explained he was leaving behind his young children all because of his smoking behaviour (*emotional arousal*). This video impacted on Richard so much that it led to his final and, importantly, successful attempt to stop smoking. His final attempt (***action***) was after a lot of thought and planning during a time where his triggers were reduced (***re-engineering***). He built upon his previous quit attempts which gave him the confidence to succeed (***self-efficacy***). Richard has now given up smoking for over 6 months (***maintenance***).

Additional learning: Think of a situation where you may know someone who has experienced a healthy lifestyle choice and apply the Transtheoretical Model to consider what their journey may have been.

Final overview and summary

- We know that health behaviour is complex, health psychology has however offered us a plethora of models and theories which have enabled us to explain, predict and facilitate health behaviour.
- The discussed theories and models contain a wide variety of components. Whilst some are unique to particular models, many share identical or overlapping characteristics.
- Behaviour change theories have demonstrated varying success. Each have their own advantages and disadvantages, which should be considered in relation to the behaviour in question and the empirical evidence to hand.

References

[1] Naidoo, J., Willis, J. (2005). *Public Health and Health Promotion.* Bailliere Tindall.

[2] Holt, E. B., Brown, H. C. (1931). *Animal Drive and the Learning Process, an Essay Toward Radical Empiricism.* New York, USA: Holt and Co..

[3] Rotter, J. B. (1954). *Social Learning and Clinical Psychology.* New York: Prentice-Hill.

[4] Bandura, A., Ross, D., Ross, S. A. (1961). **Transmission of aggression through imitation of aggressive models**. *The Journal of Abnormal and Social Psychology, 63*(3), 575.

[5]   Bandura, A., Ross, D., Ross, S. A. (1963). Imitation of film-mediated aggressive models. *The Journal of Abnormal and Social Psychology*, *66*(1), 3.

[6]   Bandura, A. (1977). *Social Learning Theory*. Englewood Cliffs, NJ: Prentice Hall; 1977.

[7]   Bandura, A. (1986). *Social Foundations of Thought and Action: A Social Cognitive Theory*. Englewood Cliffs: NJ: Prentice Hall.

[8]   Luszczynska, A., Schwarzer, R. (2005). Social cognitive theory. In: *Predicting Health Behaviour*. edn. Edited by Conner, M., Norman, P. London: Open University Press.

[9]   Bandura, A. (1982). Self-efficacy mechanism in human agency. *American Psychologist*, *37*, 122–147.

[10] Oliver, R. (1974). :Expectancy is the probability that the individual assigns to work effort being followed by a given level of achieved task performance. Expectancy Theory Predictions of Salesmen's Performance. *Journal of Marketing Research*, *11*, 243–253.

[11] Bandura, A. (1991). Social cognitive theory of self-regulation. *Organizational Behavior and Human Decision Processes*, *50*(2), 248–287.

[12] Glanz, K., Bishop, D. B. (2010). The role of behavioral science theory in development and implementation of public health interventions. *Annual Review of Public Health*, *31*, 399–418.

[13] Snead, M. C., O'Leary, A. M., Mandel, M. G., Kourtis, A. P., Wiener, J., Jamieson, D. J., Warner, L., Malotte, C. K., Klausner, J. D., O'Donnell, L. *et al.* (2014). Relationship between social cognitive theory constructs and self-reported condom use: assessment of behaviour in a subgroup of the Safe in the City trial. *BMJ Open*, *4*(12).

[14] Petosa, R. L., Suminski, R., Hortz, B. (2003). Predicting vigorous physical activity using social cognitive theory. *American Journal of Health Behavior*, *27*(4), 301–310.

[15] Guillaumie, L., Godin, G., Vézina-Im, L-A. (2010). Psychosocial determinants of fruit and vegetable intake in adult population: a systematic review. *International Journal of Behavioral Nutrition and Physical Activity*, *7*(1), 12.

[16] Armitage, C., Conner, M. (2000). Social cognition models and health behaviour: A structured review. *Psychology & Health*, *15*, 173–189.

[17] Fargher, E., Morrison, V., Hughes, D. (2012). Application of health psychology and economic behavioural models to explain medication adherence in adult patients: a systematic review of

empirical studies. *Ascertaining Barriers for Compliance: policies for safe, effective and cost-effective use of medicines in Europe Final Report of the ABC Project (Deliverable 71)*:146.

[18] Stacey, F. G., James, E. L., Chapman, K., Courneya, K. S., Lubans, D. R. (2015). A systematic review and meta-analysis of social cognitive theory-based physical activity and/or nutrition behavior change interventions for cancer survivors. *Journal of Cancer Survivorship*, 9(2), 305–338.

[19] Young, M. D., Plotnikoff, R. C., Collins, C. E., Callister, R., Morgan, P.J. (2014) Social cognitive theory and physical activity: a systematic review and meta-analysis. *Obesity reviews: an official journal of the International Association for the Study of Obesity*, 15(12), 983–995.

[20] Tierney, S., Mamas, M., Skelton, D., Woods, S., Rutter, M. K., Gibson, M., Neyses, L., Deaton, C. (2011). What can we learn from patients with heart failure about exercise adherence? A systematic review of qualitative papers. *Health Psychology*, 30(4), 401–410.

[21] Schwarzer, R., Fuchs, R. (1995). Self-efficacy and health behaviours. In: *Predicting Health Behaviour*. edn. Edited by Conner, M., Norman, P. Buckingham: Open University Press.

[22] Rosenstock, I. M. (1974). Historical origins of the health belief model. In: *The Health Belief Model and Personal Health Behavior*. edn. Edited by Becker, M. H. Thorofare, NJ: Charles B Slack, INC.

[23] Rosenstock, I. M., Strecher, V. J., Becker, M. H. (1988). Social learning theory and the health belief model. *Health Education Quarterly*, 15(2),175–183.

[24] Kirscht, J. P. (1974). The health belief model and illness behavior. In: *The Health Belief Model and Personal Health Behavior*. edn. edited by Becker, M. H. Thorofare NJ: Charles B Slack INC.

[25] Yarbrough, S. S., Braden, C. J. (2001). Utility of Health Belief Model as a guide for explaining or predicting breast cancer screening behaviours. *J Adv Nurs*, 33(5), 677–688.

[26] Johnson, C. E., Mues, K. E., Mayne, S. L., Kiblawi, A. N. (2008). Cervical cancer screening among immigrants and ethnic minorities: a systematic review using the Health Belief Model. *Journal of Lower Genital Tract Disease*, 12(3), 232–241.

[27] Bish, A., Sutton, S., Golombok, S. (2000). Predicting uptake of a routine cervical smear test: A comparison of the health belief model and the theory of planned behaviour. *Psychology and Health*, 15(1), 35–50.

[28] Green, E. C., Murphy, E. (2014). Health belief model. *The Wiley Blackwell Encyclopedia of Health, Illness, Behavior, and Society.*

[29] Galvin, K. (1992). A critical review of the health belief model in relation to cigarette smoking behaviour. *Journal of Clinical Nursing,* *1*(1), 13–18.

[30] DiMatteo, M. R., Giordani, P. J., Lepper, H. S., Croghan, T. W. (2002). Patient adherence and medical treatment outcomes: a meta-analysis. *Medical Care, 40*(9), 794–811.

[31] Taylor, D., Bury, M., Campling, N., Carter, S., Garfield, S., Newbould, J., Rennie, T. (2006). A review of the use of the Health Belief Model (HBM), the Theory of Reasoned Action (TRA), the Theory of Planned Behaviour (TPB) and the Trans-Theoretical Model (TTM) to study and predict health related behaviour change. London, UK: National Institute for Health and Clinical Excellence.

[32] Hovland, C. I., Janis, I. L., Kelley, H. H. (1953). *Communication and Persuasion; Psychological Studies of Opinion Change.* New Haven, CT: Yale University Press.

[33] Rogers, R. W. (1975). A Protection Motivation Theory of fear appeals and attitude change. *Journal of Psychology, 91,* 93–114.

[34] Plotnikoff, R. C., Higginbotham, N. (2002). Protection Motivation Theory and exercise behaviour change for the prevention of coronary heart disease in a high risk, Australian representative community sample of adults. *Psychology, Health and Medicine, 7*(1), 87–98.

[35] Plotnikoff, R. C., Higginbotham, N. (1995). Predicting low-fat diet intentions and behaviors for the prevention of coronary heart disease: An application of protection motivation theory among an Australian population. *Psychology and Health, 10*(5), 397–408.

[36] Orbell, S., Sheeran, P. (1998). 'Inclined abstainers': A problem for predicting health-related behaviour. *British Journal of Social Psychology, 37*(2),151–165.

[37] Runge, C., Prentice-Dunn, S., Scogin, F. (1993). Protection motivation theory and alcohol use attitudes among older adults. *Psychological Reports, 73*(1), 96–98.

[38] Leilani, G. (1997). Adolescents' Cognitive Appraisals of Cigarette Smoking: An Application of the Protection Motivation Theory 1. *Journal of Applied Social Psychology, 27*(22),1972–1985.

[39] Norman, P., Searle, A., Harrad, R., Vedhara, K. (2003). Predicting adherence to eye patching in children with amblyopia: an

application of protection motivation theory. *British Journal of Health Psychology*, 8(1), 67–82.

[40]   Milne, S., Sheeran, P., Orbell, S. (2000). Prediction and intervention in health-related behaviour: A meta-analytic review of Protection Motivation Theory. *Journal of Applied Social Psychology*, 30,106–143.

[41]   Floyd, D. L., Prentice-Dunn, S., Rogers, R. W. (2000). A meta-analysis of Protection Motivation Theory. *Journal of Applied Social Psychology*, 30, 407–429.

[42]   Fishbein, M. (1980). Theory of reasoned action: some applications and implications. In: *Nebraska Symposium on Motivation.* edn. Edited by Howe, H., Page, M. Lincoln, NB: University of Nebraska Press.

[43]   Azjen, I. (1985). From intentions to action: a theory of planned behaviour. In: *Action Control: From Cognitions to Behaviors.* edn. Edited by Kuhl, J., Beckham, J. New York: Springer, 11–39.

[44]   Azjen, I. (1991). The theory of planned behavior. *Organizational Behavior and Human Decision Processes*, 50,179–211.

[45]   McDermott, M. S., Oliver, M., Simnadis, T., Beck, E., Coltman, T., Iverson, D., Caputi, P., Sharma, R, (2015). The Theory of Planned Behaviour and dietary patterns: A systematic review and meta-analysis. *Preventive Medicine*, 81, 150–156.

[46]   Cooke, R., Dahdah, M., Norman, P., French, D. P. (2016). How well does the theory of planned behaviour predict alcohol consumption? A systematic review and meta-analysis. *Health Psychology Review*, 10(2),148–167.

[47]   Bashirian, S., Hidarnia, A., Allahverdipour, H., Hajizadeh, E. (2012). Application of the theory of planned behavior to predict drug abuse related behaviors among adolescents. *Journal of Research in Health Sciences*, 12(1), 54–60.

[48]   Hagger, M. S., Chatzisarantis, N. L., Biddle, S. J. (2002). A meta-analytic review of the theories of reasoned action and planned behavior in physical activity: Predictive validity and the contribution of additional variables. *Journal of Sport and Exercise Psychology*, 24(1), 3–32.

[49]   Topa, G., Moriano, J. A. (2010). Theory of planned behavior and smoking: Meta-analysis and SEM model. *Substance Abuse and Rehabilitation*, 1, 23.

[50]   Giles, M., McClenahan, C., Cairns, E., Mallet, J. (2004). An application of the Theory of Planned Behaviour to blood donation: the importance of self-efficacy. *Health Education Research*, 19(4), 380–391.

[51] Sheeran, P., Taylor, S. (1999). Predicting intentions to use condoms: a meta-analysis and comparison of the theories of reasoned action and planned behavior1. *Journal of Applied Social Psychology*, *29*(8), 1624–1675.

[52] Armitage, C., Conner, M. (2001). Efficacy of the Theory of Planned Behaviour: A meta-analytic review. *British Journal of Social Psychology*, *40*, 471–499.

[53] McEachan, R., Conner, M., Taylor, N. J., Lawton, R. (2011). Prospective prediction of health-related behaviours with the Theory of Planned Behaviour: a meta-analysis. *Health Psychology Review*, *5*(2), 97–144.

[54] Webb, T. L., Sheeran, P. (2006). Does changing behavioral intentions engender behavior change? A meta-analysis of the experimental evidence. *Psychological Bulletin*, *132*(2), 249–268.

[55] Sniehotta, F. F., Presseau, J., Araújo-Soares, V. (2014). Time to retire the theory of planned behaviour. *Health Psychology Review*, *8*(1), 1–7.

[56] Prochaska, J. O., DiClemente, C. C. (1982). Transtheoretical therapy: Toward a more integrative model of change. *Psychotherapy: Theory, Research & Practice*, *19*(3), 276.

[57] Aveyard, P., Griffin, C., Lawrence, T., Cheng, K. K. (2003). A controlled trial of an expert system and self-help manual intervention based on the stages of change versus standard self-help materials in smoking cessation. *Addiction*, *98*(3), 345–354.

[58] Marshall, S. J., Biddle, S. J. (2001). The transtheoretical model of behavior change: a meta-analysis of applications to physical activity and exercise. Annals *of Behavioral Medicine: A Publication of the* Society *of* Behavioral Medicine, *23*(4), 229–246.

[59] Horwath, C. C., Nigg, C. R., Motl, R. W., Wong, K. T., Dishman, R. K. (2010). Investigating fruit and vegetable consumption using the transtheoretical model. *American Journal of Health Promotion: AJHP*, *24*(5), 324–333.

[60] Johnson, S. S., Paiva, A. L., Cummins, C. O., Johnson, J. L., Dyment, S. J., et al. (2008). Transtheoretical model-based multiple behavior intervention for weight management: effectiveness on a population basis. *Preventive Medicine*, *46*(3), 238–246.

[61] Arden, M. A., Armitage, C. J. (2008). Predicting and explaining transtheoretical model stage transitions in relation to condom-carrying behaviour. *British Journal of Health Psychology*, *13*(4), 719–735.

[62] Weinstock, M. A., Rossi, J. S., Redding, C. A., Maddock, J. E. (2002). Randomized controlled community trial of the efficacy

of a multicomponent stage-matched intervention to increase sun protection among beachgoers. *Preventive Medicine*, *35*(6), 584–592.

[63] Hall, K. L., Rossi, J. S. (2008). Meta-analytic examination of the strong and weak principles across 48 health behaviors. *Prev Med*, *46*(3), 266–274.

[64] Bridle, C., Riemsma, R. P., Pattenden, J., Sowden, A. J., Mather, L., Watt, I. S., Walker, A. (2005). Systematic review of the effectiveness of health behavior interventions based on the transtheoretical model. *Psychology & Health*, *20*(3), 283–301.

[65] Sutton, S. (2001). Back to the drawing board? A review of applications of the transtheoretical model to substance use. *Addiction*, *96*(1), 175–186.

[66] Sutton, S. (2005). Another nail in the coffin of the transtheoretical model? A comment on West. *Addiction*, *100*(8), 1043–1046.

[67] Povey, R., Conner, M., Sparks, P., James, R., Shepherd, R. (1999). A critical examination of the application of the Transtheoretical Model's stages of change to dietary behaviours. *Health Education Research*, *14*(5), 641–651.

4 Health behaviours of children and adolescents

Contents

Introduction

The current most prevalent causes of death are no longer communicable diseases but those that are related to lifestyle, such as coronary heart disease and obesity. If we consider health in a global sense, then childhood and adolescence are important periods for making an impact on the future health of the world. Why? Because it is health behaviours that we adopt during this period that can be predictive of our overall health in adulthood [1] for example:

- There is increasing evidence that eating in the absence of hunger in young children is associated with binge eating in adolescence [2].
- Early onset of alcohol use in adolescence is associated with sustained and heavier alcohol use [3].
- There is also evidence to suggest that positive health behaviours such as eating a healthy diet and being active are also continued in adulthood [4].

So, questions that health psychologists might ask are: how do we promote health behaviour in children? And what is the best age to target our interventions?

If we consider where our health is shaped then it could be said to begin in the womb, from the genes that define our make-up and that are also influenced by the health behaviour of our mothers. But it is not just genes that shape our future, but the way that we develop and learn about the world and our interaction within the environments in which we are situated. Child and adolescent health is complex. These are distinct periods of development where there is a reliance on others and also competing developmental challenges that can impact health and wellbeing. Therefore this chapter will address health within the context of human development, and take a biopsychosocial approach in considering how factors interrelate and impact health.

The main aims of this chapter are to consider childhood and adolescence in relation to developmental changes and consider how these changes can impact health behaviours and subsequent health. To this end, developmental theories will be drawn upon to help to explain and understand how physical growth, cognitive development and social interaction all interrelate to help to explain certain health behaviours during these key developmental periods. Examples from empirical research will be used to examine these relationships with a focus on eating behaviour in children, and risky behaviour in adolescence. As childhood and adolescence reflect major milestones in development, research methods will be discussed and also the ways in which these are used to gather information to help us understand behaviour. Having gained an understanding of what might influence behaviours, the focus will then shift to intervention and an introduction to specific theoretical models that can help in understanding and predicting health behaviour in these age groups.

Children's health in context

Why is childhood so important for future health?

Well, we could start by considering the idea that childhood is an important period of learning and cognitive development. It is within this time frame that many of our health behaviours are learnt, repeated and subsequently become habitual [5] e.g. tooth brushing. Any habit, whether healthy or unhealthy is formed through a repetition of that behaviour. To understand this process, we need to consider the role of our brain and memory. According to research [6], when a behaviour is performed then a mental association between the situational cue and the behaviour is created e.g. getting ready for bed and tooth brushing. If this behaviour is repeated then this forms an association between the cue (getting ready for bed) and the response (tooth brushing) in memory. This means that in the future when a situational cue is encountered then this activates the behaviour and further strengthens the association. Repeating behaviours in a consistent manner in consistent situations will result in the behaviour becoming automatic [7] and therefore a habit. The cue-response relationships can be strengthened (reinforced) through rewards. These rewards can be **external** such as praise or financial rewards, or ***internal***, such as a sense of achievement. External rewards might seem a favourable option to strengthening a cue response and can be used to change behaviour. However, they only seem to be effective if they are not the goal of the behaviour [8] e.g. in the tooth brushing example giving a financial reward such as pocket money for tooth brushing would not sustain behaviour over a long period of time if the pocket money became the goal, and not the tooth brushing behaviour. Intrinsic (internal) rewards, however, such as the satisfaction or pleasure of carrying out the behaviour in question are more likely to reinforce the behaviour and strengthen the cue-response [7] e.g. the feeling of a clean and fresh mouth when teeth are brushed. Behaviour needs to be consistent over a period of time to become established. In sum, healthy habits can be dependent on the situational cues, responses and reinforcement. However, this is rather simplistic and does not take into consideration the complexities of behaviour such as the interaction with others, mood and the stage of development e.g. in the tooth brushing example, communication with the supervising adult, being tired or grumpy or distracted with toys may interfere with tooth brushing behaviour.

Health behaviours can be viewed as a complex interrelationship between biological factors (e.g. genetics, physiological mechanisms of body systems) and psychological (e.g. learning, mood, behaviour, individual differences) and social factors (e.g. socio economic status, environment, relationships). Therefore a biopsychosocial approach [9] is required in understanding and intervening within health. Childhood and adolescence are unique periods of rapid development and so health has to be considered within the context of these changes. Developmental theories fit within this biopsychosocial framework and describe psychological factors such as cognitive development (e.g. intelligence, reasoning, memory) [10] and the formation of identity and relationships (e.g. attachment) [11]. Social psychological theories explain the impact of individual differences (e.g. personality, gender), environments and relationships between these factors, and biological theorists attempt to understand the impact of the developing brain and body. Although these are separate disciplines to some extent, these factors do not occur in isolation but impact on each other. Therein, to understand health behaviour in this developmental period health psychologists need to consider the child within the context of their age and their cognitive abilities when conducting research.

There are a number of different theories in relation to how children develop that focus on either cognitive or social development. These theories can help us to understand children's behaviour and also to consider what methods might be the most suitable to use in researching behaviour, and subsequently in the application of research to change behaviour.

As an example we could consider the work of Piaget [10], a well-known developmental psychologist. Piaget [10], looked at intellectual and cognitive development. He maintained that children go through stages of development (see Table 4.1) and was one of the first psychologists to consider that children think differently to adults. However, these stages may not occur exactly at the time points mentioned or be completely independent of each other. Children are not merely small adults and methods and practices designed for adults may not yield the required results. For example, if you are asking a 5-year-old to solve a hypothetical scenario then they may struggle. Research and intervention therefore have to be designed in an age appropriate manner. Interventions for early years may for example be better targeted at parents or primary care givers rather than the child as they are providing the environment needed for growth and development. On the other hand, teenagers seem to be more independent from their primary care givers and may be more capable of making up their own minds, and so interventions may directly target them and their peer group.

Methods of research in children and adolescents

So, when considering how to conduct research with young children and adolescence it is important to consider the period of

Table 4.1 Piaget's stages of development

Stage	Age	Description
Sensiromotor	0–2 years	The child interacts with the environment and learns form an interaction between the sensory information and motor abilities such as manipulating objects
Preoperational	2–6/7	Can reason but only simply with focus on one salient feature. Perceptions of appearance important and tend to be egocentric
Concrete	6/7- 11/12	Beginning to problem solve using logic, but thinking still concrete (applied to real objects) and unable to think in abstract terms
Formal Operations Stage	11–12 onwards	Can think logically and hypothetically

child development and pick appropriate methods to match the cognitive and physical ability of the child/adolescent e.g. a pre-schooler in the sensorimotor stage would not be able to independently complete a questionnaire. There are a number of methods that can be used depending on the research question that is being asked and the needs of the group that are the participants. Data may be gathered at one time point (cross sectional research) or at intervals over a longer period (longitudinal research). Cross sectional research can be useful in providing a snap shot at one particular time point, whereas longitudinal studies allow the researcher to observe patterns over a longer period of time.

The data itself can be collected in a variety of ways and will also vary according to the research question in mind. The researcher may use objective measures such as height, weight or make use of technology to measure physical activity or collect physiological data. Alternatively, they may choose more subjective measures and want to find out more about individual experiences through the use of self-report questionnaires. These can be qualitative in the form of interviews, focus groups or narratives, or they can be quantitative with the use of scales and questionnaires, where people rate how they feel or their reaction to particular statements. However, if a child is very young then they will not have the capacity to respond to this type of research and so researchers may be reliant on adult others (such as parents, teachers) to complete questionnaires or use other methods. One such method is an observational study. This involves observing behaviour either live or using video and can be more reliable than parent questionnaires, where there may be social desirability to come across well or be reliant on memory. This is a method that has been used widely to observe eating behaviour in children and in the next section we will consider the importance of understanding eating behaviour in children and what influences this behaviour and consider the methodology employed.

Why is eating behaviour in children important?

Diet, for example, is an important factor when considering overall health. Malnutrition impacts growth and development and being underweight, overweight or obese is associated with poorer health throughout life. Changes in the way people live over the decades has seen an increase in more sedentary lifestyles and an increase in obesity. The global prevalence of childhood obesity increased by over 5 per cent between 1975 and 2016, although this has now plateaued in higher income countries [12]. If a child is obese then they are more likely to develop physical health problems such as CVD and Type 2 diabetes later in life. Not only does obesity affect physical health and affect overall longevity, but it also poses a risk to mental health, as those that are obese are more likely to suffer with low self esteem [13].

In the UK, reducing childhood obesity is a key aim of Government Health Policy. Childhood obesity rates are monitored annually by the National Child Measurement Programme (NCMP) [14], which measures the height and weight of around one million school children in England every year. The data collected provides a detailed picture of the prevalence of child obesity. The figures for 2012/13, showed that 18.9 per cent of children in Year 6 (aged 10–11) were obese and a further 14.4 per cent were overweight [14]. In 2016/2017 the number of children in Year 6 that were obese had risen to 20 per cent. Of children in Reception (aged 4–5), 9.6 per cent were obese. The obesity rates are highest for those children living in deprived areas with 12.7 per cent of reception children being classified as obese in the most deprived areas, compared to 5.8 per cent in the least deprived areas [14]. In Year 6, 26.3 per cent of children were obese in the most deprived areas and 11.4 per cent in the least deprived. Obesity is greater amongst boys than girls in both age groups [14]. These figures are particularly worrying, as it seems that younger generations are becoming obese earlier and are at risk of obesity in adulthood. It is therefore important to understand the factors that may affect eating behaviour in children in order to apply theory to the design of effective interventions to promote healthier lifestyles across the lifespan.

Understanding eating behaviour

Eating behaviour is complex. There is a biological need to eat as the body needs food for energy, growth and repair, but there are also psychosocial factors that can affect eating such as food availability, palatability and mood. Eating habits can become established in childhood and are influenced by a variety of factors such as genes, what foods are made available, learning eating behaviours through reinforcement, by watching significant others such as parents' and friends' eating behaviours and other influences such as advertising.

Biological factors

Health can be impacted from conception with non-modifiable genes that pre-dispose an individual to various conditions. When we consider obesity there is growing evidence that there are a number of genes that may predispose a person to become obese [15; 16; 17]. It is not possible to modify genes but if we consider obesity to run in families, then it is important to support families in adopting healthy eating practices in avoiding premature death. This could begin in the very early years of life. There is a certain complexity in that parents not only provide these genes, but also the environment in which to develop. Support for an interaction between genes and the environment come from longitudinal research that describes how multiple genes that coupled with easy access to highly palatable food leads to obesity [17]. Therefore it is not biological factors or pre-disposition alone but an interrelationship between genes and other factors such as the environment.

In our western society there is increasing attention paid to the obesogenic environment which refers to the availability of highly palatable foods that are rich in fat and sugar that are considered to be contributing to the obesity epidemic [18]. The availability of highly palatable food is an important factor in obesity because intrinsic factors such as satiety cues that indicate fullness, may be overridden. Evidence for this comes from studies that have introduced highly palatable snacks after a meal and monitored consumption. It would seem that satiety is ignored and that there is a tendency to consume snacks despite reporting fullness [19]. In one example it was observed that the more obese children consumed more snacks [17].

Psychosocial factors

Early years and the role of learning

Social factors encompass both the environment and others within that environment such as cultural aspects, socio-economic status, educational status, social norms, peers, friends, parents and how close they are. It is considered that it is a combination of these factors within the environment that contributes to high calorific intake and sedentary behaviour and constitutes what has become known as an obesogenic environment [20]. We have considered the availability of food, but also need to consider the role of significant others involved in providing the environments that may shape eating behaviours. Early years are important for establishing healthy eating habits. For example, a group of researchers [21] conducted a longitudinal study and found that there was a positive relationship between fruit and vegetable intake at six months and at age 7. Children who were exposed to home-cooked vegetables and raw fruit at 6 months were more likely to eat fruit and vegetables at age 7. This would suggest that early intervention to increase fruit and vegetable exposure in weaning babies would have a positive impact on their fruit and vegetable intake in subsequent years. Over the last 10–15 years there has been increasing amount of attention and literature with regard to the timing and approach to weaning, with baby-led weaning growing in popularity [22]. Baby-led weaning is different to trad-itional approaches in that the baby self-feed family food rather than being spoon-fed purées [23]. This is perceived to result in better appetite control as mothers are more likely to have breastfed for longer and be more responsive to their babies' needs. In response mother's have perceived that babies are less fussy and have more control over their own appetite. Baby-led weaning has been found to be significantly positively associated with the mother's educational status with higher education associated with greater responsiveness, longer breastfeeding and adopting the baby-led weaning approach [24]. In contrast early weaning is associated with lower educational and socio-economic status [25] and confusion over what is healthy and not healthy eating despite motivation for healthiness. Traditional purée weaning is associated with high levels of restrictiveness and lower satiety responsiveness and in one study babies were significantly heavier in this group compared to birth weight [23]. In comparison baby led weaning infants have lower levels of food responsiveness (desire to eat) and higher satiety responsiveness. High levels of food responsiveness and low satiety associated with being overweight [26].

How eating is reinforced is also important, such as learning and reinforcement and by observing others and modelling behaviours. Research in the 1990s demonstrated that there was indeed a relationship between parent's fat intake and level of obesity and children's obesity and fat intake [27]. Parental influ-ence is significant in shaping eating behaviour and parenting styles and controlling feeding practices can inhibit the child's ability to self-regulate food consumption and can contribute to obesity in later life [28]. The extrinsic (external) control of feeding by parents, such as restriction, monitoring and pressure to eat are considered to undermine hunger and satiety cues which then affects the intrinsic ability to self-regulate [29]. This can then lead to the ignoring of intrinsic satiety cues and to instead respond to extrinsic cues such as the availability of highly palatable foods (sweets, crisps, chocolate, pasties, biscuits, cakes, fast food, sugary beverages). A study was conducted and found that 81 per cent of children who reported that they were full or very full went on to consume palatable snacks [30]. This has become known as eating in the absence of hunger. If we learn to override satiety cues in childhood, then this pattern of eating in the absence of hunger can continue and predict problems with eating in adolescence. For example, researchers [2] found that eating in the absence of hunger in girls aged 7 predicted self-reported binge eating at age 15. Eating in the absence of hunger at age 7 was also associated with elevated body mass index (BMI), negative mood, maladaptive eating and weight related cognitions.

A focus on interventions

Healthy eating is an important issue and seems to stem back into infanthood. Delaying weaning until six months, being responsive to the child and not providing external pressure or control and introducing a side range of foods seem to be crucial for establishing health eating behaviours. There have been a number of strategies to improve eating behaviours such as structured eating practices in childhood [31]. A structured approach would allow access to palatable foods, but there would be limited availability of these foods in the home. There would also be routines established with regard to access that are consistent and flexible. This would also be in conjunction with serving child-sized amounts of food at mealtimes in consideration of the child [31]. Other interventions have focused on increasing the amount of fruit and vegetables eaten (see the example from the research). One such example is the Food Dudes Programme [32]. This programme is based around modelling behaviour, reward and repeated exposure to fruit and vegetables in a DVD series. The food dudes, which are animated children, act as the role models and are shown to eat fruit and vegetables. A study in Milan [32] with 560 6–9-year-olds demonstrated significant increase in liking for fruit and vegetables four months after watching videos and eating fruit and vegetables every day for 10 days.

So with this in mind what can be done to tackle obesity on a wider scale?

There have been a number of government related strategies and widespread campaigns to promote healthier eating and prevent obesity. One of the most well-known campaigns was started by Jamie Oliver (a TV chef), who wanted to make school dinners healthier [33]. Later this led to the ban of certain junk foods within schools by the then Labour Government, with the most infamous being the Turkey twizzler. The effectiveness of the campaign included a drastic shift to healthier school meals and improved educational outcomes [34].

There are several public health strategies that have been planned to prevent childhood obesity [35]. This includes a plan to reduce sugar intake by introducing a soft drinks industry levy to reduce the amount of sugar in soft drinks and to reduce the sugar in food commonly consumed by children by 20 per cent such as children's cereals. There have also been public health campaigns and schemes to encourage healthy eating such as the healthy start scheme, school fruit and veg and nursery milk [36; 37]. TV campaigns have included Change 4 Life [36] and other campaigns around palatable snacks with recommendations to only consume palatable snacks twice a day not exceeding 100kcals [38].

Having considered that there are many factors that can influence food intake, it is clear that establishing healthy practices in children is important in tackling the obesity crisis. If we learn to override satiety cues and rely on external control then this can become more problematic later in life. Interventions need to meet the developmental needs and there are differences in the types of intervention that are appropriate for targeting early feeding practices and those that might be aimed at pre-schoolers or those within early years and primary educational settings.

So far, we have considered children's health behaviour and used the example of eating behaviour to consider how health behaviour is shaped in childhood through the interrelationship between biological and psychosocial factors. We have also

---

Box 4.1

An example from research:
Owen, Kennedy, Hill and Houston-Price (2018) conducted an intervention study to explore whether looking at picture books of fruits and vegetables before a taste test supported parents in introducing new fruits and vegetables to preschoolers diets.

Background

This was an extension to previous research that had indicated that books that contained photos or pictures of vegetables that were both familiar or unfamiliar increased willingness to taste unfamiliar vegetables (Houston-Price, Butler & Shuba, 2009; Heath, Houston-Price & Kennedy, 2014 as cited in Owen et al., 2018). They hypothesised that children would demonstrate an increased liking for the unfamiliar food following exposure to a picture book.

Method

The participants were 105 18–24-month-old children. Each child was randomised to a fruit picture book group, a vegetable picture book group or a control group with no picture book.

Prior to the start of the study parents were given a number of questionnaires on fruit and vegetable familiarity, likes, dislikes, frequency and fussiness. Parents were also asked to identify a fruit and vegetable that the child refused to eat but they would like them to eat. Those in the fruit and vegetable groups were then sent a picture book containing the target fruit or vegetable that contained a picture and a farm to table-like story. The parents were asked to read the book for five minutes every day for 14 days. This was then followed by 15 days of taste exposure to the target fruit and veg. The parents then completed the questionnaires again and then again after a further three months.

Results

The results indicated that there was an increase in the liking of vegetables in the vegetable group but there were no significant results for the fruit group as compared to the control, which indicated that looking at pictures of vegetables prior to consumption increased the liking of those vegetables compared to just taste alone.

Conclusion

The authors concluded that familiarising young children with vegetables through picture books is beneficial in increasing the likelihood of liking and consumption.

briefly considered strategies that can be employed to target eating behaviour from a young age to prevent the onset of obesity and associated complications to health and wellbeing. We have seen how behaviours that commence in childhood may affect future health into adulthood. Therefore behaviours that become established in our young lives can be continued and affect health into adulthood. An example of such a behaviour is smoking. Smoking initiation is highest in adolescents with a marked increase in uptake in under 16s since 1990 [40] If young people reach the age of 20 as non-smokers then they are less likely to start. Adolescence seems to be a key developmental point for the uptake of risky behaviours – but why?

The period of adolescence is a unique stage of development. It is considered to be a stage of transition between childhood and adulthood and is characterised by marked extremes of emotional states [41]. Adolescence is a transitional period that includes changes in physiology, cognitive development and the development of identity, which can all impact health and wellbeing. With so many complex developmental changes going on at this time, it may come as little surprise that this period of development is associated with an uptake of risky behaviours, such as poor eating habits, smoking, risky sexual behaviour (including the non-use of condoms) and substance misuse. Let us go on to consider risky behaviours in a bit more detail.

A biopsychosocial approach to understanding risk behaviour

Biological

Genes also pre-dispose an individual to the uptake of risky behaviours associated with addictive substances (such as nicotine) [42], and subsequently these substances may affect further development of the brain. The brain is going through a period of structural change during adolescence with changes in hormones and to the neurons and chemical pathways inside the different areas of the brain. Impulse control seems to be one of the last areas of control during development, which may predispose individuals to initiate substance use. Using substances stimulates brain chemicals and can affect future functioning as these adapt to the substance's effects. This may subsequently result in permanent changes to the structure of the central nervous system and interfere with 'normal' development [43].

Often, the onset of adolescence is associated with the onset of puberty. Pubertal timing has seen a shift, in that it seems to be occurring earlier and has been linked with increased risk of uptake in smoking in adolescence [44; 40]. As well as puberty, there are also a number of other changes including changes in the structures of the pathways in the brain [44; 45], which may also both affect and be affected by behaviour. In fact the grey matter within the brain where all the cell bodies are located does not begin to resemble an adult's brain until around the early 20s

[44]. This means that adolescents are not mini-adults and therefore adult models of health behaviour may not be suitable for adolescents.

Psychosocial factors

It is a unique period for the influence of peers because as well as physiological changes, it is also a period where there is an increase in peer interactions and novelty and risk-taking behaviours. Peer pressure is often implicated in the uptake and maintenance of risky behaviour in adolescents, such as alcohol and other substance use. However, the behaviour of friends and friendship groups can also influence behaviour, with friendship often being the most significant factor when it comes to understanding and explaining risky behaviours in adolescence [46]. In a qualitative study with peer groups of similar age, the most predominant theme was related to the behaviour of their closest friendship group [47].

Why are friends so important?

Adolescence is a time of trying to maintain individuality whilst concurrently trying to fit in with the group, associated with a preoccupation with social images [48; 49]. Erikson [48] viewed adolescence as a period of transition from childhood into adult roles. He maintained that it was a time of striving in search of identity and is famous for coining the term identity crisis. It is during this period of development when individuals gain more of a sense of self with more emphasis on internal characteristics, such as their own beliefs and values as a result of thinking and reflecting about their own desires, thoughts and motives for self-definition. It is also a time when peer friendships and peer interactions gain importance and they work together to gain autonomy from their parents [50]. Peers become integral to the process of self-definition, which is especially important in the 11–16-year-old age group as this is a time where the influences of friends are more important than their parents and when romantic relationships are not yet as prominent [50; 51; 45].

The influence of parents/carers

On one hand, adolescents are considered to be going through a period of cognitive development called the formal operations stage of development. Piaget [10] proposed that at this stage of development the individual is capable of hypothetical deductive reasoning, which essentially means that in their minds they can consider many different possibilities and can move between ideas freely. They are also deemed capable of moral reasoning and self-regulation. Parents play an important part in adolescent risk behaviour through the influence of their own health behaviours, which they model to their offspring, their parenting style and the quality of their communication with their adolescent child can influence risk behaviours e.g. research [52] has found that a higher quality of communication between parents and adolescents was associated with lower odds of adolescent smoking. When parents are permissive and exert less parental control then this seems to be related to substance use [53]. Recent research suggested that 17 per cent of parents allowed their children to drink underage [54]. The focus on harm reduction programmes such as Mentor UK and M–Pact [55] has been parental permissiveness and behaviour. An under researched area though is the unpacking of the idea of permissiveness. Parents can be complicit in the supply of alcohol or spaces in which to drink may be in the interest of safety [47], although more work needs to be conducted in order to understand this more fully.

Intervening in risky behaviours

As we have already suggested, adolescence is associated with the uptake of risky behaviours and there are many factors that can influence behaviour during this period of development. Risky behaviour can be thought of as a complex interrelationship between biological factors, psychological factors and social factors. Interventions therefore need to take these factors into consideration and a theory applied to the behaviour to effect change [56].

When designing intervention to target risk behaviour in adolescents it is important to first consider the behaviour and what is already known about the behaviour to enable the targeting of behaviour change techniques to evoke change. Let us consider an example of this in relation to adolescent alcohol use.

Alcohol use in adolescents

The first step is to consider the behaviour and risk to health. Why is there a need to intervene?

1. What is the problem?

Alcohol use in adolescents has been declining since 2003 [57], but the level of drunkenness has not declined [58]. Alcohol is often the first substance of use and in the UK, 4 per cent of 11 to 15-year-olds stated that they drank alcohol at least once a week irrespective of gender. The figures also showed that drinking alcohol seemed to increase with age with 0.5 per cent of 11-year-olds stating that they drank regularly (at least once a week) increasing to 10 per cent of 15-year-olds [57]. The greatest increase in frequency and prevalence of alcohol use in adolescents seems to occur around the age of 13–14 and this seems to be a key transitional point [57].

Alcohol use is widely accepted in UK culture, but early onset can have negative short-term effects such as risk-taking behaviour and also long-term effects e.g. researchers [59] have reported an association between alcohol use and premature death in 16–24-year-olds. This was more prevalent in males (21%) compared to 9 per cent of females. Alcohol use of a certain level may also lead to other risky behaviour. This is particularly related to the way that information is processed following alcohol use and adolescents may act in a way that is not characteristic of their usual behaviour, for example, alcohol use is related to risky sexual activity and the non-use of condoms [60], or heavy episodic drinking (binge drinking). This behaviour then increases the probability of sexually transmitted infections and unplanned pregnancy. Often reports of drunkenness do not match the amount of alcohol consumed and adolescents tend to show insensitivity to the sedative effects of alcohol.

In the long term, early onset of drinking in adolescence is associated with increased drinking amounts and regular drinking in adulthood [61; 62] and is associated with poorer mental health and social harms [62]. As this is also a period that includes changes to brain physiology through the pruning of dendrites, drinking could also alter brain pathways. Long-term harmful use is also associated with problems with memory.

2. What influences alcohol use in adolescence?

Having established that there is a need for intervention it is important to consider what influences alcohol use. It is useful to consider this using the biopsychosocial approach.

Biological factors

We have already considered that there may be a genetic link and biological maturational changes that may affect uptake. Of course there are also individual differences in the way that alcohol affects the individual, but in general terms it sedates the individual, which affects processing, decision making and reaction times. Alcohol myopia [63] and the subsequent effect on processing can mean that the individual becomes more respondent to salient cues in the environment, which can result in more drinking.

Influence of others

The perception of drinking norms amongst peers has long been associated with alcohol use. Research has indicated that adolescents may misperceive and overestimate the amount that other peers are drinking, which may increase their own alcohol use [64]. Other researchers have found that having an alcohol-using peer increases the risk of early onset drinking (initiating drinking when young) [65]. As previously stated, we know that friendship groups are particularly important during this stage of development and greater closeness in networks is associated with increased use, even in younger adolescents. For example, one study [66] found 14 per cent of 11-year-olds had consumed alcohol and were more likely to drink alcohol if their friends were drinking.

Positive expectancies

These are the personal beliefs relating to alcohol use, whether behavioural, cognitive or emotional [67]. These expectancies can be positive e.g. 'it will remove my inhibitions', or negative e.g. 'it will make me feel sick'. Positive expectancies are consistently significantly related to the initiation and maintenance of alcohol use [68]. These expectancies can differ and seem to become more positive in the transition between childhood and adolescence [69]. They can also be related to other factors such as positive images and become more positive after initiation. So, they appear to be related to personal experiences and may be influenced by others and the environment.

Parental influence

Parental behaviour and their attitudes towards alcohol may affect alcohol use. In a cohort study of 10,498 participants in the UK [66] it was found that those participants who had mothers that drank were more likely to also drink. The effect was not the same for fathers. Other studies have found that there is a strong association between parental alcohol use and positive alcohol expectancies, even if they had not yet begun drinking themselves [70]. Parenting itself can also have an effect, such as communication between the parent and adolescent. For example, in the millennium cohort study [66] it was found that frequent battle of wills and unhappiness at home were linked to alcohol use as well as a lack of supervision on weekdays and weekends. Parenting is also related to access to alcohol and there has been work in relation to permissiveness and drinking. Early sipping (under age 13) was more common in households with more permissive parenting styles [71].

Affect and personality factors

Individual difference factors such as personality and affect (mood) can also contribute to our understanding of why some adolescents may be more inclined to drink alcohol. Personality characteristics that have been linked to alcohol use have been impulsivity, sensation seeking, anxiety sensitivity and hopelessness [72].

Impulsivity is the tendency to act without considering the consequences and this tends to peak during the adolescent period of development. Sensation seeking is a little different to impulsivity as this is the preference of novel and exciting experiences [45]. Hopelessness is linked with drinking behaviour as it seems to be related to coping with negative emotions and vulnerability [73].

These factors are not exhaustive and human beings are complex and so these factors also do not occur independent of each other, but serve to give some indication of what factors might affect alcohol use that could be used to target interventions to prevent risky drinking and promote sensible drinking. Theoretical frameworks provide the basis for health psychology interventions and yet there are few that capture the more impulsive tendencies of adolescents. The next part of the chapter will consider models that could be used in intervention design with adolescents.

3. Choosing theory appropriate to the needs of the target group

As outlined in previous chapters, health psychologists use theoretical models to understand the antecedents to health behaviours and to subsequently provide a framework for intervention. If we know that certain factors predict certain behaviours then targeting these factors should produce a change in behaviour.

The need for a dual processing approach in predicting adolescent behaviour

Whilst there are a number of theoretical models that predict health behaviour in adults, these tend to be more rational and suggest a reasoned path to behaviour through a weighing up of the pros and cons of that particular behaviour (see Chapter 3). However, is all behaviour reasoned? Strack and Deutsch [74] argue that it is not, and propose that people do not always act in a way that is representational of their underlying values and beliefs. They therefore argue that a dual processing approach is needed to explain both a reasoned and rational pathway to behaviour and a more impulsive pathway.

What is the dual processing approach?

Smith and Decoster [75] described a theoretical two-system model of memory, a slow schematic system and rapid processing system.

1. The slow schematic system could be considered as reasoned, as within this system an individual can call upon and also reflect on experiences and knowledge in relation to a situation or decision.
2. The rapid processing system is a dual system that operates in tandem and meets the needs of more novel experiences and can be related to emotional factors and impulse processes.

    The dual process theory takes into account cognitive (see Figure 4.1), motivational and behavioural mechanisms, where behaviour is not considered to be about anticipated consequences, but related to factors that are beyond rational control. If we consider the reflective decisional pathway for a moment we can relate this to the expectancy value models that have been previously discussed. The reflective decisional process is about weighing up the probability and the value of the consequences of behaviour, and reaching a preferred option. It is proposed that once the decision has been made, the appropriate behavioural frameworks are activated through an intention. However, this system does not operate in isolation, but interacts with the impulsive system, which activates schemata through spreading activation, which can originate from peripheral input (such as the environment, others etc.) or reflective

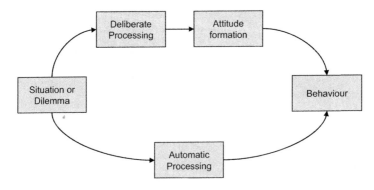

Figure 4.1 A simple depiction of Smith and DeCoster's [75] dual processing approach

processes, but unlike the decisional process this is spontaneous and requires little cognitive effort. This dual processing approach may then explain impulsive behaviours such as impulsive eating, but there is also growing evidence that some health related behaviours are automatic reactions to certain stimuli [76]. This is an important consideration when planning interventions to consider strategies to deal with these unconscious processes.

How do children and adolescents differ from adults?

While the dual process approach is relevant to both adults and children and adolescents, there are differences in memory and experience that can affect the decisional pathway and lead to greater impulsivity. Let us consider the role of experience. Memory and schemata (the way that memory is organised) are important when considering child and adolescent behaviour, and key to health psychologists designing health interventions.

Schemata are frameworks in which information is categorised and stored and according to Piaget [10] are constantly changing as we are presented with new information through the processes of accommodation and assimilation:

- Assimilation
  - Is about taking new information into an existing schema by activating and using a pre-existing schema and making adjustments by adding in new information e.g. we might know that a tomato is red and round, but are then confronted with a plum tomato and this is added to the schema of tomato.
- Accommodation
  - Is about adding to the schema if the previous experience is not sufficient. This is when existing knowledge is not enough. If we consider the tomato example, a child may know that tomatoes are red and can be different shapes, but may one day encounter tomatoes that are different in colour such as yellow and have to accommodate these by changing the schema that all tomatoes are red.

Adolescents then differ from adults when it comes to risky health behaviours as they may have knowledge about them, but may lack experience. Circumstances that are novel may then produce behaviour that is more reactive to their surroundings and external cues due to a lack of internal cues. Coupled with a developing brain with maturational changes that suggest a peak in impulsivity during the period of adolescence [43] helps to explain the uptake of risky behaviours during this period of development. The timings of this peak may also be different according to gender, with females seeming to peak more towards the age of 16 and males around 18. There may also be individual differences within the decline of impulsivity as the individual progresses towards adulthood that may leave them more susceptible to risk behaviour. Research has indicated that the rate of decline in impulsivity is associated with increased susceptibility to alcohol misuse. For example, in a longitudinal study, researchers [77] found in their sample of 15–16-year-olds that there was an increased susceptibility in alcohol use in those participants with the most gradual decline in impulsivity. This link has also been replicated across a student sample aged 18–25 [78]. This is without even considering the effect of alcohol on the brain and how this may interfere with processing and increasing the likelihood of relying on situational cues. Therefore, reasoned models of behaviour that are applied to adult behaviours may not be as appropriate for children and adolescent behaviour or predict more risky impulsive behaviours such as smoking, drinking and substance use. A dual processing approach could therefore be a suitable model to consider when seeking to understand health behaviour, especially risk behaviour, and for targeting interventions.

The Prototype Willingness Model

The Prototype Willingness Model (PWM) [79; 80] is a dual processing approach that was developed specifically to account for the less reasoned, more impulsive health risk behaviour that is exhibited by adolescents. It has been used to investigate a number of behaviours such as alcohol use, sexual activity and driving. This model suggests decisions are based on both mood and heuristics (decision-making) [81]. and unlike models such as the Theory of Planned Behaviour [82], which assumes that not all behaviour is reasoned, but proposes an alternative, reactionary pathway in response to a situation.

Within the model the reasoned pathway is consistent with an expectancy value approach and the closest predictor of the health behaviour is an intention to perform that behaviour. Antecedents, or precursors to intention are considered to be attitudes towards the given behaviour, perceived vulnerability, subjective norms (whether significant others approve of the behaviour) and the behaviour of peers. The divergent path to behaviour is considered to be via a willingness to engage in the behaviour should the opportunity arise.

In essence the model proposes that risk behaviour is the result of a social reaction to the social circumstances. Gibbons and Gerrard [80; 81] suggest that through this reactionary pathway the deliberation of the potential consequences are truncated and that how the individual is feeling has more of an impact. In this way the behaviour is not planned, but there may be a willingness to engage in the behaviour in the right set of circumstances. This would align with the automatic processing suggested within the dual processing approach as previously described. The model also proposes that behavioural willingness is also preceded by the images or prototypes of the person who typically engages in the behaviour, both healthy and unhealthy, positive or negative. Also considered is the favourability of this image and how similar the image is to the self. However, one cannot assume that positive drinker images represent a goal to adolescents as they tend to rate themselves more positively, but in fact some research suggests that it is non-drinker images that are more representative of their ideal selves [83]. The favourability of drinker prototypes has been linked with adolescent alcohol use, for example, in a longitudinal study higher favourability of drinker prototypes was linked to a greater willingness to use alcohol and later alcohol use [83]. Therefore behaviour is associated with positive prototype images of those that engage in that behaviour and a willingness to engage should the risk opportunity presents itself.

The concept of willingness is associated with automatic processing in that there is no reflective weighing up of pros and cons of the behaviour. For example, one group of researchers [84] found that if adolescent participants are asked to read about the negative consequences of taking non-prescription stimulants then they reported less willingness to engage in non-prescription stimulant use. So if adolescents are asked to consider the potential negative consequences of, for example, drinking or smoking then this may reduce their willingness. The issue here is that it is difficult to measure behavioural willingness as in fact you are asking people to consider whether they would be willing, which could be considered to be a deliberation. However, information and consideration of potential consequences in high-risk situations such as how to say no to a cigarette or refuse more alcohol may build upon schemata and make these more readily available in similar situations.

Overall, studies have indicated that the Prototype Willingness Model does indeed extend the expectancy value models, and is more successful in predicting behaviour, especially in relation to alcohol use in the adolescent age group [85]. This would suggest that this would be a useful framework on which to base future adolescent alcohol interventions.

Having considered the need for intervention and then evaluated the relevant theory, the subsequent stages of intervention design would then be to consider how to target the specific behaviours. Health psychologists map behaviour change techniques to theoretical constructs to evoke behaviour change. Previous interventions have attempted to alter prototypes by manipulating images with some success e.g. one study showed that activities which highlighted negative images of young smokers was successful in reducing willingness to smoke [86]. To date, interventions using the prototype willingness have not clearly specified the behaviour change techniques employed. In order to address this there has been recent literature that has attempted to link the prototype willingness model with behaviour change techniques in planning health behaviour change interventions in both healthy eating [87] and alcohol use [88], although, however, as yet the success of these interventions has not been evaluated.

Summary of chapter

Childhood and adolescence are important periods of development for establishing positive health behaviours. Childhood behaviours can impact future health in adulthood and there seems to be a risk for establishing harmful behaviours such as tobacco and alcohol use during the interval of adolescence. It is important to view childhood and adolescence as being uniquely different to adulthood and consider that methods that are used for adults may not be easily transferable. There is a need to consider maturation and the differences in processing to be able to be successful in targeting behaviour change interventions.

References

[1]   Gustafsson, P. E., Janlert, U., Theorell, T., Westerlund, H., & Hammarström, A. (2012) Do peer relations in adolescence influence health in adulthood? Peer problems in the school setting and the metabolic syndrome in middle-age. *PLOS ONE* 7(6): e39385.

[2] Balantekin, K. & Birch, L. & Savage, J. (2016). Eating in the absence of hunger during childhood predicts self-reported binge eating in adolescence. *Eating Behaviors*. 24, 7–10.

[3] McVie, S. & Bradshaw, P. (2005). The Edinburgh Study of Youth Transitions and Crime (7) Edinburgh: Centre for Law and Society, The University of Edinburgh.

[4] Hallal, P., Victoria, C. G., Azevedo, M. R. & Wells, C. K. (2006). Adolescent physical activity and health. *Sports Medicine*, 36(12), 1019–1030.

[5] Gardner, B., Lally, P., & Wardle, J. (2012). Making health habitual: the psychology of habit formation and general practice. *British Journal of General Practice*, 62(605): 664–666.

[6] Wood, W. & Neal, D. T. (2009). The habitual consumer. *Journal of Consumer Psychology*, 19, 579–592.

[7] Lally, P. & Gardner, B. (2010). Promoting habit formation. *Health Psychology Review*, 7(1), 137–158.

[8] Dickinson, A. (1985). Actions and habits: The development of behavioural autonomy. *Philosophical Transactions of the Royal Society of London. B, Biological Sciences*, 308(1135), 67–78.

[9] Engel, G. L. (1977). The need for a new medical model: A challenge for biomedicine. *Science*, 8196(4286), 129–136.

[10] Inhelder, B. & Piaget, J. (1958). *The Growth of Logical Thinking from Childhood to Adolescence.* London: Routledge and Kegan Paul.

[11] Ainsworth, M. D. . & Bell, S. M. (1970). Attachment, exploration and separation: Illustrated by the behaviour of one-year-olds in a strange situation. *Child Development*, 41(1), 49–67.

[12] Abarca-Gómez, L., Abdeen, Z. A., Hamid, Z. A. et al. (2017). Worldwide trends in body-mass index, underweight, over-weight, and obesity from 1975 to 2016: a pooled analysis of 2416 population-based measurement studies in 128.9 million children, adolescents, and adults. *Lancet*, 390(10113), 2627–2642.

[13] van Grieken, A., Renders, C. M., Wijtzes, A. I., Hirasing, R. A., & Raat, H. (2013). Overweight, obesity and underweight is associated with adverse psychosocial and physical health outcomes among 7-year-old children: The "Be active, eat right" study. *PLoS ONE*, 8(6), e67383.

[14] The National Child Measurement Programme Operational Guidance 2018. Public Health England.

[15] Choquet, H., & Meyre, D. (2011). Genetics of obesity: What have we learned? *Current Genomics*, 12(3), 169–179.

[16] Walley, A. J., Blakemore, A. I. F., Froguel, P. (2006). Genetics of obesity and the prediction of risk for health. *Human Molecular Genetics*, 15(2).124–130.

[17] Wardle, J. & Carnell, S. (2009). Appetite is a heritable phenotype associated with adiposity. *Annals of Behavioral Medicine*, 3(suppl 1), 525–530.

[18] Yach, D.. Stuckler, D. Brownell, K. D. (2006). Epidemiologic and economic consequences of the global epidemics of obesity and diabetes. *Nature Medicine*, 12(1), 62–66.

[19] Lansigan, R. K., Emond, J. A., & Gilbert-Diamond, D. (2014). Understanding eating in the absence of hunger among young children: a systematic review of existing studies. *Appetite*, 85, 36–47.

[20] Townshend, T., & Lake, A.(2017). Obesogenic environments: current evidence of the built and food environments, *Perspectives in Public Health*, 137(1), 38–44.

[21] Coulthard, H., Harris, G. & Emmet, P. (2010). Long-term consequences of early fruit and vegetable feeding practices in the United Kingdom, *Public Health Nutrition*, 13(120),2044–2051.

[22] Brown, A., Jones, S. W., & Rowan, H. (2017). Baby-led weaning: The evidence to date. *Current Nutrition Reports*, 6(2), 148–156.

[23] Brown, A. & Lee, M. D. (2013). Early influences on child satiety-responsiveness: the role of weaning style. *Pediatric Obesity*, 10(1), 57–66.

[24] Brown, A. (2017). No difference in self-reported frequency of choking between infants introduced to solid foods using a baby-led weaning or traditional spoon-feeding approach. *Journal of Human Nutrition and Dietetics*, 31, 396–504.

[25] Lovelace, S., Rabiee-Khan, F. (2013). Food choices made by low income households when feeding their pre-school children; a qualitative study. Maternal and Child Nutrition, 11(4), 870–881.

[26] Johnson, S. L., & Birch, L. L. (1994). Parents' and children's adiposity and eating style. *Pediatrics*, 94, 653–661.

[27] Birch, L. & Fisher, J. (1998). Development of eating behaviors among children and adolescents. *Pediatrics*, 101, 539.

[28] Rollins, B.Y., Loken, E., Savage, J. S., Birch, L. L. (2014). Maternal controlling feeding practices and girls' inhibitory control interact to predict changes in BMI and eating in the absence of hunger from 5 to 7 y. *American Journal of Clinical Nutrition*, 99, 249–257.

[29] Faith, M. S., Scanlon, K. S., Birch, L. L., Francis, L. A. & Sherry, B. (2012). Parent-child feeding strategies and their relationships to child eating and weight status, *Obesity*, 12(11), 1711–1722.

[30] Harris, H., Mallan, K. M., Nambiar, S., & Daniels, L. A. (2014). The relationship between controlling feeding practices and boys' and girls' eating in the absence of hunger. *Eating Behaviors*, 15(4), 519–522.

[31] Rollins B. Y., Savage, J. S., Fisher, J. O. & Birch, L. L. (2016). Alternatives to restrictive feeding practices to promote self-regulation in childhood: A developmental perspective. *Pediatric Obesity*, 11(5), 316–332.

[32] Laureah, M., Bergamasch, V., Pagliarini, E. (2014). School-based intervention with children. Peer modelling, reward and repeated exposure reduce food neophobia and increase liking of fruits and vegetables. *Appetite*, 83, 26–32.

[33] Jamie Oliver www.feedmebetter.com/ acccessed 28.12.2018

[34] Berlot, M. & James, J. (2009). Healthy school meals and educational outcomes. *Institute for Social and Economic Research.* London.

[35] Cabinet Office, Department of Health and Social Care, HM Treasury, and Prime Ministers Office, 10 Downing Street (2017): Childhood Obesity: A plan for action

[36] Health Start www.healthystart.nhs.uk/ accessed 4.1.2019.

[37] Public Health England 2015: Change 4 Life. London.

[38] Change 4 Life www.nhs.uk/change4life/food-facts/healthier-snacks-for-kids/100-calorie-snacks accessed 4.1.2019.

[39] Owen, L. H., Kennedy, O. B., Hill, C., & Houston-Price, C. (2018). Food familiarization through picture books helps parents introduce vegetables into toddlers' diets. *Appetite*, 128, 32–43.

[40] Marcon, A., Pesce, G., Calciano, L., Bellisario, V., Dharmage, S. C., Garcia-Aymerich, J. et al. (2018). Trends in smoking initiation in Europe over 40 years: A retrospective cohort study. *PLoS ONE* 13(8), e0201881.

[41] Larson, R. W., Moneta, G., Richards, M., Wilson, S. (2002). Continuity, stability and change in daily emotional experience across adolescence. *Child Development*, 73, 1151–1165.

[42] Macarea, C., Duccia, F., Zhanga, Y. Ruggeria, B., Jiaa, T., Kaakinene, M. et al. (2018) A neurobiological pathway to smoking in adolescence: *TTC12-ANKK1-DRD2* variants and reward response. *European Neuropsychopharmacology*, 28, 1103–1114.

[43] Spear, L. P. (2000). The adolescent brain and age-related behavioral manifestations. *Neuroscience and Biobehavioral Reviews*, 24, 417–463.

[44] Westling, E., Andrews, J. A., & Peterson, M. (2012). Gender differences in pubertal timing, social competence, and cigarette use: a test of the early maturation hypothesis. *The Journal of Adolescent Health: Official Publication of the Society for Adolescent Medicine*, 51(2), 150–155.

[45] Windle, M., Spear, L. P., Fuligni, A. J., Angold, A., Brown, J. D., Pine, M., Smith, G. T., Gedd, J. & Dahl, R. E. (2011). Transitions into underage and problem drinking: Developmental processes and mechanisms between 10 and 15 years of age. *Pediatrics*, 121(4), 5273–5289.

[46] Ali, M. M., & Dwyer, D. S. (2011). Estimating peer effects in sexual behaviour among adolescents. *Journal of Adolescence*, 34, 183–190.

[47] Wood, L., & McMurray, I. (2018). Perceptions of alcohol use in UK 12–14 year olds, *Drugs and Alcohol Today*,18(4), 262–271.

[48] Erikson, E. H. (Ed.). (1963). *Youth: Change and Challenge*. New York: Basic Books.

[49] Gerrard, M., Gibbons, F. X., Reis-Bergan, M., Trudeau, L., Vande Lune, L. S. and Buunk, B. (2002) Inhibitory effects of drinker and non-drinker prototypes on adolescent alcohol consumption. *Health Psychology*, 21(6), 601–609.

[50] Bulowski, W. M., Motzoi, C. & Meyer, F. (2009). Friendship as process function and outcome in K. H. Rubin, W. M. Lukowski and B. Laursen (eds) *Handbook of Peer Interactions, Relationships and Groups*. New York: The Guildford Press.

[51] Fuglini, A. J. & Eccles, J. E. (1993). Perceived parent-child relationships and early adolescents' orientation towards peers. *Developmental Psychology*, 29(4), 622–632.

[52] Leeuw, R., Scholte, R,. Vermulst, A., Engels, R. (2010). The relation between smoking-specific parenting and smoking trajectories of adolescents: How are changes in parenting related to changes in smoking? *Psychology & Health*, 25, 999–1021.

[53] Becoña, E . Martinez, Ú., Calafat, A. Fernández-Hermida, J. R., Juan, M., Sumnall, H., Mendes, F. & Gabrhelík, R. (2013). Parental permissiveness, control, and affect and drug use among adolescents. *Psicotherma*, 25(3), 292–298.

[54] Maggs, J., & Staff, J. (2018). Parents who allow early adolescents to drink. *Journal of Adolescent Health*, 62(2), 245–247.

[55]   Bax, S. (2013). M-PACT: supporting families dealing with addiction (www.ssj.org.uk/blog/m-pact-supporting-families-dealing-addiction: accessed 16.3.2018).

[56]   Bartholomew, L. K., Parcel, G. S., Kok, G., & Gottlieb, N. H. (2006). *Planning Health Promotion Programs: An Intervention Mapping Approach.* San Francisco, CA: Jossey-Bass.

[57]   National Statistics (2017). Statistics on Alcohol England 2017, available at www.content.digital.nhs.uk/catalogue/PUB23940/alc-eng-2017-rep.pdf (accessed 21.11.2017)

[58]   Brooks, F., Magnusson, J., Klemera, E., Spencer, N. & Morgan, A. (2011). *HBSC England National Report. Findings from the 2010 HBSC study for England.* Hatfield: University of Hertfordshire.

[59]   Jones, L. & Bellis, M. A. (2013). *Updating England-Specific Alcohol-Attributable Fractions, Centre for Public Health.* Liverpool: Liverpool John Moores University.

[60]   Phillips-Howard, P. A., Bellis, M. A., Briant, L. B., Jones, H., Dwoning, J., Kelly, I. E., Bird, T. & Cook, P. A. (2010). Wellbeing, alcohol use and sexual activity in young teenagers: Findings from a cross sectional survey in school children in North West England. *Substance Abuse Treatment, Prevention, and Policy,* 5, 27.

[61]   McVie, S. & Bradshaw, P. (2006). *The Edinburgh Study of Youth Transitions and Crime (7),* Edinburgh: Centre for Law and Society, The University of Edinburgh.

[62]   McCambridge, J., McAlaney, J., Rowe. R. (2011). Adult consequences of late adolescent alcohol consumption: a systematic review of cohort studies, *PLoS Med,* 8: e1000413.

[63]   Moss, A. C. & Albery, I. P. (2009). A dual-process model of the alcohol-behavior link for social drinking. *Psychological Bulletin,* 516–530.

[64]   Perkins, H. W. (2007). Misperceptions of peer drinking norms in Canada: Another look at the "reign of error" and it's consequences among college students. *Addictive Behaviors,* 32, 2645–2656.

[65]   Hahm, H. C., Kolacyk, E., Jang, J., Swenson, T. & Bhindawala, A. M. (2012). Binge drinking trajectories from adolescence to young adulthood: The effects of peer social network, *Substance Use and Misuse,* 47(6), 745–746.

[66]   Kelly, Y., Goisis, A., Sacker, A., Cable, N., Watt, R., & Britton, A. (2016). What influences 11 year olds to drink? Findings from the Millenium cohort study. *BMC Pulic Health,* 16, 169.

[67]   Jones, B. T., Corbin, W. & Fromme, K. (2001). A review of expectancy theory and alcohol consumption. *Addiction,* 96, 57–72.

[68] Jester, J. M., Steinberg, D. B., Heitzig, M.M. & Zucker, R. A. (2015). Coping expectanciees, not enhancement expectancies, mediate trauma experience effects on problem alcohol use: A prospective study from early childhood to adolescence. *Journal of Studies on Alcohol and Drugs*, 76(5), 781–789.

[69] Colder, C. R., O'Connor, R. M., Read, J. P. Eiden, R.D., Lengua, L. J. Hawk JR, L. W. Wieczorek, W. F. (2014). Growth trajectories od alcohol information processing and associations with escalation of drinking in early adolescence. *Psychology of Addictive Behaviors*, 28(3), 69.

[70] Kuntsche, E. & Kuntsche, E. (2018). Even in early childhood offspring alcohol expectancies correspond to parental drinking. *Drug and Alcohol Dependence*, 183, 51–54.

[71] Colder, C. R., Shyhalla, K., & Frndak, S. E. (2018). Early alcohol use with parental permission: Psychosocial characteristics and drinking in late adolescence. *Addictive Behaviors*, 76, 82–87.

[72] Conrod, P. J., Pihl, R. O., Stewart, S. H., & Dongier, M. (2000). Validation of a system of classifying female substance abusers on the basis of personality and motivational risk factors for substance abuse, *Psychology of Addictive Behaviors*, 14(3), 243–256.

[73] Woicik, P. A., Stewart, S. H., Pihl, R. O., & Conrod, P. J. (2009). The substance use risk profile scale: A scale measuring traits linked reinforcement specific substance use profiles. *Addictive Behaviors*, 34, 1042–1055.

[74] Strack, F. & Deutsch, R. (2004). Reflective and impulsive determinants of social behavior. *Personality and Social Psychology Review*, 8(3), 220–247.

[75] Smith, E. R. & DeCoster, J. (2000). Dual-process models in social and cognitive psychology: Conceptual integration and limits to underlying memory systems. *Persoanlity and Social Psychology Review*, 4(2), 108–131.

[76] Heatherton, T. F. & Wagner, D. D. (2011). Cognitive neuroscience of self-regulation failure. *Trends in Cognitive Science*, 15, 132–139.

[77] Stewart, S. H., Conrod, P. J., Marlatt, G. A., Comeau, M. N., Thrush, C., & Krank, M. (2005). New developments in prevention and early intervention for alcohol abuse in youths. *Alcoholism; Clinical and Experimental Research*, 29(92), 278–286.

[78] Littlefield, A. K., Sher, K. J. & Steinley, D. (2010). Developmental trajectories of impulsivity and their association with alcohol use and related outcomes during emerging and young adulthood. *Alcoholism Clinical and Experimental Research*, 34(8),1409–1416.

[79] Gibbons, F. X., & Gerrard, M. (1995). Predicting young adults' health-risk behaviour. *Journal of Personality and Social Psychology*, 69, 505–517.

[80] Gibbons, F. X., Gerrard, M. (1997). Health images and their effects on health behaviour. In Buunk, B. P., & Gibbons, F. X. (eds), *Health, Coping, and Well-being: Perspectives from Social Comparison Theory*. Mahwah, NJ: Erlbaum.

[81] Gerrard, M., Gibbons, F. X., Houlihan, A. E., Stock, M. L. & Pomery, E. A. (2008) A dual-process approach to heatlh risk decision making: The prototype willingness model. *Developmental Review*, 28, 29–61.

[82] Ajzen, I. (1991). The theory of planned behaviour. *Organizational Behavior and Human Decision Processes*, 50, 179–211.

[83] Gerrard, M., Gibbons, F. X., Reis-Bergan, M., Trudeau, L., Vande Lune, L. S., & Buunk, B. (2002). Inhibitory effects of drinker and non-drinker prototypes on adolescent alcohol consumption. *Health Psychology*, 21, 601–609.

[84] Stock, M. L., Litt, D. M., Arlt, V., Peterson, L. M. & Sommerville, J. (2013). The prototype/willingness model, academic versus health-risk information, and risk cognitions associated with non-medical prescription stimulant use among college students. *British Journal of Health Psychology*, 18, 490–507.

[85] Todd, J., Kothe, E., Mullan, B. & Monds, L. (2016). Reasoned versus reactive prediction of behaviour: A meta-analysis of the prototype willingness model. *Health Psychology Review*, 10(1), 1–24.

[86] Andrews, J. A., Gordon, J. S., Hampson, S. E., Christiansen, S. M., Gunn, B., Slovic. P. & Severson, H. H. (2011). Short-term efficacy of click city[R]: tobacco: Changing etiological mechanisms related to the onset of tobacco use, *Prevention Science*, 12(1), 89 102.

[87] Dohnke, B., Deveitt, T. & Steinhiber, A. (2018). A prototype-targeting intervention for the promotion of healthy eating in adolescents: Development and evaluation using intervention mapping. *Health Education*, 10, 1108.

5   Stress

Contents

Chapter overview

This chapter is devoted to the topic of stress and to the consideration of the potential link between stress and ill health. In order to appreciate stress and illness the chapter will take a biopsychosocial approach. We will start by considering the concept of stress and then move on to the biological mechanisms of the stress response, and how these mechanisms may affect health and wellbeing. We will then take a more psychological approach and consider key theories that link stress and health, before considering the importance of the appraisal of stress. In doing so we will also draw links between biological mechanisms and psychological factors in considering individual differences in bodily responses. We will then introduce the concept of psychoneuroimmunology and the link between stress and immune functioning, drawing on evidence and examples from literature. These examples will include how stress might increase susceptibility to the common cold, the effect it may have on the healing process and how it might affect inflammation and alter the production of antibodies. We will also consider how stress can indirectly affect health through behaviours such as illness behaviours and health behaviours such as smoking. The chapter will then go on to focus on coping with stress, the concept of resilience and the role of health psychology in measuring stress and stress management.

Introduction

Stress is a term that is commonly used in contemporary society, and is often linked to health and wellbeing. However, what do we mean by stress? It is a rather simplistic term for what is actually a multifaceted phenomenon. It is a term that can be traced back to Middle English where it is thought that it was used to denote the hardship or force put upon a person [1]. It has since been adopted in the field of engineering as the pressure or tension exerted upon a material object and in psychology, it is a term used to explain the mental/emotional tension that results from demanding circumstances.

In human behaviour, stress has been studied widely from a range of perspectives such as an evolutionary function in terms of survival, how genes and the environment may interact and explain individual variations in response [2], and how it might be assessed or measured. The concept of stress is complex and not easily defined and so this chapter takes a biopsychosocial approach in examining the biological mechanisms of stress and considers how psychosocial influences may interact with these mechanisms. It also provides an evaluation of some of the available literature with regard to the potential link between stress and ill health.

What is stress?

Let's start by considering the psychological definition of stress in more detail. The general definition of stress is that it is an experience/situation that is appraised as being a threat at the same time as coping resources are appraised as being inadequate [3]. To pinpoint stress into a single definition is challenging, as it is dependent on a number of factors, such as cultural, individual differences, environmental factors and physiological mechanisms. It is therefore perhaps best considered as an umbrella term that includes a range of different factors such as psychosocial factors and environmental factors and their effect on psychological or physical wellbeing.

Models of stress

Fight or flight

Early models of stress were based around experiments of the physiological mechanisms of the stress response. These theories focused on the element of the stress response as a means for survival e.g. evolutionary theory suggests that the stress response is necessary to prepare the body to meet the physiological demands that are posed by a potential threat. Within this context it is considered to be short intense emergency reaction that enables the organism to either flee or fight [4; 5; 6; 7]. Through the work of Walter Canon [4; 5; 6; 7] this became known as the fight or flight response. This response has been likened to lighting a match, in that it is quick and short-lived [8].

What happens in the body during the fight or flight response?

In physiological terms when the organism is presented with a stressful stimulus (the stressor) this activates an emotional response in the amygdala which then in turn activates the hypothalamus (the portion of the brain that controls homeostasis). The hypothalamus stimulates the autonomic nervous system through the sympathetic adrenal medullary (SAM) pathway (see Figure 5.1 and follow the left hand pathway), made up of the sympathetic nervous system and the parasympathetic nervous system. The stimulation of the sympathetic nervous system prepares the body for action, and when activated stimulates the release of adrenalin and noradrenalin from the adrenal medulla (which sits on the top of the kidneys) through sympathetic nerves releasing acetylcholine. These hormones then cause an increase in heart

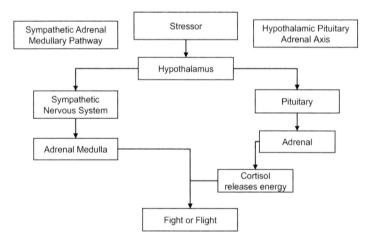

Figure 5.1 A diagram of the SAM and HPA stress pathways

rate and breathing, constrict blood vessels and tighten muscles. The organism is then in a state of alert, and blood and oxygen requirements may cause symptoms such as upset tummies and as more blood is diverted to leg and arm muscles be aware of a thumping heat rate. When the stressor has passed then it is assumed that the organism returns to a 'normal' state or set point.

Canon [4; 5; 6; 7] favoured the homeostatic theory and presumed that the parasympathetic nervous system worked in tandem with the sympathetic nervous system to restore homeo-stasis and return the body to a set point. This theory would suggest that mechanisms within the body detect and correct any deviations to a set point. However, this is now considered to be an over simplified explanation which does not fully capture the complexity of the mechanisms of stress and in more recent years there has been a movement away from the homeostatic theory [9]. However, there is still a consensus within the literature that the sympathetic nervous system mobilises the body in response to stress and that the function of the parasympathetic nervous system is to restore energy to the body by reducing the heart rate and increasing ingestion.

Biological Model of Stress – Seyle's General Adaption Syndrome

The biological understanding of the physiological mechanisms of stress was influenced by the work of Selye [10] who found stress was not only related to activation of the SAM pathway and the autonomic nervous system, but also involved activation of the Hypothalamic Pituitary Adrenal (HPA) pathway. His theory became known as the General Adaption Syndrome (GAS). This second stress pathway involves activation of the hypothalamus, which stimulates the production of adrenocorticotropic hor-mone (ACTH), which in turn triggers the production of cor-tisol. Cortisol is a corticosteroid, which activates the release of stored sugar from the liver and insulin from the pancreas – this makes you hungry and more likely to snack on high sugar foods and store fat. Cortisol is also considered to suppress the immune system, but more on this later. Whereas the SAM pathway had been likened to striking a match, then the HPA pathway has been likened to lighting a fire; it takes more effort and lasts longer [8].

Selye first offered a definition of stress in which he described it as a general neuroendocrine response [11]. He challenged this definition later as he noticed that it affected systems beyond the endocrine system such as the cardiovascular system. From observations on rats, which he injected with nocuous agents, he noticed a set of similar effects which was initially called the General Adaption Syndrome (GAS), but later he called 'stress'. These effects were assimilated into a series of three stages.

1. **Stage 1 – Alarm Reaction**
    The alarm reaction refers to the first 6–48 hours following the stressor when the sympathetic branch of the autonomic nervous system is activated and the adrenal glands are stimulated to secrete cortisol and adrenalin. In the rats, Selye observed that this resulted in organ shrinkage (e.g. in the liver, thymus and lymph glands) and also caused a decrease in the amount of body fat. The rat's body temperature also decreased. These symptoms were considered to be energy conserving and align with the idea of a preparedness to flee or fight [11]. In this way the stage one response is considered similar to the fight or flight response as described by Canon.

2. **Stage 2 – Resistance**
    The second stage was considered to be the stage of resistance. After 48 hours the rats seemed to recover, and the stress hormones had reduced. They seemed to be adapting to the threat. However, he also found that there was evidence that there were changes as a result of the event, such as elevated blood glucose levels and elevated blood pressure [11].

3. **Stage 3 – Exhaustion**
    The stage of exhaustion Selye described was characterised by depleted resources and insufficient energy to cope with the continued stress. He found that chronic stress or continued exposure to a stressor resulted in adrenal exhaustion and high levels of cortisol. Some of the rats even died [10].

It was therefore proposed that the excessive, persistent or repeated activation of the SAM and HPA pathways were biological evidence that supported the concept of stress. The impact of the physiological reaction was considered to be the primary pathway in connecting events to physical outcomes and linking it to health such as wear and tear on the cardiovascular system. However, this is a very simplistic stimulus-response model that assumes that everyone responds to stressors in the same way – but do they?

Transactional Theory of Stress

The problem with stimulus-response models of stress such as Selye's model is that it is assumes that the individual is passive, and that stress response exists independent of the stressor. However, what might be stressful for some people may be exciting for others. The transactional model of stress is all about the importance of the cognitive appraisal of events.

Is it stress?

The fight or flight response is the arousal of the body in response to a potential stressor, but is this always negative? or could it be positive? Let us consider the example of bungee jumping. Some people find this fun and exhilarating while for others it may cause fear and anxiety, however, in both cases it is likely that there will be some activation of the physiological systems. Physiological models are important, but the fight or flight model is perhaps too simplistic as it does not take into consideration the individual interpretation of the meaning of the stressor.

How an individual appraises the potential stressor is important. Human beings are not simply passive, but interact with their environment. In the transactional model of stress Lazarus and Folkman [12] theorised that when an external or an internal event is considered a demand then this signals a need to cope, which is then weighed up in terms of the resources required. Stress within this theory is defined as when the event exceeds the available coping resources and affects wellbeing. Stress within this framework is a complex phenomenon and is affected by a range of factors. At the crux of the model is appraisal, which accounts for individual differences.

The Transactional Model [12] (see Figure 5.2) states that when a person encounters an event or demand, then there is an appraisal of this event or demand, which they termed primary appraisal [12]. This is the process of determining whether the stimulus is a threat or a challenge. The demand is evaluated in terms of meaning, relevance and significance, or in other words, does this matter? and by how much? This may not be a conscious weighing up but may occur in the subconscious and be compared to similar experiences/events. They [12] then propose that there is a second stage of appraisal, the secondary appraisal, which is the weighing up of the different coping strategies. In other words, what coping sources are available and evaluate their availability [9]. This means that it can be affected by learning, previous experience, memory, expectations and also be continually updated. However, this model has come under some criticism

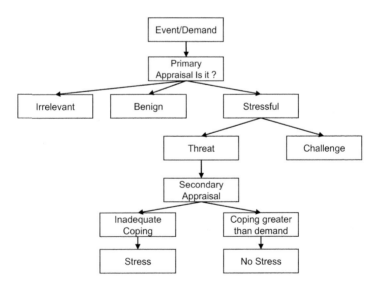

Figure 5.2 A diagram of Lazarus and Folkman's Transactional Theory of Stress

for how appraisal can be measured (primary appraisal is unconscious) and evaluated, it does offer a reasonable explanation for individual differences in the effects of stress when presented with similar stressors. It is all about appraisal!

Is there a link between stress and health?

To answer this, we first need to consider the potential mechanisms of the stress response and the relationship between these physiological mechanisms and individual differences in appraisal of stressors, coping resources and behaviours. There is now considerable evidence that stress can affect health both indirectly and directly. The indirect pathway is through health behaviours, including maladaptive coping behaviours such as increased smoking, drinking and eating high fat foods. The direct route is through the physiological mechanisms of stress and the subsequent altered physiological states, including changes in the immune system. In other words, individuals who experience negative stressful life experiences may be more at risk of illness.

However, the concept of stress is rather broad and there have been attempts to quantify stressors and how they might affect health. This originally stemmed from clinical observation, which found that sick people were more likely to have experienced serious life events such as bereavement. This led to work by Holmes and Rahe [13] who tried to identify what types of events and experiences might make people ill. To do this they asked 5,000 people who had recently been ill to come up with a list of events that they considered to be the most stressful. Based on these ratings they developed the Social Readjustment Rating Scale (SRRS), as a way of quantifying their significance to health outcomes using a consensus approach. Within the scale are 43 examples of events and associated life change unit scores e.g. death of a spouse is at the top of the scale and is equivalent to 100 life change units. This became the life events theory [13], and what they found was that the higher the life change unit scores were (e.g. being fired from work – 47 LCU, in-law troubles 29 LCU, changing residence 20 LCU) the higher the risk to health.

In a study of 88 physicians 70 per cent of those scoring over 300 life change units reported ill health [14]. Subsequently, they also found that cancer patients were more than twice as likely to have reported negative life events. There has been some debate about the link between life events and cancer in the literature and more recent evidence suggested that women may have a tendency to attribute their breast cancer to psychological factors such as stress [15].

On the whole this type of research seems to suggest that there may be a link between stress and ill health, but there are some issues to be considered. Because the research tends to be retrospective (asking people to recall events), there may be some bias as they try to make sense of their illness. For example in the previous example where women were reported to attribute the onset of breast cancer to psychological factors such as stress [15] as compared to a very large prospective study [16] of around 106,000 participants (1,788 developed breast cancer) where there was no link found between adverse life events in the previous five years and subsequent cancer.

The role of daily hassles

What we have gleaned so far is that although individuals may perceive life events to be important in explaining the stress-illness link, they have not been demonstrated to be strong predictors of future illness. But could it be that because we might be coping with these major events and our stress response is already stimulated it is the daily hassles in our lives that add extra stress and are related to illness? Researchers [17; 18] have found that daily hassles such as missing your train, losing your car keys, having an argument, being stuck in traffic and late for an appointment are more predictive of subsequent illness than life events. So let's consider the effect of the physiological stress response over time.

Allostatic load

Allostasis refers to the physiological adaption of the body systems to acute stress, and the return to a pre-stress level. This would be considered to be the activation of the sympathetic nervous system and return to homeostasis in Canon's homeo-static model.

However, the question is:

If there is a repeated activation of the stress response does it ever return to a 'normal' level?

Allostatic load therefore refers to the long-term impact of the effects of stress on the cardiovascular, metabolic, neural, behavioural and cellular levels when the body is forced to adapt to the stressful stimulus.

If then, people have many stressful events in their lives, this may cause wear and tear on the body through repeated activation. In some people the body does not recover well from the stress activation or fails to turn off the stress response efficiently. The way that the hormones respond also relates to whether this response is protective or indeed damaging. Prolonged, repeated activation can result in body systems not working as effectively. If we consider circumstances where after a stress response there is inadequate coping, then the response will not stop, which will put pressure on systems in the body. This type of chronic stress and repeated activation of the stress response can result in an impairment of adaptive mechanism and result in wear and tear on the body. This is otherwise known as allostatic load. Subsequently, this may affect the person's ability to cope with any new stressors [19; 20].

Support for this theory comes from some prospective research, where researchers [21] found that those who had been identified as having higher allostatic load at the start of the study were at greater risk of dying 10 years later. What does this mean? Well, there appears to be four situations that are associated with allostatic load, these are when there are repeated hits, where there is a lack of adaption to the stressor, where there is a prolonged response to a stressor or where there is an inadequate response. So, it is the flexibility of the physiological systems in response to SNS and HPA activation that can affect the individual's ability to cope with stressors [22], and is therefore subject to individual differences.

How might stress be linked to ill health?

In addition to the wear and tear on the body caused by the stress response and allostatic load, people may also behave differently when under stress. When people experience stressful events or negative emotions then they may also engage in behaviours that make them feel better (emotionally) but may not be healthy [23]. Some examples might include people who smoke may smoke more when feeling stressed, or people may drink alcohol or eat more fast food [24]. Although the effects of these behaviours may not be acute, in the long term these may be detrimental to an individual's overall health. Therefore, when considering the link between stress and illness there are potentially two routes, the direct route and the indirect route (see Figure 5.3). In this chapter we are looking at the potential direct route.

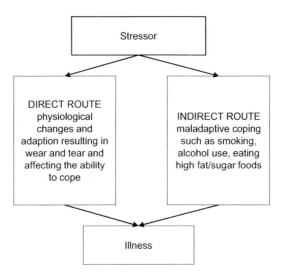

Figure 5.3 The direct and indirect routes between stress and illness

The potential direct route between stress and illness

The direct pathway between stress and illness comes from the prolonged chronic stress response, which produces a prolonged production of epinephrine and cortisol. This prolonged state may result in high blood pressure (permanent state of arousal), changes in the immune response (cortisol) and changes in disease processes. However, not everyone who becomes stressed becomes ill and this is very much dependent on coping and individual differences e.g. individual differences in HPA activation can influence an individual's susceptibility to disease. Some people may respond more rapidly and have a greater biological response than others. This is of interest because those individuals that have a greater reaction to stress (high stress reactivity) tend to be more at risk of cardiovascular disease, and cardiovascular related mortality [25].

Stress reactivity

How quickly an individual physiologically responds to a stressor is dependent on their emotional (affective) response [26]. Heightened activation has been associated with poorer outcomes and individuals who respond more strongly with increased negative feelings over and over again are more vulnerable to problems with their health. This could be particularly problematic for those who have chronic illnesses such as asthma, arthritis or diabetes e.g. higher levels of cortisol from heightened reactivity [27] can increase the amount of glucose in the blood, which can be problematic for diabetes control. Changes have also been seen in antibody responses and to immune system inflammatory markers [28], which could impact inflammatory conditions such as arthritis. Because physiological reactions also affect areas of the brain involved in decision-making and coping, then this may also affect behaviours such as smoking, alcohol use and risk-taking, further increasing health risk. The question is then, if high stress reactivity is related to poorer health, what about low stress reactivity? Well, it would seem that either extreme, with high or low reactivity would be suggestive of some dysregulation

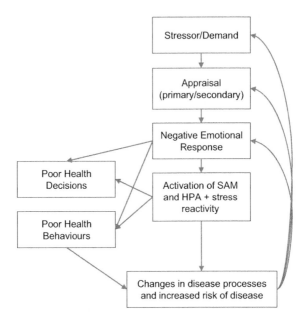

Figure 5.4 Simplified diagram of some potential relationships between stress, stress reactivity and health

within the body systems and may have negative consequences [29]. Some evidence suggests that low reactivity can also affect cognition and motivation and is associated with poorer health behaviours such as alcohol use, or eating high calorie foods [29; 30] (see Figure 5.4 for a simplified diagram).

So far, we have considered the complexity of the stress response and how our thoughts and feelings affect the physiological activation of the physiological systems, but also how this activation may also affect our thoughts and motivations and health behaviours. In doing so we have demonstrated the complexity of the interrelationships between biopsychosocial factors. We are now going to move on to consider the effects of stress on the immune response, subsequent health and the multidisciplinary approach in understanding these relationships.

Psychoneuroimmunology/
psychoneuroendocrinology

The link between psychological wellbeing and the immune system is well evidenced and psychoneuroimmunology (PNI) is the study of the interrelationship between the central nervous system, immune system and endocrine system [31]. The term psychoneuroimmunology was coined by Robert Ader [32], who when studying a classical conditioning paradigm in the 1970s inadvertently conditioned the immune system [32]. He did this in an experiment with rats by pairing a sugar solution with a drug that made the animals sick. The animals soon learned not to drink the sugar solution. However, when he stopped giving the drug the rats not only continued to avoid the sugar solution but some of them died, which was an unexpected result. Ader [32] concluded that this result was because the conditioning, which affected higher order processes in the brain, had also affected the immune system. This then led to the now blooming field of psychoneuroimmunology.

Since Ader's early work, numerous studies have been conducted to observe the effects of stress on the immune system functioning, the susceptibility to illnesses and wound healing. In order to examine the susceptibility to illness researchers have conducted a number of studies on the effect of stress on the common cold and flu e.g. in one study, participants were exposed to respiratory viruses and a variety of stressors, and it was found that those that reported greater amount of stress also reported more clinical symptoms [33]. There may also be direct effects on the immune system such as changes to the number of specific cells such as natural killer cells [34]. Evidence for these changes come from studies that observe immune changes during stressful periods e.g. one set of researchers looked at NK cells in students and found that there was a decrease in natural killer cell activity during exam stress [34]. Effects on the immune system may also interfere with wound healing, for example, in one study [35] the researchers observed wound healing rates in periods of stress and relaxation. The experiment was conducted on volunteer dental students who received a punch biopsy (small hole) to their soft palate (soft bit at the back of the roof of the mouth) during exams and also during the summer break. The researchers found that the punch biopsy healed more quickly during the summer break as compared to exams, which suggested that stress can delay wound healing.

These examples then have demonstrated that there is a potential link between the immune system and stress, but does not really tell us much about whether there is a difference between different types of stressors. Further studies have found that there is a difference in the way that the immune system responds in response to acute stress and chronic stress. Understanding these differences can help health psychologists to work with clients in preventing and managing stress. We will start with a brief introduction to the immune system.

The brief overview of the immune system

The immune system is a network of tissues and cells that protect the body from foreign invaders [36]. The immune system does not act autonomously but is linked to other bodily systems, such as the sympathetic nervous system. The structure of the immune system means that there are links throughout the body and in brief consists of the tonsils, lymph nodes (neck, armpits, tummy and groin) and lymphatic vessels (carry lymph), the thymus gland, bone marrow and spleen. The bone marrow is where white blood cells (see Figure 5.5), are produced and the thymus, which is large in childhood and diminishes with age, is important in the process of maturing and differentiating the T-cells.

The body is constantly under attack, for example, from bacteria, viruses and pollution. The immune system's defence works like a team with two systems consisting of the innate immune system and adaptive immune system. The innate system is non-specific and protects against a wide range of threats e.g. macrophages such as phagocytes recognise and attack foreign invaders. The adaptive system, on the other hand, is more specific and is involved in resistance against particular invaders such as viruses, with specific T-cells.

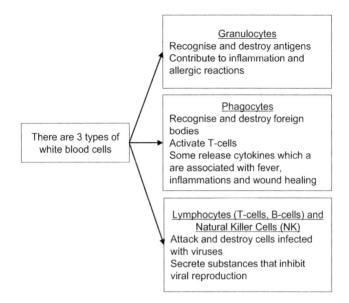

Figure 5.5 An overview of the different types of white blood cells and their basic functions

A simplified explanation of the nervous system is that it consists of the innate and adaptive systems. The innate system is the first line of defence and includes organs such as the skin and filters such as the hair follicles in the nose, natural antimicrobial substances such as sebum, sweat, interferon (chemicals that are produced by cells invaded by viruses), inflammatory responses and surveillance. Surveillance includes Natural Killer (NK) cells that patrol the body and recognise cells that have been infected or mutated by markers. The non-specific nature of the innate system includes phagocytes (macrophages and neutrophils) that are the first line of the cellular defence. Very simply, the purpose of the first defence is to attach and engulf any foreign cells, debris and damaged body cells. After they have ingested the threat, they then display the antigen on their surface, which stimulates

T-lymphocytes and activates an immune response. Inflammation is the collection of neutrophils and macrophages at the site of injury or infection. Macrophages also release cytokines that have broad effects such as fever, inflammation and promote wound healing. These cytokines can cross the blood brain barrier, which means that there is a connection between the immune system and the central nervous system. Immune responses generate an immunological memory, which means that future responses will be faster and more powerful. In sum, the natural/innate system is a generalised response in a short time frame, that results in inflammation from the various roles of the cells involved. This also takes a lot of energy.

Specific immunity, on the other hand, is less speedy and has greater specificity. Lymphocytes have a receptor cell that responds to one invader. When these cells are activated it can take several days for a full defence. T-cells include T-helper cells that amplify the response, T-Cytotoxic cells which recognise when a cell has been infected by a virus or has been compromised and destroys them and B cells (which produce proteins and antibodies) that neutralise toxins.

The potential pathways between stress and the immune system

When experiencing acute stress (as described above) changes occur in the immune system that provide the first line of defence against any potential invading pathogens.

There is some evidence that in the short term there may be immune enhancement in response to stress. This evidence comes from animal studies and so has to be treated with some caution, but studies have demonstrated cell re-distribution due to the initial activation of the stress pathways (fight or flight) to the skin [37]. This response fits within an evolutionary perspective and the adaptive response (fighting or fleeing), and the preparation of the body for potential injury as a result. In the short term this is critical in protecting us from disease and infections.

However, in long-term chronic stress there may be poorer immune functioning. Early theories in relation to chronic stress and immunity suggested that chronic stress induced a global immunosuppression due to corticosteroids [10]. This theory postulates that when an individual is exposed to a major stressor over a long period of time there is an adaption to the increased levels of cortisol in immune cells which become less responsive to it. The result of this is that the body is unable to reduce the inflammatory response and in studies on the common cold, people were more likely to develop a cold [38]. It is important to note that inflammation is a normal reaction and in the short term, such as when there is injury, it promotes an influx of immune cells to the site of injury, and promotes healing [39], but it is long-term inflammation that can be harmful [40].

However, when trying to uncover the mechanisms of this response, there do seem to be variations in immune responses and to different types of stress [41]. A meta-analysis [41], which included an analysis of 293 studies with a total of 18, 941 participants, found that acute stressors such as public speaking induced an increase in immune parameters. Brief stressors such as exams did not demonstrate any significant change in blood markers, but there was a shift in cytokines (inflammatory marker produced by macrophages). The analysis of studies looking at stressful events did not demonstrate reliable or consistent changes, but there did seem to be a decrease in NK cells and an increase in cortisol in response to loss and bereavement and in a small number of studies there was an increase in natural and specific immune responses in response to trauma, such as a natural disaster. In chronic stress, such as studies looking at carers, then there was evidence that both natural and specific immune responses were being negatively affected, leaving that group more vulnerable to illness.

So, we stated earlier that it was important for health psychologists to understand the potential relationships between stress and illness, in order to be able to apply health psychology theory in helping to reduce the negative effects of stress. Now that we have more understanding of how stress may be linked to ill health, it is important to consider other factors that may moderate this relationship.

What moderates the relationship between stress and illness?

Coping

As we have discovered, the stress reaction is complex and involves different mechanisms that are dependent on the duration and the type of the stressor, and also on the individual appraisal of the stressor and availability of coping resources. The way that people cope, or their coping style may be related to their disposition. This could mean that some people may actively confront the problem, whilst others may avoid the problem, or somewhere in between.

Avoidance is reminiscent of Freudian coping mechanisms where people may avoid negative feelings by repressing them and banishing them to the unconscious [42]. This way of coping is distinguishable from those that may try to reduce negative feelings by approaching or trying to control the event. So how does this link to illness? People that use avoidance techniques such as repression may be more prone to heart disease and cancer [43]. However, this relationship is not simplistic as these same sets of people may also engage in healthy behaviours that they perceive are under control. So coping style may only partly explain the relationship between stress and illness, because maybe coping is also about the type of stressor and the situation.

As we have seen, coping is central to the transactional theory of stress [12], which posits that coping can change over time and is also in response to the demands that are made. The ways that someone copes may be problem-focused, where a person acts to reduce the effects of the stressor. This could be, for example, making a revision plan before an exam, or a to do list with tasks that can be crossed off when completed. Or, coping could be emotion-focused, in an attempt to deal with the emotions that result in response to a stressful event. Central to the way a person may cope is an appraisal of the situation. But how do we measure or assess how a person may cope? There have been attempts to measure coping, for example, Lazarus and Folkman [12; 44] came up with a way of measuring coping, based on their transactional model and the appraisal of the situation known as the Ways of Coping Checklist [44]. To give you an idea of this measure, it consists of eight subscales that measure:

- confrontive coping (such as standing their ground)
- distancing (such as carrying on as if nothing happened)
- self-control (such as keeping feelings to oneself)
- seeking social support (such as talking to someone)
- accept responsibility (such as stern self-talk)
- escape-avoidance (such as wishing the situation was over or would go away)
- planful problem-solving (such as knowing what needs to be done and putting in effort)
- positive re-appraisal (such as finding new faith)

However, the potential limitations of this measure are that although the situation is important so are the characteristics of the individual within the situation. People are likely to use a range of strategies at their disposal and so both dispositional coping styles and the situation are important. The COPE scale [45] is an alternative measure of stress that measures both dispositional styles and strategies for coping:

- Active coping (taking action or steps to reduce stressor)
- Planning (developing strategies to deal with the stressor)
- Suppression of competing activities (avoid distraction from other things)
- Restraint (avoiding rushing in but a desire to act)
- Seeking social support for help and assistance (instrumental aid)
- Seeking social support for understanding and moral support
- Focusing on and letting go of emotion
- Behavioural disengagement (reducing efforts to deal with the stressors)
- Mental disengagement (distraction with activities)

- Positive reinterpretation and growth (trying to view stressor more positively)
- Denial (refusing to acknowledge that the stressor exists)
- Acceptance (accepting that there is a stressful situation)
- Turning to religion (seeking comfort and support in religion)
- Alcohol/Drug abuse (avoidance of the problem using substances to feel better)
- Humour (making light of the situation)

These measures of coping are still popular and widely used, but what is difficult about measuring coping is supposing that people might select coping strategies, when in fact people may adapt and shift to balance out their desires and needs [46]. This shifting is known as coping flexibility. Coping flexibility then is the ability to switch from a coping strategy that is not working and implement a new coping strategy [47]. Coping flexibility therefore is about modifying coping behaviour effectively in response to each stressful event or situation. Ineffective coping strategies can lead to dysfunction and the inability to cope. Why is this important? Well, this has implications for stress management interventions to help people to recognise when a particular strategy is not working and to increase their coping flexibility.

Why are some people more resilient to stress than others?

What makes people resilient and protects them against adverse effects are things such as positive affect, individual control, positive affect, social support, confidence in their own ability (self-efficacy), having a purpose in life and a high self-esteem [38].

Resilience is considered to be an adaptive response to stress that enables an individual to cope [48]. It is not a trait, but a set of behaviours and thoughts and actions that affect the capability of the individual to limit the negative effects of a stressor, and the physical capacity to recover [49]. It is a dynamic process and includes both psychological and physiological relationships between the brain and the immune system [38]. The concept of resilience originated in work with children who were considered to be at high risk of for future development of mental health problems. Some children who were at high-risk did not go on to develop psychological disorders [50]. A systematic review of the literature on resilience in long-term carers of those with dementia has indicated that those that are higher in resilience are less likely to experience depression and have greater physical health [51].

Diet also seems to affect resilience through the brain/gut axis. Diverse microbes in the gut that come from a diet rich in fibre, especially from vegetables such as onions, garlic, leeks, Jerusalem artichokes seems to be related to resilience [52]. Fast food and drugs such as antibiotics can interfere with these microbes and cause an imbalance. This type of imbalance has been found to be associated with symptoms of depression [52], although the exact mechanisms are not yet clearly understood. Other researchers have found that the Mediterranean diet seems to be associated with greater resilience [53] and diets generally rich in fruit, veg, grains and fish. Therefore, eating well seems to be an important factor in the relationship between stress and illness, but so too are social relationships. Let's consider the role of social support in coping and resilience to stress.

Social support

Human relationships are really important and there is a wealth of literature on the topic of social support and the way that it buffers the stress response. Social support encompasses a range of concepts from social integration, the quality of relationships and social networks. Research on social support has looked at self-reported relationships such as social networks, it's also looked at marital status, perceived support and social integration [54]. Social support can be defined as the provision of instrumental (material) or emotional (psychological) support for the purpose of increasing an individual's ability to cope with stress [55]. Good social support providers are those that are able to restore feelings of security [54].

Social support is an important factor in understanding the relationship between stress and health as it has been shown to moderate the effects of both acute and chronic stress. In a review of the literature researchers have found that social integration into a social network and high quality relationships were more predictive of mortality than lifestyle factors, such as smoking or exercise [56]. The stress buffering effects are seen when there is a match between the needs of the person and the perceived functions of the available support [57]. The type of support that helps people to thrive has been referred to as source of strength support. Thriving refers to aspects of life such as happiness and life satisfaction, having a purpose and meaning, and positive self-regard and resilience, deep and meaningful relationships and faith in humanity and subsequently physical health and longevity. People thrive when they are able to cope with stress and emerge stronger and relationships are fundamental to thriving. Source of strength support provides a refuge and relief from burdens during times of adversity and also provides an environment where it is safe to express negative emotions and provide reassurance and comfort, understanding and acceptance and provides instrumental aid and shields the person from the stressor [54].

Caring from families can also buffer the effects of stress through both psychological and functional support, which can enhance psychological wellbeing [58]. So, we can see that there is evidence that social support decreases the risk of mortality and there have been some inroads into some of the potential physiological mechanisms. Inflammatory cytokines seem to play an important role in chronic inflammatory diseases [59]. Chronic inflammation has been linked to a wide range of health issues in the modern age including diabetes and autoimmune diseases [60]. As social support has been demonstrated to buffer the stress reactions, it may also reduce the inflammatory response that is induced by stress. Being ill with induced inflammation can lead to social withdrawal, but also can increase sensitivity to positive social experiences [61]. A meta-analysis of 41 studies with 73,037 participants found that social support and social integrations were related to lower levels of pro-inflammatory cytokines [62]. This is interesting because it offers a link between social relationships and social support and the physiological processes of the stress response in the development of illness or health problems.

However, not all relationships are positive and relationships themselves may be the source of stress or the chronic stressor. Being understood and cared for and being validated can contribute to the quality of the relationship and to the overall wellbeing [63]. It may be that partners may either over-provide or under-provide support [64] or provide the wrong support which may add additional stress, rather than buffering the effects of stress. In a lab discussion with participants about their marital problems, researchers [65] found changes in the immune functioning and elevated blood pressure even when there was self-reported marital satisfaction. So, relationships are complex and can either enhance or buffer the stress response or may contribute to immune functioning dysregulation.

How do we measure stress?

There are numerous ways that health psychologists can measure stress and stress responses. Objective measures tend to be physiological measures and can be helpful if there is a baseline for comparison but are often more invasive. Subjective measures help us to understand the individual perspective but may be subject to bias (see Table 5.1). A combination of methods may provide a more reliable picture.

Table 5.1 Objective and subjective measures of stress.

Objective Measures	*Subjective Measures*
Cardiovascular Reactivity	Questionnaires
Immune markers (NK cells, Pro-inflammatory cytokines)	Dairy studies
	Prospective and longitudinal studies
Galvanic skin response	Interviews
Cortisol	

Stress management

Biofeedback

The purpose of biofeedback is to help the individual to learn how to regulate their physiological state. Usually it consists of data being collected from a number of biosensors that monitor physiological variables such as breathing, heart rate and blood pressure. They are then given feedback from a clinician and from monitors that help them to achieve an optimal breathing rate that regulates the stress response i.e. activation of the sympathetic nervous system. In a review of 14 studies on the effectiveness of biofeedback it was found that there were improvements that suggested that it could be a useful stress management intervention, but that there was inconsistency in design and effectiveness of these interventions in the literature, and so more good quality research is needed [66].

Emotional expression relaxation, guided imagery and music

There are a wide number of stress-reducing techniques that may be helpful in reducing psychological distress and improve immune functioning, e.g it has been found that disclosing traumatic events, and problems that are emotionally disturbing can enhance immune functioning. In one study [67] it was found that participants who wrote about traumatic events for 20 minutes every day for four days had improved immune functioning. Other techniques that may reduce the physiological stress response have also been researched, such as relaxation, guided imagery and music (to name but a few).

Singing, playing an instrument or listening to music can have effects on the mood, arousal and promote wellbeing e.g. relaxing music can reduce the heart rate and blood pressure that is associated with the stress response [68]. There are individual differences to consider when using music for stress reduction as music preferences may influence the effect. Some music may be stimulating and increase heart rate, while other types such as non-rhythmic, low pitch music may soothe and decrease sympathetic arousal [69; 70]. In one randomised controlled trial over 13 weeks it was found that guided imagery and music also decreased cortisol levels [71]. Taking part in group music may also affect the immune system. Evidence comes from studies that have looked at the effects of group drumming and singing on the immune system [70]. In one study looking at group drumming [72], it was found that participants demonstrated positive immune and neuroendocrine effects including an increase in natural killer cells. So music may boost the innate immune system and reduce inflammation, in another study on choral singers [73] it was found that there was a significant decrease in cortisol and an increase in antibodies after rehearsal, although cortisol did increase during performance.

Mindfulness

In brief, mindfulness-based stress reduction is a form of meditation that is based on Buddhist mindfulness meditation and is mainly characterised by being present in the moment and acceptance and awareness of any internal or external sensations or experiences. It involves scanning the body with the mind gradually and focusing and accepting any sensations or feelings within the body, whilst also concentrating on breathing. It also involves acknowledging any thoughts that pop into the head and any distractions without any judgement. It also involves Hatha yoga techniques, which are simple stretches and postured and breathing exercises that relax the body. Usually people are encouraged to practice these techniques for 45 minutes a day. In a review and meta-analysis of 10 studies to examine the benefits on stress reduction, it was found that there was a significant stress reduction compared to controls. It also enhanced spirituality, reduced overthinking and psychological symptoms such as anxiety [74].

Exercise

The benefits of exercise are well documented, and the effects of exercise on stress management are manifold. Exercise improves sleep quality, boosts the release of positive endorphins that improve mood and reduces levels of adrenalin and cortisol associated with the stress response. Regular exercise can also increase strength and stamina and so individuals may feel more able to cope with the demands that are placed upon them. Evidence suggests that physical activity can diminish the stress response and also improve recovery e.g. resistance training has been shown to affect heart rate and a more rapid return to a baseline and to reduce inflammation. Regular exercise has also demonstrated improvements in the amount of harmful by-products of the stress response and to improve immune functioning and resilience [75].

Overall, there are a number of stress-reducing strategies that can be employed to reduce the physiological effects of stress, decrease inflammation, boost immunity and positively impact psychological outcomes.

Box 5.1 CASE STUDY

A woman in her 50s has been referred to you because she has been putting on weight, has difficulty in sleeping and is feeling irritable and fatigued. She currently works full time as a teaching assistant, has two teenage children and supports her elderly mother in caring for her father who has dementia. On initial examination her GP has found that her blood pressure is high and a finger prick test indicated that her blood glucose levels are also raised. The GP has arranged further tests.

On initial consultation with you she tells you that she has little time for herself and although she would like to do more exercise, she is struggling to balance all of the demands. She used to belong to choir, but hasn't been for ages as she has been so tired. You discuss these aspects and together make an action plan.

Following her consultation:

She has decided to try going back to choir as she remembers how much she enjoyed it. She is also going to monitor her steps and try to just start with increasing the amount of walking she is doing throughout the day such as walking to the local park to eat her lunch everyday instead of staying in the staff room where there may be cakes or treats. These are small steps, but she feels that they are achievable.

When you next see her, she tells you that she is starting to feel better and that she is really enjoying being back at choir and sleeps really well after that. She has successfully managed to increase her walking and this has boosted her confidence and has made her consider her diet more too. Although the GP is still monitoring her, her blood pressure has started to come down and her blood glucose levels are within the normal range.

Chapter summary

In this chapter we have considered the stress response as the activation of the HPA and Sam pathways, and we have also observed the possible link between stress and illness through psychoneuroimmunology. However, stress is complex and the bi-directional nature of bodily systems have provided insight into how systems can be affected, adapt and change through an interaction between physiological systems and lifestyle. Modern lifestyles, such as the wide use of screens and the disruption to the circadian rhythms and changes to the environment have evolved more quickly than the physiological systems can cope with. Some researchers [76] believe that this has affected the flexibility of the way the body adapts to stress and has affected resilience.

It has long been considered that stress employs a top down approach in that stress triggered a cascade of hormones stimulated by the hypothalamus via the sympathetic nervous system and hypothalamic pituitary adrenal axis (see Figure 5.2). However, more recently, with the advance of technology, imaging studies have demonstrated that there is a response from a network of cortical and limbic areas of the brain, which are associated with the appraisal and physiology of stress and the concept of homeostasis may be outdated.

There has been more focus in recent years on the bi-directional nature of the relationships between the immune system and the brain, and there is more evidence to suggest that the psychological states have an influence on the immune system and that the immune system influences psychological states. Chronic inflammation and infections tend to trigger symptoms in various parts of the body and induce behavioural changes such as fatigue or inability to concentrate or sleep (due to proinflammatory cytokines). This may also influence how people behave in a social context and they may be more sensitive to threat or positive feedback. Stress is therefore a multi-faceted phenomenon that requires a biopsychosocial approach in understanding how it may affect illness. However, we cannot state unequivocally that stress causes illness, as we have seen there is evidence that it may increase susceptibility to illness. The role of the health psychologist is to understand the complex interrelationship of factors that can affect stress and to design interventions that may reduce the negative effects of stress and promote wellbeing.

References

[1]   Simpson, J., & Weiner, E. (1989). Stress. *Oxford English Dictionary*. Oxford: Oxford University Press. Retrieved from www.oxforddictionaries.com/definition/english/stress

[2]   Boyce, W. T., & Ellis, B. J. (2005). Biological sensitivity to context: I. An evolutionary-developmental theory of the origins and functions of stress reactivity. *Developmental Psychopathology*, *17*, 271–301. DOI: 10.1017/S0954579405050145

[3]   Cohen, S., Gianaros, P. J., & Manuck, S. B. (2016). A stage model of stress and disease. *Perspectives on Psychological Science*, *11*(4), 456–463. DOI: 10.1177/1745691616646305

[4]   Cannon, W. B. (1929). Organization for physiological homeostasis. *Physiological Reviews*, *9*, 399–431.

[5]   Canon, W. B. (1932). *The Wisdom of the Body*. London: Kegan Paul, D. Appleton & Co.

[6]   Cannon, W. B. (1931). The effects of progressive sympathectomy on blood pressure. *American Journal of Physiology*, *97*, 592–595.

[7]   Cannon, W. B. (1939). *The Wisdom of the Body*. New York: W. W. Norton.

[8]   Clow, A. (2001). The physiology of stress. In F. Jones & J. Bright (Eds), *Stress, Myth, Theory and Research.*. London, UK. Pearson Education, 47-51.

[9]   Gianaros, P. J., & Jennings, J. R. (2018). Host in the machine: A neurobiological perspective on psychological stress and

cardiovascular disease. *American Psychologist*, 73(8), 1031–1044. DOI:10.1037/amp0000232

[10] Selye, H. (1956). *The Stress of Life*. New York: McGraw-Hill Book Company.

[11] Szabo, S.,ƒTache, Y., & Somogyi, A. (2012). The legacy of Hans Selye and the origins of stress research: a retrospective 75 years after his landmark brief "letter" to the editor# of nature. *Stress*, 15(5), 472–478. DOI:10.3109/10253890.2012.710919

[12] Lazarus, R. S. & Folkman, S. (1984). *Stress, Appraisal, and Coping*. New York: Springer.

[13] Holmes, T. H. & Rahe, R. H. (1967). The social readjustment rating scale. *Journal of Psychosomatic Research*, 11(2), 213–218.

[14] Holmes, T. H. & Masuda, M. (1974). Life change and illness susceptibility. In B. S. Dohrenwend & B. P. Dohrenwend (eds.), *Stressful Life Events: Their Nature and Effects*. New York: John Wiley, pp. 45–72.

[15] Dumalon-Canana, J. A., Hutchinson, A. D., Prichard, I., & Wilson, C. (2014). What causes breast cancer? A systematic review of causal attributions among breast cancer survivors and how these compare to expert-endorsed risk factors. *Cancer Causes Control*, 25(7), 771–785. DOI: 10.1007/s10552-014-0377-3

[16] Schoemaker, M. J., Jones, M. E., Wright, L. B., Griffin, J., McFadden, E., Ashworth, A. & Swerdlow, A. J. (2016). Psychological stress, adverse life events and breast cancer incidence: a cohort investigation in 106,000 women in the United Kingdom. *Breast Cancer Research*, 18, 71. DOI: 10.1186/s13058-016-0733-1

[17] Kanner, A. D., Coyne, J. C., Schaefer, C., & Lazarus, R. S. (1981). Comparison of two modes of stress measurement: Daily hassles and uplifts versus major life events. *Journal of Behavioral Medicine*, 4(1), 1–39. DOI: 10.1007/BF00844845

[18] DeLongis, A., Coyne, J. C., Dakof, G., Folkman, S., & Lazarus, R. S. (1982). Relationship of daily hassles, uplifts, and major life events to health status. *Health Psychology*, 1(2), 119–136. DOI: 10.1037/0278-6133.1.2.119

[19] Ganzel, B. L., Morris, P. A., & Wethington, E. (2010). Allostasis and the human brain: Integrating models of stress from the social and life sciences. *Psychological Review*, 117(1), 134–174. DOI:10.1037/a0017773

[20] Schulkin, J. (2004) *Allostasis, Homeostasis, and the Costs of Physiological Adaptation*. Cambridge, MA: Cambridge University Press.

[21]   Hwang, A-C,. Peng, L-N., Wen, Y-W., Tsai, Y-W., Chang, L-C., Chiou, S-T., Chan, L-K. (2014). Predicting all-cause and cause-specific mortality by static and dynamic measurements of allostatic load: a 10-year population-based cohort study in Taiwan. *Journal of the American Medical Directors Association, 15,* 490–496. DOI: 10.1016/j.jamda.2014.02.001

[22]   Russo, S. J., Murrough, J. W., Han, M. H., Charney, D. S., & Nestler, E. J. (2012). Neurobiology of resilience. *Nature Neuroscience, 15*(11), 1475–1484. DOI:10.1038/nn.3234

[23]   Cohen, S. & Herbert, T. B. (1996). Health psychology: Psychological factors and physical disease from the perspective of psychoneuroimmunology. *Annual Review Psychology, 47,* 113–142. DOI:10.1146/annurev.psych.47.1.113

[24]   Steptoe, A., Lipsey, Z., & Wardle, J. (1998). Stress, hassles and variations in alcohol consumption, food choice and physical exercise: A diary study. *British Journal of Health Psychology, 3*(Part 1), 51–63. DOI:10.1111/j.2044–8287.1998.tb00555.x

[26]   Carroll, D., Ginty, A. T., Der, G., Hunt, K., Benzeval, M., & Phillips, A. C. (2012). Increased blood pressure reactions to acute mental stress are associated with 16-year cardiovascular disease mortality. *Psychophysiology, 49*(10), 1444–1448. DOI:10.1111/j.1469-8986.2012.01463.x.

[27]   Jacobs, N., Myin-Germeys, I., Derom, C., Delespaul, P., van Os, J., & Nicolson, N. A. (2007). A momentary assessment study of the relationship between affective and adrenocortical stress responses in daily life. *Biological Psychology, 74,* 60–66. DOI:10.1016/j.biopsycho.2006.07.002

[28]   Sin, N. L., Graham-Engeland, J. E., Ong, A. D., & Almeida, D. M. (2015). Affective reactivity to daily stressors is associated with elevated inflammation. *Health Psychology, 34,* 1154 –1165. DOI::10.1037/hea0000240

[29]   Lovallo, W. R. (2011). Do low levels of stress reactivity signal poor states of health?. *Biological Psychology, 86*(2), 121–128. DOI:10.1016/j.biopsycho.2010.01.006

[30]   Carroll, D., Ginty, A. T., Whittaker, A. C., Lovallo, W.R., & de Rooij, S. R. (2017). The behavioural, cognitive, and neural corollaries of blunted cardiovascular and cortisol reactions to acute psychological stress. *Neuroscience and Biobehavioral Reviews. 77,* 74–86. DOI:10.1016/j.neubiorev.2017.02.025

[31]   Kiecolt-Glaser, J. K., Gouin, J. P. & Hantsoo, L. (2010). Close relationships, inflammation and health. *Neuroscience and*

Biobehavioral Reviews, *35*, 33–38. DOI: 10.1016/j.neubiorev. 2009.09.003

[32]   Ader, R., Cohen, N. & Felten, D. (1995). Psychoneuroimm unology: interactions between the nervous system and the immune system. *The Lancet*, *345*(8942), 99–103. DOI: 10.1016/ s0140-6736(95)90066–7

[33]   Cohen, S., Tyrrell, D. A., & Smith, A. P. (1991). Psychological stress and susceptibility to the common cold. *The New England Journal of Medicine*, *325*(9), 606–612. DOI:10.1056/ NEJM199108293250903

[34]   Kiecolt-Glaser, J. K., Garner, W., Speicher, C., Penn, G. M., Holliday, J., Glaser, R. (1984). Psychosocial modifiers of immuno-competence in medical students. *Psychosomatic Medicine*, *46*(1), 7–14. DOI:10.1097/00006842-198401000-00003

[35]   Marucha, P. T., Kiecolt-Glaser, J. K., Favagehi, M. (1990). Mucosal wound healing is impaired by examination stress. *Psychosomatic Medicine*, *60*(3), 362–365. DOI:10.1097/00006842-199805000-00025

[36]   O'Connor, T. G., Moynihan, J. A., & Caserta, M. T. (2014). Annual research review: The neuroinflammation hypothesis for stress and psychopathology in children--developmental psychoneuro-immunology. *Journal of Child Psychology and Psychiatry*, *55*(6), 615–631. DOI:10.1111/jcpp.12187

[37]   Dhabhar, F. S. (2002). A hassle a day may keep the doctor away: Stress and the augmentation of immune function, *Integrative and Comparative Biology*, *42*(3), 556–564, DOI:10.1093/icb/42.3.556

[38]   Dantzer, R., Cohem, S., Russo, S. J., & Dinan, T. G. (2018). *Resilience and immunity. Brain Behaviour and Immunity*, *74*, 28–42. DOI:10.1016/j.bbi.2018.08.010

[39]   Abbas, A. K., Lichtman, A. H., & Pillai, S. (2016). Basic Immunology: Functions and disorders of the immune system (5th Ed.) St Louis, MO: Elsevier.

[40]   Hunter, C. A., & Jones, S. A. (2015). IL-6 as a keystone cyto-kine in health and disease. *Nature Immunology*, *16*, 448–457. DOI:10.1038/ni.3153

[41]   Segerstrom, S. C., & Miller, G. E. (2004). Psychological stress and the human immune system: a meta-analytic study of 30 years of inquiry. *Psychological Bulletin*, *130*(4), 601–630. DOI:10.1037/ 0033-2909.130.4.601

[42]   Byrne, D. (1961). The repression-sensitization scale: rationale, reliability. and validity. *Journal of Personality*, *29*, 334–349. DOI:10.1111/j.1467–6494.1961.tb01666.x

[43]   Myers, L. B. (2010). The importance of the repressive coping style: findings from 30 years of research. *Anxiety Stress and Coping*, *23*(1), 3–17. DOI:10.1080/10615800903366945

[44]   Folkman, S. (2013). Ways of Coping Checklist (WCCL). In: Gellman, M. D., Turner, J. R. (eds) *Encyclopedia of Behavioral Medicine*. Springer: New York, NY.

[45]   Carver, C. S., Scheier, M. F., & Weintraub, J. K. (1989). Assessing coping strategies: A theoretically based approach. *Journal of Personality and Social Psychology*, *56*(2), 267–283. DOI:10.1037/0022-3514.56.2.267

[46]   Kashdan, T. B., & Rottenberg, J. (2010). Psychological flexibility as a fundamental aspect of health. *Clinical Psychology Review*, *30*(7), 865–878. DOI:10.1016/j.cpr.2010.03.001

[47]   Kato, T. (2012) Development of the coping fexibility scale: Evidence for the coping felxibility hypothesis. *Journal of Counselling Psychology*, *54*(2), 262–273. DOI:10.1037/a0027770

[48]   Oken, B. S., Chamine, I., & Wakeland, W. (2015). A systems approach to stress, stressors and resilience in humans. *Behavioural Brain Research*, *282*, 144–154. DOI:10.1016/j.bbr.2014.12.047

[49]   Anisman, H. (2015). *Stress and your health: From vulnerability to resilience*. Wiley-Blackwell. DOI:10.1002/9781118850350

[50]   Cicchetti, D. (2010). Resilience under conditions of extreme stress: a multilevel perspective. World Psychiatry: Official Journal of the World Psychiatric Association (WPA), *9*(3), 145–154. DOI:10.1002/j.2051–5545.2010.tb00297.x

[51]   Dias, R., Santos, R. L., de Sousa, M. F. B., Nogueira, M. L., Torres, B., Belfort, T., & Dourado, M. C. N. (2015). Resilience of caregivers of people with dementia: a systematic review of biological and psychosocial determinants. *Trends in Psychiatry and Psychotherapy*, *37*(1), 12–19. Epub January 30. DOI:10.1590/2237-6089-2014-0032

[52]   Jiang, H., Ling, Z., Zhang, Y. et al. (2015). Altered fecal microbiota composition in patients with major depressive disorder. *Brain Behavour Immunity*, *48*,186–194. DOI:10.1016/j.bbi.2015.03.016

[53]   Bonaccio, M., Di Castelnuovo, A., Costanzo, S. et al. (2018). Mediterranean-type diet is associated with higher psychological resilience in a general adult population: findings from the Molisani study. *European Journal of Clinical Nutrition*, *72*(1), 154–160. DOI:10.1038/ejcn.2017.150

[54]   Feeney, B. C., & Collins, N. L. (2015). New look at social support: A theoretical perspective on thriving through relationships.

Personality and Social Psychology Review, *19*(2), 113–147 DOI:10.1177/1088868314544222

[55] Cohen, S. (2004). Social relationships and health. *American Psychologist* 59, 676–684. DOI:10.1037/0003-066X.59.8.676

[56] Holt-Lunstad, J., & Smith, T. B. (2012). Social relationships and mortality. *Social and Personality Psychology Compass*, *6*, 41–53. DOI:10.1111/j.1751-9004.2011.00406.x

[57] Cohen, S., & Wills, T. A. (1985). Stress, social support, and the buffering hypothesis. *Psychological Bulletin*, *98*(2), 310–357. DOI:10.1037/0033-2909.98.2.310

[58] Almeida, J., Subramanian, S. V., Kawachi, I., Molnar, B. E. (2011). Is blood thicker than water? Social support, depression and the modifying role of ethnicity/nativity status. *Journal of Epidemiology and Community Health*, *65*(1), 51–56. DOI:10.1136/jech.2009.092213

[59] Kiecolt-Glaser, J. K., Gouin, J. P., & Hantsoo, L. (2010). Close relationships, inflammation, and health. *Neuroscience and Biobehavioral Reviews*, *35*(1), 33–38. DOI:10.1016/j.neubiorev.2009.09.003

[60] Soysal, P., Stubbs, B. Lucato, P. Luchini, C., Solmi, M., Peluso, R., Sergi, G., Isik, A. T., Manzato, E., Maggi, E., Maggio, S., Prina, A. M., Cosco, T. D., Wu, Y. T., Veronese, N. (2016). Inflammation and frailty in the elderly: A systematic review and meta-analysis. *Ageing and Research Reviews*, *31*, 1–8. DOI:10.1016/j.arr.2016.08.006

[61] Eisenberger, N. L., Moiemi, M., Inagaki, T. K., Muscatell, K. A., & Irwin, M. R. (2017). In sickness and in health: The co-regulation of inflammation and social behaviour. *Neuropsychopharmacology Reviews*, *42*, 242–253. DOI: 10.1038/npp.2016.141

[62] Uchino, B. N., Trettevik, R., Kent de Grey, R. G., Cronan, S., Hogan, J. & Baucom, B. R. W. (2018). Social support, social integration, and inflammatory cytokines: A meta-analysis. *Health Psychology*, *37*(5), 462–471. DOI: 10.1037/hea0000594

[63] Reis, H. T., Clark, M. S., & Holmes, J. G. (2004). *Perceived* partner responsiveness as an organizing construct in the study of intimacy and closeness. In D. J. Mashek & A. P. Aron (Eds.), *Handbook of Closeness and Intimacy* (pp. 201–225). Mahwah, NJ: Lawrence Erlbaum Associates Publishers.

[64] Brock, R. L., & Lawrence, E. (2014). Intrapersonal, interpersonal, and contextual risk factors for overprovision of partner support in marriage. *Journal of Family Psychology*, *28*(1), 54–64. DOI:10.1037/a0035280

[65]   Kiecolt-Glaser, J. K., Malarkey, W. B., Chee, M. et al. (1993). Negative behavior during marital conflict is associated with immunological down-regulation. *Journal of Psychosomatic Medicine*, *55*(5), 395-409. DOI:10.1097/00006842-199309000-00001

[66]   De Witte, N. A. J., Buyck, I. & Van Daele, T. (2019). Combining biofeedback with stress management interventions: A systematic review of physiological and psychological effects. *Applied Psychophysiology and Biofeedback*, *44*, 71–82. DOI:10.1007/s10484-018-09427-7

[67]   Pennebaker, J. W., Kiecolt-Glaser, J. K., Glaser, R. (1988). Disclosure of traumas and immune function: health implications for psychotherapy. *Journal of Consulting and Clinical Psychology*, *56*(2), 239-245. DOI:10.1037//0022-006x.56.2.239

[68]   de Witte, M., Spruit, A., van Hooren, S., Moonen, X. & Stams, G-J. (2020). Effects of music interventions on stress-related outcomes: a systematic review and two meta-analyses, *Health Psychology Review*, *14*(2), 294–324. DOI: 10.1080/17437199.2019.1627897

[69]   Rentfrow, P. J., Goldberg, L. R., & Levitin, D. J. (2011). The structure of musical preferences: a five-factor model. *Journal of Personality and Social Psychology*, *100*(6), 1139–1157. DOI:10.1037/a0022406

[70]   Chanda, M. L., Levitin, D. J. (2013). The neurochemistry of music. *Trends in Cognitive Science*, *17*(4),179–193. DOI:10.1016/j.tics.2013.02.007

[71]   McKinney, C. H., Antoni, M. H., Kumar, M., Tims, F. C., & McCabe, P. M. (1997). Effects of guided imagery and music (GIM) therapy on mood and cortisol in healthy adults. *Health Psychology*, *16*(4), 390–400. DOI:10.1037//0278-6133.16.4.390

[72]   Bittman, B. B., Berk, L. S., Felten, D. L., et al. (2001). Composite effects of group drumming music therapy on modulation of neuroendocrine-immune parameters in normal subjects. *Alternative Therapies in Health and Medicine*, *7*(1), 38–47. PMID: 11191041

[73]   Beck, R. J., Cesario, T. C., Yousefi, A. & Enamoto, H. (2000). Choral singing, performance perception, and immune system changes in salivary immunoglobulin A and cortisol. *Music Perception*, *18*(1), 87–106. DOI:10.2307/40285902

[74]   Chiesa, A., & Serretti, A. (2009). Mindfulness-based stress reduction for stress management in healthy people: a review and meta-analysis. *Journal of Alternative and Complementary Medicine*, *15*(5), 593–600. DOI:10.1089/acm.2008.0495

[75] Huang, C. J., Webb, H. E., Zourdos, M. C., & Acevedo, E. O. (2013). Cardiovascular reactivity, stress, and physical activity. *Frontiers in Physiology, 4*, 314. DOI:10.3389/fphys.2013.00314

[76] Rao, R., & Androulakis, I. P. (2019) The physiological significance of the circadian dynamics of the HPA axis: Interplay between circadian rhythms, allostasis and stress resilience. *Hormones and Behaviour, 110*, 77–89. DOI:10.1016/j.yhbeh.2019.02.018

6 Adjusting to chronic illness

Contents

Chapter overview

In Chapter 2 we considered the biopsychosocial factors that can affect the aetiology of chronic illness. In this chapter we will focus on how people may adjust to chronic illness and self-manage their condition. We will start by considering what we mean by chronic illness and the consequences of living with a chronic illness. We will then move on to consider how people may react to a diagnosis of chronic illness and how it may affect coping. We will consider the impact on the family and informal care-givers and factors that may affect quality of life. We will then move on to consider some specific self-management interventions using examples from coronary heart disease, Type 2 diabetes and irritable bowel syndrome.

Introduction

Improvements in healthcare have seen a rise in life expectancy, but although people may be living longer, it does not necessarily mean that they are in good health and often may be living with one or more chronic illnesses. This makes chronic illness a major heath concern accounting for 71 per cent of worldwide deaths, with 15 million people in England alone [1], with long term health conditions, 58 per cent of those being in the over 60 age bracket. They make up 70 per cent of all hospital in-patient admissions and 50 per cent of GP appointments [1].

With chronic illness the focus of treatment is in the management of symptoms and in slowing down deterioration and reducing disability. In doing so, there has been a shift away from the biomedical approach of adhering to a medical regime, devised around the disease/illness, onto self-management. Self-management can be considered to be the individual's ability to manage their own symptoms, treatment, physical and psychological consequences of the illness and associated lifestyle changes. Therefore, in this chapter we will focus on how people may adjust to chronic illness and the role of the health psychologist in developing psychosocial interventions to support individuals in being able to self-manage their condition.

What are chronic illnesses?

Let's start by considering that chronic illnesses are those that are long lasting in nature and often can be life-limiting and impact a person's quality of life. Currently, the leading cause of death worldwide is coronary heart disease, whilst in the UK cancer is the second principle cause of death. However, it is asthma which is the most common chronic disease and arthritis which is the main cause of physical disability [1]. There are many different chronic illnesses with varying symptomology and disability, but they all share some common factors when it comes to adjustment and self-management. Let's consider what it might be like to live with a chronic illness.

Living with a chronic disease has widespread emotional, social and physical consequences, not only to the individual with the illness, but also on their wider family network [2]. Also, many people are not just living with one chronic illness but often have other co-morbidities (more than one chronic illness). Day-to-day living with chronic disease has a significant impact on the person's identity, their family and their quality of life, as once a chronic illness has been diagnosed there is no return to a 'normal' state, and so it requires an adjustment to a new set of circumstances [3]. Not only may individuals need to cope and adjust with a diagnosis and new self, the treatment itself may damage health or affect body image and sense of self e.g. chemotherapy, surgery, colostomy, side effects of steroids and psychological consequences may be depression.

The consequences of living with a chronic illness

The consequence of living with a chronic illness is a lifetime of managing symptoms, treatment and any debilitation caused by the illness. Some people will need to monitor physiological parameters such as blood sugar levels, others may need their blood testing regularly and have to spend time in phlebotomy clinics to monitor side effects of drugs such as blood clotting factors. In adhering to medical regimes, some may have to inject themselves with insulin or cope with emptying and applying colostomy bags. There may be an increased dependence on others [4] or indeed withdrawal. It may also affect the person's ability to do their job and so may result in financial

Box 6.1

Frank Shontz (1975) – reactions to diagnosis with a chronic illness.

Shock – an emergency-like reaction that can leave the person bewildered, on autopilot and feeling detached. The shock may be short lived or persist for a period of weeks.

Encounter – during this phase the individual may not be able to think straight and have feelings of grief and loss, they feel helpless and overwhelmed.

Retreat – at this stage the individual may be using defensive strategies such as avoidance and denial to cope, but as symptoms continue to develop or there is confirmation of the diagnosis the individual begins to consider that adjustments need to be made and they will begin to contact reality a bit at a time.

difficulties. When a person is newly diagnosed with a chronic illness they may experience a sense of loss or grief of their former self, both in terms of their state of health and also their self-image. They may also experience a sense of loss of control of the disease itself and also a loss of independence [5]. In a sense it is grieving for a former self and coming to terms with a new self, but this may not happen immediately, and individuals may go through a sequence of reactions following diagnosis of a chronic illness [6].

It is important to consider the reactions to the diagnosis as this may affect adjustment and self-management. If an individual is in a state of shock, they may not be able to process information on how to manage their illness, or indeed if they are in denial they may refuse to adopt lifestyle changes or adhere to any treatments. According to researchers [7] adjusting to, and coping with, a chronic illness is an ongoing process as the condition may alter and change. Coping in this sense is not short lived or about returning to a pre-illness state, but adjusting to a new state [8]. Adjustment and coping is made up of both general and disease-related adaptive tasks [7; 9]. The general tasks are around preparing for a future that is less certain, maintaining social relationships and sense of their own competence and self-image whilst also managing symptoms, any treatment and relationships with healthcare providers [7].

Coping requires major lifestyle changes

Many chronic diseases, as we have seen in previous chapters, are related to lifestyle factors such as lack of exercise, obesity, smoking and alcohol use, and many outcomes can be improved with changes to these lifestyle factors. However, when a person is diagnosed, they must find new ways of coping, as previous patterns of coping may further exacerbate symptoms e.g. drinking alcohol, eating highly palatable foods or smoking. Most people will eventually reach adjustment, but some people may fail to adjust or take longer. People may also experience a host of somatic symptoms such as fatigue, lethargy, difficulty in concentrating and depressive symptoms that may be due to inflammatory processes as a consequence of their illness [10], and may make lifestyle changes more difficult. Symptoms may be further exacerbated by repression or denial that can increase the physiological stress response [11] (see Chapter 5). Positive coping on the other hand is associated with improved wellbeing and self-management as demonstrated by interventions that increase knowledge, coping skills, improve adherence and work/life balance [12].

Impact of chronic illness on family

Research suggests that chronic illness has a profound effect on family members and family functioning [13]. In fact, because there is no return to normal then the chronic illness also becomes part of the family's identity. The family can have beneficial and harmful effects on the way that someone adjusts to and manages their chronic illness. Let's consider an example (see Box 6.2).

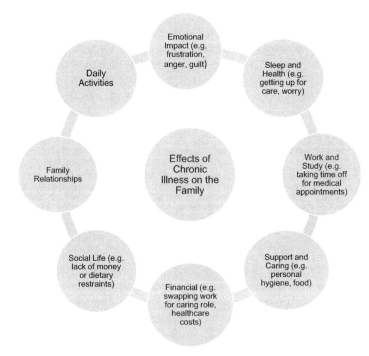

Figure 6.1 Themes identified

Box 6.2

Alfred is 62 and has been with his partner for 40 years. Alfred's partner works in a supermarket and tends to do all the food shopping. Alfred has recently been diagnosed with Type 2 diabetes and has been advised to cut out refined sugar from his diet and cut down on his carbohydrate intake. Alfred's partner keeps bringing home high sugar and high carbohydrate snacks and treats despite Alfred asking them not to. When Alfred tries to talk to his partner about it, they just shrug and say the occasional treat won't hurt. Alfred is finding it difficult to stick to his new diet because all of these tasty treats are available.

The effects of a family member with chronic illness can have a negative effect on family relationships, but there can also be positive effects such as becoming closer and pulling together.

In a qualitative study of interviews with 133 family members across 26 medical specialities, who were mostly female and partners, spouses or parents of the individual with the chronic illness, key themes were identified around the impact of the chronic illness on the family (see Figure 6.1).

Quality of life

Quality of life is a term that is often used, but what does it actually mean? There have been several attempts to define it, but as it is subjective it is very difficult to define. The World Health Organisation (WHO) considers it to be an individual's perception of their life based on their own set of values and culture and in consideration of their individual expectations, standards and goals. There have been attempts to measure quality of life using objective measures and it is often cited as an outcome when considering the effectiveness of psychosocial interventions. The World Health Organisation has a cross cultural assessment tool called the WHOQOL (100), which assesses six domains:

1. PHYSICAL HEALTH: Pain, sleep, energy.
2. PSYCHOLOGICAL: Self-esteem, memory, learning.
3. LEVEL OF INDEPENDENCE: Activities of daily living.
4. SOCIAL RELATIONSHIPS: Social support, personal relationships.
5. RELATION TO ENVIRONMENT: Safety, finances, home, leisure.
6. SPIRITUAL/RELIGIOUS/PERSONAL BELIEFS

There are many factors that can influence perceptions of quality of life:

a) Demographics such as age, gender.
b) Individual differences such as personality characteristics and coping style.

c) Chronic illness such as the symptoms and disease processes e.g. impairment in cognition or speech.
d) The availability of treatment or indeed the toxicity of treatment or side effects.
e) Psychosocial factors such as social support, affect, role conflict, environment.

These factors are important because the link between the level of disability and the underlying pathology of the disease is often not directly related and can be moderated by psychosocial factors such as affect, social support and environmental factors [14]. Therefore, interventions that aim to improve psychosocial outcomes may also improve perceptions of quality of life.

Mindfulness and gratitude

Some studies have focused around the areas of positive psychology such as mindfulness and gratitude in improving quality of life. Research [15] has found that people with higher levels of mindfulness and acceptance of thoughts and emotions are often more likely to give more positive self-assessments. Others [16] have looked at the differences in those that score high and low in mindfulness and gratitude and found that mindful individuals tend to report higher quality of life and greater life satisfaction. They also reported sleeping better, reported less stress and were higher in gratitude. Grateful individuals also reported a higher level of quality of life.

Social support

There is an array of literature around the impact of social support on health outcomes. Actual or perceived social support has been associated with improved outcomes and positive effects on cardiovascular, neuroendocrine and immune responses [17] and psychological factors such as affect [18]. In a review of the literature on the impact of social support on Type 2 diabetes self-management [19], favourable results were found. In 14 out of the 37 papers reviewed there were positive outcomes of social support on management. Eleven of the studies showed an increase in self-management behaviours such as taking prescribed medicines. The research also indicated that different groups of people showed a preference for different types of support (e.g. telephone or group support), suggesting that social support interventions should be tailored to individual needs. This suggests that interventions to improve social support may be beneficial, but that different types of support may be more beneficial than others. In support of this statement research that was conducted on creating peer support for cancer patients demonstrated that it was helpful for those that did not have support but that it had detrimental effects in those who already had support [20].

Self-management

If a person has a chronic illness then self-management is a daily responsibility over the course of the illness. Self-management is the individual's ability to manage the symptoms, treatments physical and psychological consequences and the lifestyle changes that are associated with living with a chronic illness. In order to understand self-management from individual's perspective researchers [21] have conducted some qualitative work with chronic illness patients and found that self-management included three tasks, the first of which was **medical and behavioural management,** such as taking medication or changing exercise, dietary, or other behaviours such as smoking e.g. for someone with CHD this may mean eating a low fat diet, avoiding certain vegetables that may interact with their medication and stopping smoking or cutting back on alcohol. The second was **role management** and this might mean changing being able to maintain or creating new and meaningful roles e.g. for someone who is a window cleaner and has inflammatory bowel disease this may mean changing jobs for something that allows full access to toilet facilities. The third and final task was **emotional management** and being able to deal with emotions such as guilt, fear, anger, frustration and anxiety that may accompany a chronic illness diagnosis.

Box 6.3 Lorig and Holman [22] described six self-care management skills

Problem solving
Recognise and identify the problem
Define the problem and form a mental representation
Develop a solution strategy
Organise knowledge
Allocate mental and physical resources
Monitor progress towards their goal
Evaluate a solution (Bransford & Stein, 1993; Sternberg, 1986; Hayes, 1989)

Decision-making
Which can be affected by cognitive and personal biases

Resource utilisation
Making use of the resources that are available

Forming a partnership with the healthcare provider
Action planning
Behaviour change and action planning to set and monitor goals

Self-tailoring

This requires the individual to apply a number of skills.
So, according to this model, then problem solving is a key skill in self-management, but this may also be affected by the chronic illness e.g. if the individual is fatigued or has brain fog or high blood sugar, which may also have an affect on their cognitive abilities. Confidence in their ability (self-efficacy) to carry out self-management tasks seems to be an important factor. Higher levels of self-efficacy have also been linked to motivation to carry out the tasks [23]. In a more recent meta-synthesis of 101 qualitative studies, key categories in self-management were identified as focusing on the illness needs, activating resources

and living with the chronic illness [24]. It was also found that addressing emotional needs was important in improving outcomes. Having more than one chronic illness may complicate things further, and individuals may have difficulty in prioritising needs [25].

Self-management is important as successful self-management further increases the individual's confidence and reduces anxiety and improves health outcomes such as increasing physical functioning [26]. It may also reduce the burden to the NHS and the number of unplanned hospital admissions [27] and adherence to medication. The role of health psychologists is therefore to design interventions that target these key areas to improve self-management and health outcomes. In this next section we will consider self-management interventions using examples of coronary heart disease, Type 2 diabetes and irritable bowel disease.

Education based interventions or psychological interventions?

Education or information-based interventions tend to focus on illness management [28]:

1. Recognising symptoms
2. Correct use of medication
3. Diet
4. Exercise
5. Smoking cessation
6. Managing stress
7. Communicating effectively with healthcare providers

There has been some success with these types of intervention in terms of managing symptoms and increasing a sense of control [29]. Psychological/psychosocial interventions tend to target a range of outcomes and use a variety of techniques [30], and are aimed at either the patient themselves, the patient's carer or both [31]. Health psychology interventions can be categorized into three different types:

1. Those that help patients to manage their condition to improve or maintain health and slow disease progression.
2. Those that aim to treat psychophysiological disorders such as pain.
3. Those that address psychological adjustment such as depression and anxiety [32].

Cardiac rehabilitation

Cardiac rehabilitation is offered by hospitals free of charge following heart attack or heart surgery. Cardiac rehabilitation usually consists of education about illness management and an exercise programme. The most popular form of delivery is a group-based intervention. In 2018, the uptake of cardiac rehabilitation was 59 per cent of all eligible in Wales, 50 per cent of England and 39 per cent in Northern Ireland [33]. On the whole, women were less likely to attend than men and only 40 per cent were likely to attend from the most deprived areas. Out of those that attended 76 per cent completed the programme. The reasons for dropping out were stated as being too ill to continue, which was mostly older participants or that they had returned to work. However, for those who were able to attend there were benefits. Before attending the cardiac rehabilitation programme 44 per cent had not met the recommended guidance for the amount of exercise per week, but this increased to 73 per cent post intervention. Similar programmes are run by insurance companies in the USA. The following example is used to demonstrate the level of commitment required from the participants in attending and adopting lifestyle changes to manage CHD (see Box 6.4).

These types of interventions tend to be group-based and focus on behaviour, but other types may be more individualised and focus on psychological factors such as illness cognitions, which are thoughts and beliefs around the illness itself. As we have seen in previous chapters people vary in their beliefs about the causes of illness and this can affect their ability or willingness to change their behaviours, resulting in poorer outcomes. Psychologists are able to work one to one with clients using motivational interviewing techniques or CBT to challenge beliefs that may

Box 6.4 Lifestyle intervention programme [34]

This is an example of a multi-site cardiac lifestyle intervention. The number of participants in this intervention were 293 women and 576 men.

The intervention took place onsite (as opposed to in the home) twice a week for three months.

The intervention itself consisted of lectures, cooking demonstrations, an hour of supervised exercise, an hour of stress management, an hour of group support and they would also eat a meal that was consistent with the diet guidelines, which was a plant-based wholefood diet that was low in fat.

The stress management component consisted of yoga, progressive muscle relaxation and guided imagery and they were instructed in this for an hour every day.

They were also asked to exercise for three hours a week and spend at least 30 minutes within their prescribed heart rate boundary and to keep a food diary.

The results indicated that adherence was high at three months with 74 per cent sticking to the diet, 79 per cent to the exercise and 47 per cent to the stress management.

There was also significant improvement in weight loss, blood pressure, cholesterol levels and perceived levels of stress across all participants.

Participants also demonstrated a decrease in depressive symptoms, improved metabolic function and weight loss.

These results suggest that multi-factor interventions that focus on diet, exercise and stress management may be beneficial to CHD patients.

be preventing them from managing their chronic illness. These types of intervention may focus on challenging irrational beliefs and enhancing the individual's ability to cope. CBT in particular attempts to help patients out of a vicious cycle of symptom perpetuation and inactivity. One such intervention following a myocardial infarction (heart attack) focused on changing beliefs and consisted of 3 x 40-minute sessions with a psychologist [35]. In the first session the focus was around the symptoms and the individual's beliefs about the cause. In the second session, more time was spent exploring the individual's beliefs about the causes, but also the psychologist assisted the patient to develop a plan that would help them to minimize their risk. In the third session they reviewed the action plan together then discussed any concerns in relation to the medication and also around how to distinguish between symptoms such as breathlessness that is associated with complications and breathlessness associated with exercise. At the follow-up appointment the patients were more likely to report more positive views about their heart attack, were better prepared to leave hospital, returned to work faster and also reported lower rates of angina symptoms [35].

Diabetes self-management

Similar to other chronic illnesses, self-management of Type 2 diabetes requires radical changes to lifestyle, adherence to medication, regular monitoring, or blood sugar levels, eyes and feet due to microvascular complications and communicating effectively with healthcare professionals. A validated structured education programme DESMOND (diabetes education and self-management for ongoing and newly diagnosed), is recommended by the National Institute for Clinical Excellence (NICE) as a multi-cultural self-management education programme for Type 2 diabetics. The DESMOND programme offers a toolkit of resources that promotes self-management and is focused around education and skills management [36], and consists of 6-hour education sessions over one day or two half days given by trained educators.

The core programme involves education on the physiology of diabetes in a group-based session and tips on diet and exercise, with the aim of empowering the individual and making them the expert. Empowerment is a key health educating philosophy and is structured around the belief that it is the individual who has the necessary skills, attitudes and self-awareness to influence their own behaviour [37]. Indeed, empowerment has demonstrated significant effects and reduction in blood glucose levels as measured by HbA1c. A systematic review [38] of randomised controlled trials evaluating these types of intervention, identified 10 randomised controlled trials with a total of 3,728 participants. Seven out of the 10 studies demonstrated a reduction in HbA1c and 3 demonstrated changes in self-management behaviours. It seemed that the people who benefitted the most were those who were poorly controlled, with greater HbA1c reductions. The most effective interventions seemed to be those that combined face to face and telephone interaction and those that were tailored to specific cultures.

However, although these interventions are effective in reducing biomedical factors such as reduction in lipids, weight loss, improvements in blood pressure measures and in psychosocial factors such as depression, there is still an issue of uptake. Barriers to attendance may be linked to the timing of the sessions e.g. clashes with work or social activities, or it may be the time commitment due to the length of the course, or they may feel that they don't need it. In an attempt to address some of the issues with face-to-face interventions some researchers have developed online interventions. A Cochrane review of computer based self-management interventions [39] compared 16 randomised controlled trials and found that there was no significant difference between the intervention group and control group when it came to assessment of depression and health related quality of life, but there was a greater reduction in HbA1c. This may therefore be a useful avenue to explore for those who are unable to attend face-to-face sessions. Based on the evidence from the cardiac rehabilitation literature, incorporating some stress management techniques, guided imagery or yoga may be useful in targeting depression. More recent interventions have specifically targeted diet and the reduction of carbohydrates and this is gaining momentum not only within literature, but also on social media and support sites.

Carbtoxicity and low carbohydrate diets in type 2

Ketogenic diets have increased in popularity among people with Type 2. This was sparked by research from Professor Roy Taylor [40]. He noticed that after bariatric surgery and a large amount of weight loss, people's blood sugar levels returned to normal. He then hypothesised that Type 2 diabetes was caused by the excess amounts of fat around the liver and pancreas that was interfering with responses to insulin and causing too much glucose to be released by the liver. This has since been confirmed with magnetic resonance imaging. The implications are that for some people, losing weight can reduce their symptoms to the point where they are considered to be in remission and/or reduce the need for medication. The original study [41] was on 11 people who went on a very low calorie diet of around 800 calories for eight weeks. After the eight weeks it was found that the participants had lost fat from around their liver and pancreas and their insulin levels had returned to normal.

So what has happened since?

Following on from this work the DiRECT trial [42], a larger scale cluster randomised study of 306 participants from 49 primary care trusts in Scotland and Tyneside was conducted. The aim of the study was to compare a weight management programme with the usual best practice. All of the participants were overweight and were not on insulin. Participants in the intervention group were given a formula diet, which was between 825 and 850 calories a day for three to five months with stepped re-introduction of food commencing from two to eight weeks. Twenty-four per cent of those in the intervention group achieved a 15kg weight loss. A total of 68 people in the intervention group managed to achieve remission (no indication of raised plasma glucose levels) compared to only six in the comparison group. It was also noted that the more weight that they lost, the more likely they were to be in remission. These results suggest that very low-calorie diets may be a successful treatment for those with Type 2. However, is it possible to achieve the same results through diet modification, rather than using meal replacements?

The focus has shifted onto low carbohydrate diets and the concept of carbotoxicity. This is because excess sugar is stored in the liver and as fat around the organs and so theoretically restricting carbohydrates will encourage the body to use this fat for energy. This should result in weight loss and a reduction of inflammation and insulin resistance and should theoretically also reduce blood sugar levels. In an attempt to examine whether there is a difference between low calorie diets and carbohydrate-restricted low calories diets a systematic review and meta-analysis of 25 randomised controlled trials (2,412 participants) was carried out [43]. It was found that low carbohydrate diets resulted in greater reductions in blood sugar levels three months later and this was greatest for those diets where carbohydrates made up less than 26 per cent of the daily intake.

What are the implications?

Well this means that low carbohydrate diets could form part of self-management interventions for those at risk of, and for those with Type 2. There is evidence that this has been successful in some interventions e.g. in one intervention study [44] that involved restriction of carbohydrates, alongside other behaviour change techniques such as goal setting, peer support and behavioural self-monitoring, half of the participants lost 5 per cent of their body weight and at least half also reduced their medication.

What about exercise?

Evidence suggests that exercise is an important factor in the management of blood sugar levels and so interventions need to also consider the role of exercise in self-management e.g. a systematic review was conducted of lifestyle interventions [45]. This review compared 18 studies, including 14 randomised controlled trials across USA, Europe and Asia that focused on diet, exercise and education in Type 2 diabetes. What they found was that there was a lot of similarity across these interventions and that those who included exercise were more successful in terms of managing blood sugar levels. Interventions that included exercise also had the greatest impact, but like many health behaviours the exercise was not always sustained over time. Dietary interventions, like the previous studies mentioned tended to demonstrate significant differences in overall BMI, but the study concluded that none of the interventions were of greater value, and therefore what is needed is multiple behavioural change interventions. The role of a health psychologist in Type 2 management is to try to combine the best evidence into behavioural change interventions that are tailored to the needs of the individual and promote weight loss and exercise to support self-management and even remission.

So far we have considered diseases of lifestyle that can be prevented and managed with changes to lifestyle and building on self-management skills and the reduction of stress. However, there is a group of chronic illnesses that do not quite fit into this category and where symptoms may be unpredictable and appear less under personal control. There are many illnesses that would fit under this umbrella including autoimmune conditions such as multiple sclerosis and fibromyalgia, but let's look at irritable bowel syndrome as an example.

Irritable bowel syndrome

Irritable bowel syndrome is a functional disorder that is characterised by impaired intestinal movements. What do we mean by that? It means that symptoms can vary, and some people may have diarrhoea and others constipation, or some may alternate between the two. They may also experience excessive flatus (wind), urgency to go to the toilet and incomplete emptying. It is a condition that is largely medically unexplained and affects around 11 per cent of the population [46]. Often people may undergo invasive investigations in an attempt to identify the cause of their symptoms and find that there are no structural abnormalities. The diagnosis for irritable bowel syndrome therefore is often more intuitive, going on symptoms, after ruling out other bowel conditions [47]. There are no clear aetiological pathways, but there could be a genetic link, there may be some sensitivity to allergens or inflammation amongst a host of other suggestions [48]. Some researchers have found a relationship between suppressed anger and childhood trauma and IBS [49]. Self-management of the condition may involve monitoring of diet and making changes to the diet accordingly. Some people may also be treated with medication that is usually used for treating depression.

Healthcare professionals may lack knowledge about IBS and there is some associated stigma with the condition. One researcher [50] found that 57 per cent of their sample felt that there was a degree of stigma to the condition and that healthcare professionals viewed it as being self-inflicted or all in their head. This could further be reinforced with treatments that are usually for depression. Stigma has been associated with poorer outcomes, increased healthcare utilisation, poorer health related quality of life [50] and subsequent incurred stress may further exacerbate the symptoms.

Interventions

In trying to help people to cope with IBS some researchers have looked at psychological therapy such as CBT [51]. There is some suggestion that IBS can be in part explained by psychological processing mechanisms that changes the gut-brain communication. Individuals with IBS may experience visceral hypersensitivity where there is an increased tendency to experience pain, they may also have increased anxiety and hypervigilance to bowel symptoms and central processing deficits in the regulation of pain. This may lead them to avoid social situations. Feeling pain can be stressful and further exacerbate the pain cycle and they may not be coping with the emotional factors associated, but be reliant on more problem focused coping where there is little room for control [51].

Cognitive behavioural therapy (CBT) can help by modifying behaviours and targeting dysfunctional patterns of thinking. Typically, CBT may contain some psychoeducation where individuals are taught about the link between the brain and the gut and the stress response and how this may affect symptoms. They may also be taught relaxation strategies to try and regulate the stress response such as diaphragmatic breathing. Cognitive restructuring then attempts to increase awareness of the potential distortions in patterns of thinking and again a more balanced perspective of thinking by working through examples of catastrophising and setting homework for practice. They also work with coping training to increase emotion-focused coping such as breathing technique and seeking social support. The practice scenarios then help to increase self-efficacy in scenarios that the individual has been avoiding. CBT can be very successful, and often in a short time frame, at reducing symptoms and increasing perceptions of quality of life. More psychoeducation is needed that explains the interactions between physiological systems and psychosocial factors or this may reinforce the perceived stigma [51].

Mindfulness

Mindfulness has become increasingly popular and may help individuals with IBS to develop the ability to not react to negative emotions or body sensations, which may then have an effect on hypersensitivity and overthinking. It can help by reducing the brain activation and promoting recovery as opposed to focusing on the symptoms. Mindfulness interventions teach individuals to mediate while sitting and walking. They are taught to scan the body in sequence and to bring into awareness any pain and sensation and to distinguish the sensations themselves from the thoughts of sensations. According to some researchers this moves the individual away from catastrophising and into sensory processing, and reduces the perceived severity of the symptoms, through the non-reaction to physiological sensation and cognitive emotions, thus decreasing sensitivity [52].

Summary of the chapter

In this chapter we have looked at the impact of chronic illness. Chronic illnesses are becoming increasingly more prevalent as healthcare facilities and technology advances. We have considered the many interrelating factors that can affect adjustment to chronic illness and self-management and quality of life. Many of the chronic illnesses discussed can be prevented or delayed with changes to lifestyle and health behaviours such as maintaining a healthy weight, avoiding smoking, drinking in moderation and eating a Mediterranean-based diet and we have discussed the implication of changes in diet on Type 2 remission. We have also discussed factors that may affect self-management of chronic illness and the role of psychosocial factors such as social support. We have also considered the role of health psychology in improving self-management interventions and individual outcomes and have used examples from coronary heart disease and Type 2 diabetes and irritable bowel syndrome in discussing self-management interventions.

What can we conclude?

That self-management for chronic disease is complex and requires interventions that empower the individual to understand their condition and to make changes to their dietary and exercise behaviour, and also to manage their emotions and the feelings that may threaten their sense of self. Often, self-management interventions are tailored to the individual, but chronic illnesses can also affect the wider family network and so maybe there is a need for family-oriented interventions in some instances. We can also conclude that current interventions are successful for a number of outcomes, but they are not well attended and so there is a role for health psychology in understanding barriers to uptake and tailoring interventions to individual needs.

References

[1]   Kings Fund www.kingsfund.org.uk/projects/time-think-differently/trends-disease-and-disability-long-term-conditions-multi-morbidity (accessed 3.7.2020).

[2]   Golics, C. J., Basra, M. K. A., Salek, M. S., & Finlay, A. Y. (2013). The impact of patients' chronic disease on family quality of

life: An experience from 26 specialties. *International Journal of General Medicine*, *6*, 787–798. DOI:10.2147/IJGM. S45156

[3] de Ridder, D., Geenen, R., Kuijer, R., & van Middendorp, H. (2008). Psychological adjustment to chronic disease. *Lancet*, *372*(9634), 246–255. DOI:10.1016/S0140-6736(08)*61078-8*

[4] Janssen, D. J., Franssen, F. M., Wouters, E. F., Schols, J. M., & Spruit, M. A. (2011). Impaired health status and care dependency in patients with advanced COPD or chronic heart failure. *Quality of Life Research: An International Journal of Quality of Life Aspects of Treatment, Care and Rehabilitation*, *20*(10), 1679–1688. DOI:10.1007/s11136-011-9892-9

[5] Sidell, N. L. (1997). Adult adjustment to chronic illness: A review of the literature, *Health & Social Work*, *22*(1), 5–11. DOI: 10.1093/hsw/22.1.5

[6] Shontz, E. C. (1975). *The Psychological Aspects of Physical Illness and Disability*. New York: Macmillan.

[7] Moss-Morris, R. (2013). Adjusting to chronic illness: Time for a unified theory [Editorial]. *British Journal of Health Psychology*, *18*(4), 681–686. DOI:10.1111/bjhp.12072

[8] Livneh, H. (2001). Psychosocial adaptation to chronic illness and disability: A conceptual framework. *Rehabilitation Counseling Bulletin*, *44*(3), 151–160. DOI:10.1177/003435520104400305

[9] Moos, R. H., Schaefer, J. A. (1984). The crisis of physical illness. In: Moos R.H.(eds) *Coping with Physical Illness*.Springer: Boston, MA.

[10] Dantzer, R. (2001). Cytokine-induced sickness behavior: mechanisms and implications. *Annals of the New York Academy of Sciences*, *933*, 222–234. DOI:10.1111/j.1749–6632.2001. tb05827.x

[11] de Ridder, D., Geenen, R., Kuijer, R., van Middendorp, H. (2008). Psychological adjustment to chronic disease. *Lancet*, *372*(9634), 246–255. DOI:10.1016/S0140-6736(08)61078-8

[12] Coventry, P., Lovell, K., Dickens, C., et al. (2015). Integrated primary care for patients with mental and physical multimorbidity: cluster randomised controlled trial of collaborative care for patients with depression comorbid with diabetes or cardiovascular disease. *BMJ*, *350*, h638. DOI:10.1136/bmj.h638

[13] Campbell, T. L. (2003). The effectiveness of family interventions for physical disorders. *Journal of Marital and Family Therapy*, *29*, 263–281. DOI:10.1111/j.1752-0606.1995.tb00178.x

[14] Walker, J. G., Jackson, H. J., Littlejohn, G. O. (2004). Models of adjustment to chronic illness: using the example of rheumatoid

arthritis. *Clinical Psychology Review, 24*(4), 461–488. DOI:10.1016/j.cpr.2004.03.001

[15] Kong, F., Wang, X. & Zhao, J. (2014). Dispositional mindfulness and life satisfaction: The role of core self-evalaution. *Personality and Individual Differences, 56,* 160–169. DOI: 10.1016/j.paid.2013.09.002

[16] Azad Marzabadi, E., Mills, P. J. & Valikhani, A. (2018). Positive personality: Relationships among mindful and grateful personality traits with quality of life and health outcomes. *Current Psychology.* DOI:10.1007/s12144-018-0080-8

[17] Uchino, B. N. (2006). Social support and health: a review of physiological processes potentially underlying links to disease outcomes. *Journal of Behavioral Medicine, 29*(4), 377–387. DOI:10.1007/s10865-006-9056-5

[18] Kong, F., Gong, X., Sajjad, S. et al. (2019). How is emotional intelligence linked to life satisfaction? The mediating role of social support, positive affect and negative affect. *Journal of Happiness Studies, 20,* 2733–2745. DOI10.1007/s10902-018-00069-4

[19] Strom, J. L., & Egede, L. E. (2012). The impact of social support on outcomes in adult patients with type 2 diabetes: a systematic review. *Current Diabetes Reports, 12*(6), 769–781. DOI:10.1007/s11892-012-0317-0

[20] Helgeson, V. S., & Cohen, S. (1999). *Social support and adjustment to cancer: Reconciling descriptive, correlational, and intervention research.* In R. M. Suinn & G. R. VandenBos (Eds.), *Cancer Patients and Their Families: Readings on Disease Course, Coping, and Psychological Interventions* (pp. 53–79). American Psychological Association. DOI:10.1037/10338-003

[21] Corbin, J. M., & Strauss, A. (1988). *The Jossey-Bass Health Series and the Jossey-Bass Social and Behavioral Science Series. Unending Work and Care: Managing Chronic Illness At Home.* Jossey-Bass.

[22] Lorig, K. R., & Holman, H. (2003). Self-management education: history, definition, outcomes, and mechanisms. *Annals of Behavioral Medicine, 26*(1), 1–7. DOI:10.1207/S15324796ABM2601_01

[23] Clark, N. M., & Dodge, J. A. (1999). Exploring self-efficacy as a predictor of disease management. *Health Education and Behavior, 26*(1), 72–89. DOI:10.1177/109019819902600107

[24] Schulman-Green, D., Jaser, S., Martin, F., Alonzo, A., Grey, M., McCorkle, R., Redeker, N. S., Reynolds, N., & Whittemore, R. (2012). Processes of self-management in chronic illness. *Journal*

of Nursing Scholarship: an official publication of Sigma Theta Tau International Honor Society of Nursing, 44(2), 136–144. DOI:10.1111/j.1547-5069.2012.01444.x

[25] Elliott, R. A., Ross-Degnan, D., Adams, A. S., Safran, D. G., & Soumerai, S. B. (2007). Strategies for coping in a complex world: adherence behavior among older adults with chronic illness. *Journal of General Internal Medicine, 22*(6), 805–810. DOI:10.1007/s11606-007-0193-5

[26] Challis, D., Hughes, J., Berzins, K., Reilly, S., Abell, J., Stewart, K. (2010). Self-care and Case Management in Long-term Conditions: The effective management of critical interfaces. Report for the National Institute for Health Research Service Delivery and Organisation Programme. NIHR SDO programme website. Available at: www.sdo.nihr.ac.uk/projdetails.php?ref= 08-1715-201, accessed 3.7.2020

[27] Purdy, S. (2010). Avoiding hospital admissions: what does the research evidence say? London: The King's Fund. Available at: www.kingsfund.org.uk/publications/avoiding-hospital-admissions (accessed on 3.7.2020).

[28] Clark, N. M., Becker, M. H., Janz, N. K., Lorig, K., Rakowski, W., & Anderson, L. (1991). Self-management of chronic disease by older adults: A review and questions for research. *Journal of Aging and Health, 3*(1), 3–27. DOI:10.1177/089826439100300101

[29] Helgeson, V. S., Cohen, S. (1996). Social support and adjustment to cancer: reconciling descriptive, correlational, and intervention research. *Health Psychology, 15*(2), 135–148. DOI:10.1037// 0278-6133.15.2.135

[30] Abraham, C., Michie, S. (2008). A taxonomy of behavior change techniques used in interventions. *Health Psychology, 27*(3), 379–387. DOI:10.1037/0278-6133.27.3.379

[31] Martire, L. M., Lustig, A. P., Schulz, R., Miller, G. E., Helgeson, V. S. (2004) Is it beneficial to involve a family member? A meta-analysis of psychosocial interventions for chronic illness. *Health Psychology, 23*(6), 599-611. DOI:10.1037/0278-6133.23.6.599

[32] Nicassio, P. M., Meyerowitz, B. E., Kerns, R. D. (2004). The future of health psychology interventions. *Health Psychology, 23*(2), 132–137. DOI:10.1037/0278-6133.23.2.132

[33] National Audit for Cardiac Rehabilitation (2018). www.bhf.org. uk/informationsupport/publications/statistics/national-audit-of-cardiac-rehabilitation-quality-and-outcomes-report-2018 (accessed 3.7.2020)

[34]   Daubenmier, J. J., Weidner, G., Sumner, M. D., et al. (2007). The contribution of changes in diet, exercise, and stress management to changes in coronary risk in women and men in the multisite cardiac lifestyle intervention program. *Annals of Behavioral Medicine, 33*(1), 57-68. DOI:10.1207/s15324796abm3301_7

[35]   Petrie, K. J., Cameron, L. D., Ellis, C. J., Buick, D., & Weinman, J. (2002). Changing illness perceptions after myocardial infarction: an early intervention randomized controlled trial. *Journal of Psychosomatic Medicine, 64*(4), 580-586. DOI:10.1097/00006842-200207000-00007

[36]   Davies, M. J., Heller, S., Skinner, T. C. et al. (2008). Effectiveness of the diabetes education and self management for ongoing and newly diagnosed (DESMOND) programme for people with newly diagnosed type 2 diabetes: cluster randomised controlled trial *BMJ, 336*(7642), 491–495. DOI:10.1136/bmj.39474.922025.BE

[37]   Asimakopoulou, K. G., Newton, P. & Scambler, S. (2010). 'First do no harm': the potential shortfalls of empowerment in diabetes, *European Diabetes Nursing, 7*(2), 79–81, DOI: 10.1002/edn.162

[38]   Almutairi, N., Hosseinzadeh, H., Gopaldasani, V. (2020). The effectiveness of patient activation intervention on type 2 diabetes mellitus glycemic control and self-management behaviors: A systematic review of RCTs. *Primary Care Diabetes, 14*(1),12-20. DOI:10.1016/j.pcd.2019.08.009

[39]   Pal, K., Eastwood, S. V., Michie, S. et al. (2013). Computer-based diabetes self-management interventions for adults with type 2 diabetes mellitus. *Cochrane Database of Systematic Reviews*, (3):CD008776. Published 2013 Mar 28. DOI:10.1002/14651858. CD008776.pub2

[40]   Taylor, R. (2008). Pathogenesis of type 2 diabetes: tracing the reverse route from cure to cause. *Diabetologia, 51*, 1781–1789. DOI:10.1007/s00125-008-1116-7

[41]   Lim, E. L., Hollingsworth, K. G., Aribisala, B. S., Chen, M. J., Mathers, J. C. & Taylor, R. (2011). Reversal of type 2 diabetes: normalisation of beta cell function in association with decreased pancreas and liver triacylglycerol. *Diabetologia, 54*, 2506–2514. DOI: 10.1007/s00125-011-2204-7

[42]   Lean, M. E., Leslie, W. S., Barnes, A. C. et al. (2018). Primary care-led weight management for remission of type 2 diabetes

(DiRECT): an open-label, cluster-randomised trial. *Lancet*, *391*(10120), 541–551. DOI:10.1016/S0140-6736(17)33102-1

[43] Sainsbury, E., Kizirian, N.V., Partridge, S. R., Gill, T., Colagiuri, S., & Gibson, A. A. (2018). Effect of dietary carbohydrate restriction on glycemic control in adults with diabetes: A systematic review and meta-analysis. *Diabetes Research in Clinical Practice*, *139*, 239–252. DOI:10.1016/j.diabres.2018.02.026

[44] Saslow, L. R., Summers, C., Aikens, J. E., & Unwin, D. J. (2018). Outcomes of a digitally delivered low-carbohydrate Type 2 diabetes self-management program: 1-year results of a single-arm longitudinal study. *JMIR Diabetes*, *3*(3),e12. DOI: 10.2196/diabetes.9333

[45] Seib, C., Parkinson, J., McDonald, N., Fujihira, H., Zietek, S., & Anderson, D. (2018). Lifestyle interventions for improving health and health behaviours in women with type 2 diabetes: A systematic review of the literature 2011–2017. *Maturitas*, *111*, 1-14. DOI:10.1016/j.maturitas.2018.02.008

[46] Canavan, C., West, J., & Card, T. (2014). The epidemiology of irritable bowel syndrome. *Clinical Epidemiology*, *6*, 71–80. DOI:10.2147/CLEP.S40245

[47] Agrawal, A., & Whorwell, P. J. (2006). Irritable bowel syndrome: diagnosis and management. *BMJ*, *332*(7536), 280-283. DOI:10.1136/bmj.332.7536.280

[48] Hadjivasilis, A., Tsioutis, C., Michalinos, A., Ntourakis, D., Christodoulou, D. K., & Agouridis, A. P. (2019). New insights into irritable bowel syndrome: from pathophysiology to treatment. *Annals of Gastroenterology*, *32*(6), 554–564. DOI:10.20524/aog.2019.0428

[49] Beesley, H., Rhodes, J., & Salmon, P. (2010). Anger and childhood sexual abuse are independently associated with irritable bowel syndrome. *British Journal of Health Psychology*, *15*(Pt 2), 389–399. DOI:10.1348/135910709X466496

[50] Taft, T. H., Bedell, A., Naftaly, J., & Keefer, L. (2017). Stigmatization toward irritable bowel syndrome and inflammatory bowel disease in an online cohort. *Neurogastroenterology and Motility: The Official Journal of the European Gastrointestinal Motility Society*, *29*(2). DOI: 10.1111/nmo.12921

[51] Kinsinger, S. W. (2017). Cognitive-behavioral therapy for patients with irritable bowel syndrome: current insights. *Psychology*

Research and Behavior Management, 10, 231–237. DOI:10.2147/PRBM.S120817

[52] Garland, E. L., Gaylord, S. A., Palsson, O., Faurot, K., Douglas Mann, J., Whitehead, W. E. (2012). Therapeutic mechanisms of a mindfulness-based treatment for IBS: effects on visceral sensitivity, catastrophizing, and affective processing of pain sensations. *Journal of Behavioral Medicine*, 35(6), 591–602. DOI:10.1007/s10865-011-9391-z

7   Health psychology in healthcare settings

Contents

Introduction

There are three strands to this chapter, which centrally relate to the 'healthcare setting'. Health psychology can help us understand and improve healthcare services that relate to (1) the role of communication in healthcare settings, (2) the impact of non-adherence and the role of HP in improving adherence) and (3) the impact of hospitalisation and stressful procedures on both adults and children.

Communication in healthcare settings

What is the doctor-patient relationship?

The medical consultation represents a 'central act of medicine' [1] and a fundamental process of healthcare practice. Best described as a two-way interaction between a doctor and a patient, the medical consultation is organised around the transfer of knowledge to make relevant decisions.

The doctor-patient relationship is a unique affiliation, one based on vulnerability and trust [2] Whilst at its most basic level this relationship appears to be contractual, one in which the doctor agrees to provide a high standard of care, bound by confidentiality it is very often more meaningful than this. For example, it would not be uncommon for patients to disclose very personal information, some of which may not even be known by their family members. Patient are often given bad news and have to make difficult choices, sharing their innermost fears and worries with their doctor.

This unique relationship encompasses four key elements, which together provide the foundation for the doctor-patient relationship [2] (Figure 7.1).

The doctor-patient relationship has changed dramatically over the last few decades. Szasz and Hollender (1956) proposed that there have been three basic models of the doctor-patient relationship; (a) active-passivity, (b) guidance-co-operation and (c) mutual participation [3] (Table 7.1).

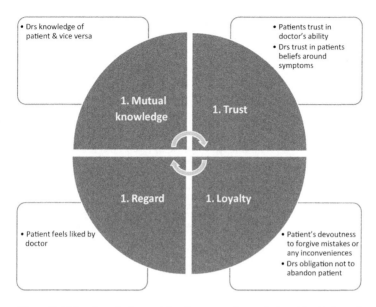

Figure 7.1 The foundations of the doctor-patient relationship (Adapted by Chipidza et al. [2])

Table 7.1 Evolvement of doctor-patient relationships

Model	What is the doctor's role?	What is the patient's role?	Relationship Prototype
Active-passivity	Doctor does something to the patient	Patient is the recipient and is unable to respond	Parent-infant
Guidance co-operation	Doctor tells patient what to do	Patient co-operates with doctor and obeys orders	Parent-Child/ adolescent
Mutual participation	Doctor helps patient to find himself	Patient is in partnership with doctor and uses expert help	Adult-Adult

The Active Passive Model [3] dominated medical practice during the late eighteenth century in response to our biomedical approach to illness. This model, paternalistic in nature, represents the idea that we as patients are passive recipients to the doctor, unable to actively contribute. The doctor is viewed as the expert and in response we as patients are helpless. The ideals of paternalism then saw the emergence of the Guidance Cooperation Model. Hippocratic doctors were focused on acting in the best medical interests of the patient. This model depicted that the doctor is in a position of power, depended upon by their patients to make the best decision. Synonymous with the 'parent-infant' relationship patients would be expected to submissively comply and accept the passive role of the infant [4].

The emergence of psychoanalytic and psychosocial theories provided an increased desire for a more reciprocal and equal relationship, where patients are viewed and treated as human beings.

> *To attend those who suffer, a physician must possess not only the scientific knowledge and technical abilities, but also an understanding of human nature. The patient is not just a group of symptoms, damaged organs and altered emotions. The patient is a human being, at the same time worried and hopeful, who is searching for relief, help and trust.*
>
> [5], p. 452

The Mutual Participation Model saw the end of paternalism and, in response to the publication of the first code of patient's rights in 1969, patients were now being viewed as responsible adults who must be involved in decision making and consent. This change in roles was centred on equal partnership and power; whereby, both parties respect each other's expertise; the doctor's knowledge and the patient's experiences and understanding.

What is the impact of a good doctor-patient relationship?

It could be argued that the success of medicine is dependent on the relationship between the doctor and the patient. As Hall

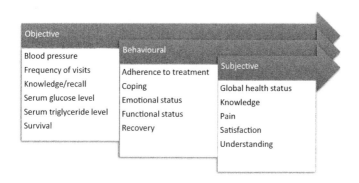

Figure 7.2 The impact of doctor–patient relationship on health outcomes (Chipidza et al. [2])

and Roter once stated, '*Medicine is an art whose magic and creative ability have long been recognized as residing in the interpersonal aspects of patient-physician relationship*' [6]. Good communication is extremely important, it provides doctors the ability to gather information, which in turn can facilitate an accurate diagnosis, counsel appropriately, give therapeutic instructions, and establish caring relationships [7].

The doctor–patient relationship can have an impact on both objective (based on an accurate and consistent measurement) and subjective (based on personal experiences and feelings) health outcomes [8] (see Figure 7.2). For example, if you experienced a poor relationship with your doctor, one where you do not feel respected or heard, this could ultimately impact on how often you visit your doctor, lead to an increase in blood pressure, and even reduce your survival rate. On a subjective level, the poor doctor-patient relationship could influence your pain tolerance, level of knowledge and understanding, and lead to a poorer quality of life. Behavioural factors and poor communication have also been linked to poor coping resources, reduced functional status and reduced adherence to treatment. Thus, it could be argued that having a good relationship with our doctor has the potential to make us healthier.

The medical consultation

Byrne and Long [9] analysed over 2,500 tape-recorded consultations from over 100 doctors in the UK and New Zealand. The researchers found that there are six stages in a consultation [9].

1. The doctor establishes a relationship with the patient.
2. The doctor attempts to discover the reason for the patient's attendance and understand any fears and concerns.
3. The doctor considers the history and conducts a verbal and/or physical examination.
4. Doctor, in consultation with the patient considers the condition.
5. The doctor and occasionally the patient consider further treatment and investigation.
6. The doctor brings the consultation to a close.

Factors that influence the medical consultation

According to Edelman [10] there are a number of competing factors that are shown to influence the medical consultation. These factors include: healthcare professional factors, patient related factors, the discrepancy between healthcare professional and patient factors alongside situational factors (see Figure 7.3).

Healthcare professional related factors

- **Profile characteristics**

Doctors will have a wide range of profile characteristics which will vary. For example, doctors will vary by age, gender, culture and where they live. They will also come with different experiences and judgements, all of which may impact on the consultation.

- **Beliefs of nature of clinical problems**

The consultation will be influenced by the doctor's beliefs, if they adopt a bio-medical or bio-psycho-social perspective to health

---

Box 7.1 Case vignette: Mr A

Mr A is 64, he was diagnosed with Type 2 diabetes mellitus when he was 34, which unfortunately has not been well controlled for many years.

As a result of this Mr A has developed peripheral neuropath, a lack of sensation in his foot which has now led to a neuropathic (diabetic) ulcer on his foot.

Mr A is finding it increasingly difficult to walk and get around and has noticed his ulcer is not healing despite getting it dressed and taking the course of antibiotics he was given.

The doctor reviewed Mr A's foot and is very concerned. The ulcer has formed black tissue (called eschar) surrounding the ulcer, a sign of a lack of healthy blood flow to the area. The doctor tells Mr A if it gets any worse and does not heal Mr A may need to have his foot amputated. More antibiotics are prescribed. Mr A shakes his head, and leaves holding his prescription.

---

and illness. For example, if a patient complains of being tired a doctor could treat this as anemia (biomedical) or as a direct result of stress (bio–psycho–social).

• **Personal knowledge of patient**

How well the doctor knows the patient will inevitably impact on the interaction. A patient with an extensive medical background with complex health problems is likely to cause more concern to a doctor compared to a patient they may consider to be 'healthy'. Likewise, a doctor will take into account the psychological state of the patient.

• **Stereotypes**

Doctors are often time limited and as a consequence may use stereotypes to help inform their judgements, this is referred to

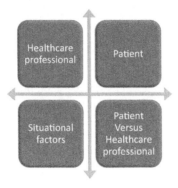

Figure 7.3 Factors that influence the medical consultation

as 'cognitive economy'. For example, a doctor may perceive a mother who has brought her young child in to be 'over reacting'.

Patient related factors

- The patient's age, gender, socio-economic status, culture, values and personality can all influence the consultation.
- Prior illness experience can also impact on the consultation. For example, someone who has had an illness in the past may have had a negative experience with a doctor. These experiences will no doubt shape their perceptions towards their current consultation, even if they are with a different doctor and for a different health condition.
- The severity of illness and emotional distress of the patient are also shown to impact on the consultation.

Patient and healthcare professional factors

The quality of interaction impacts on the patient's ability to be confident in dealing with their condition [11]. Patients have different styles of interaction depending on the healthcare professionals. For example, nurses have been traditionally viewed as more empathetic and more nurturing compared to doctors.

Patients are also likely to disclose more personal information and make more positive statements to female physicians compared to their male counterparts [12].

Situational factors

The waiting time to be seen at the consultation and the time given to the patient are all important factors, as is the environment where the consultation takes place.

What makes a good or bad medical consultation?

Think back to the last time you went to see your doctor. What was your consultation like? How would you have rated the communication between you and your doctor? It is current practice for doctors to offer 10 minutes for routine appointments. This does not seem long given that a doctor has to be able to assess the patient, diagnose and to provide treatment as needed. Therefore, doctors have a really difficult challenge in being able to balance not making the patients feel rushed with getting all the information they need to make important clinical judgements.

Shared decision making

Over the past decade of healthcare systems there has been an increased desire to involve patients more fully in decisions about their own care. We briefly considered consultation styles in doctor-patient relationships. We can think of these as lying on a spectrum from one extreme, paternalistic (clinician makes decision alone) to informed consent (patient makes decision alone). Somewhere within these two extremes lies the notion of shared decision making. This process involves at least two although often more participants, which normally involves the healthcare professional(s) and the patient. A treatment decision is made and both parties agree with the decision. Receptiveness is given by the doctor to the patient's opinions and expectations and they try to see the illness through the patient's eyes. The patient has full involvement in the decision making and planning of treatment.

Attention to the affective content of consultation of both the patient and doctor [13].

There is a growing body of evidence which suggests that shared decision making can lead to improved adherence to treatment regimes, higher levels of satisfaction and improved health outcomes [14]. According to Ford, Schofield and Hope [15] there are six stages within which in a good medical consultation can result, which highlights the importance of engaging the patient in the decision-making process.

These stages include:

1. having a **good knowledge** of research or medical information and being able to communicate this to the patient;
2. achieving a **good relationship** with the patient;
3. establishing the **nature of the patient's medical problem;**
4. gaining an **understanding of the patient's understanding;**
5. engaging the patient in the **decision-making process;**
6. **managing time.**

Some research has, however, suggested that not everyone wants to be actively involved in making a decision about their treatment. For example, a study conducted by Strull, Lo and Charles [19] examined patients' preferences for decision making among 210 hypotensive outpatients and their 50 clinicians. The results found that nearly half (47%) of patients preferred the clinician to make the decision without any participation, 33 per cent preferred the clinician to make the decision, but to consider their own opinion with less than 20 per cent stating that they would like to make the treatment themselves.

Why do you think this could be? One reason may be that some patients prefer the doctor to take the lead in decision making as they do not feel informed enough to make a decision. Also, patients may prefer to place that responsibility with someone else, particularly if they are concerned whether they will make the wrong decision. Evidence does also tell us that there is a range of characteristics that can explain if someone wants to engage in shared decision making or not. For example, those with more educational qualifications, younger, and those

Box 7.2 Key reading [16]

Background

Declining mortality rates in the UK mean higher life expectancy. In fact, one third of babies who were born in 2013 can expect to celebrate their 100th birthday [17]. This has resulted in increasing numbers of frail people who are in need of acute healthcare services, with two thirds of acute hospital beds occupied by people aged 65 years and over [18]. Older people have more complex health needs compared to the general population and there are concerns that healthcare services are not meeting these needs. As such this study aimed to gain insight into older peoples' and their relatives' views on and experiences of acute healthcare.

Methods

This study was a systematic review and synthesis of qualitative studies. This approach allows the researcher to bring together all the research available on a topic, analytically searching for research evidence from primary qualitative studies and then aims to pull all the findings together.

Figure 7.4 Image of an older person
(Source: Creative Commons)

Searching techniques were used for all relevant studies which were written in English between January 1999 and June 2008. A wide range of electronic sources were used to find the studies along with grey sources (unpublished or not commercially published). The authors found a total of 42 primary studies and one systematic review which met the inclusion criteria.

Results

The quality of technical care is often taken for granted by older patients. Patients and relatives were more likely to comment on aspects of care and experiences mediated through interpersonal relationships between staff and themselves. Findings suggested that the experience of visiting an acute hospital unearths many feelings, feelings of worthlessness and fear of not being in control of what happens. These feelings were more pronounced if the patient had impaired cognition, or communication difficulties.

Three key features of care consistently mediated these negative feelings and were linked to more positive experiences. These included;

"creating communities: connect with me"

The relationships with the healthcare professionals were an important factor in their experience. They wanted to feel connected with staff who can then provide them reassurance that they were "safe" and in good hands. Feeling connected with others including family and social networks was also important.

"maintaining identity: see who I am"

The process of becoming an in-patient resulted in a loss of identity. Patients wanted to feel that they could relate to people, remember important things and feel that staff know about their individual needs.

I can't even explain what I mean … It just seemed like they [staff] took away everything. It was just like you were at everybody's mercy, and you didn't count … When I was good and sick, it didn't matter, I guess. Their word was law.

Patient in Jacelon, 2004b, p. 31

"sharing decision-making: include me"

Many patients were not involved in decisions about their care or discharge. They tended to take a step back when important decisions were being made. This feeling of lack of control impacted on the degree to which they would anticipate a full recovery and the extent to which they trust others in control. Relatives seemed to prefer taking a more active role in decision making.

There were occasions when patients were not provided with important information, for example where death is imminent.

I know that something's up, I mean they used to be checking my blood pressure and temperature and taking blood samples and doing all sorts of tests. Now they do nothing and during the ward round they look at me and smile and say nowt, oh I know what's going on alright.

Patient in Costello, 2001, p.64

It was also not uncommon for relatives to feel excluded by staff from explanations and decision making.

Conclusion

These findings emphasise the importance of interpersonal relationships for both older people and their relatives when communicating with healthcare professionals in medical settings. This review also highlighted the importance for "relationship-centred" approaches to care, that is, the need for open and connected communication with patients and relatives, laying a degree of importance on the creation of reciprocal relationships with staff to provide an increased sense of security, significance and belonging.

with more experience with symptoms are more likely to want to be involved in decision making [14].

Older people, as an example, are often not involved in decisions about their care or discharge and tend to take a step back with relatives seeming to prefer to take a more active role in decision making. However, by not including the patient it can lead to them feeling isolated, as demonstrated in the key reading. Active participation is not uniformly desired, and this preference should be respected. Therefore, patient–centred decision making has to be concordant with the patient's values, needs and preferences. Regardless, ensuring that open and connected communication is provided to patients will serve to provide an increased sense of security and control.

Summary

Successful and unsuccessful communication has a major impact on adherence to treatment and patient satisfaction. For effective doctor-patient communication there must be mutual respect and exchange of ideas that are not just one sided. Doctors and patients perhaps value different aspects of the consultation, which can sometimes lead to confusion about what is an ideal doctor and consultation. There is also not a uniform consultation preference among patients, which can be influenced by a range of socio-demographic factors. Therefore, doctors should tailor their approach to the patient preference.

Concordance, adherence and compliance

What is adherence?

Think back to the last time you went to the doctors and were prescribed medication. Perhaps you have to take medication daily for an existing medical condition? Did you take all your medication as prescribed? If you have missed your medication (don't worry most of us have) then think back to some of the reasons why.

Perhaps you simply forgot, we would call this unintentional nonadherence. If this was the reason you would not be alone, in fact research suggests that around 50–70 per cent of cases of not taking medicines as prescribed is related to forgetfulness, carelessness or circumstances beyond the individual's control [20]. Those most likely to fall into this category include those who are older (aged 70 years+), those on complex medication regimes, those on new medication such as an antibiotics and patients who have existing and . However, there are still many patients (around 30–50%), who make a deliberate decision not to take medications as prescribed, this is referred to as intentional nonadherence. We will consider why later.

You might also question why does adherence matter? Poor adherence produces significant health losses through inadequate symptom management e.g., patients with Parkinson's who do not take their medication regularly as described have diminished mobility, increased fluctuations [21] and more hospital admissions [22, 23, 24]. There are also vast cost implications; conservative estimates of unused medicines in the NHS exceed £100 million annually. Non-adherence is also associated with a twofold increase in inpatient costs [25] and accounts for 23 per cent of nursing home and 8–11 per cent of hospitalisation admissions [24, 26, 27] and that doesn't include all the added unnecessary doctor visits, diagnostic tests and treatments.

What psychological factors predict adherence?

There has been a range of theories developed to help us conceptualise how adherence can be predicted. One of the earliest theories is the Cognitive Hypothesis Model of Compliance developed by Ley [28] (Figure 7.5). This theory suggests that our understanding and our memory are central in predicting if we will comply to a medical regime or not. A longitudinal study conducted by Miller et al. [29] followed 128 HIV infected patients who were receiving treatment and found that poor recall was associated with lower adherence and lower levels of literacy. This, therefore, emphasises the importance of checking patients'

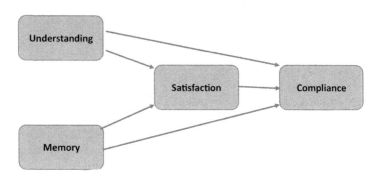

Figure 7.5 Ley's Cognitive Hypothesis Model of Compliance (Ley [28])

understanding when putting patients on new or complex medication regimes. Other factors that have been shown to influence recall have included: anxiety, medical knowledge, intellectual ability and primacy effect; but, surprisingly perhaps, is not found to be influenced by age [30].

According to Ley, this theory also suggests that patient satisfaction plays an integral role when an individual makes a decision to take medication as directed. Ley [28] found that around 40 per cent of patients were dissatisfied with their treatment, with a further 28 per cent dissatisfied with their GP practice [28], which negatively influenced their adherence behaviour. There is also strong and consistent evidence that there is a strong relationship between patient dissatisfaction and non-adherence with medical regimens [31] with a good quality doctor-patient relationship shown to promote adherence behaviour [32].

According to Ley, there are three strategies based on this theory that can be used to increase adherence, these include:

- **Maximising satisfaction with the process of treatment**
  - Ensuring there is sufficient time in the consultation to fully discuss relevant issues, guaranteeing that patients see the same health professional on repeat visits, and providing good accessibility to healthcare professionals.

- **Maximising understanding of the condition and its treatment**
  - problems arise if a health professional 'leads' a consultation, or a patient does not think through information they may need before leaving and check a patient's understanding of mediation regime.
- **Maximising memory for information given**
  - Provide patients the most important information early or late in the flow of information to maximise primacy and recency effects, ensure that the importance of the medication is emphasised.

The Perceptions and Practicalities Approach (PAPA)

One of the biggest criticisms of Ley's Cognitive Hypothesis model was that whilst it uncovered some important aspects around adherence it did not differentiate between different types of adhering behaviour. In other words, are the reasons for not adhering the same for patients who simply forget (unintentional) compared to those who avertedly choose not to comply (intentional). In response to this Horne [33] developed the Perceptions and Practicalities Approach (PAPA) model. This theory is based on a necessity concerns framework, which suggest that the higher the necessity (of the medication) and the lower the concerns (of

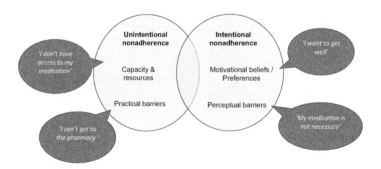

Figure 7.6 The Perceptions and Practicalities Approach Model (Horne [33])

the medication) the more likely they are to adhere (Figure 7.5). These beliefs have been shown to predict adherence across many long-term health conditions including: asthma [34], Diabetes, Cancer & coronary heart disease [35], HIV [36] and Rheumatoid arthritis [37]. Therefore, taking account of patients' necessity beliefs and concerns could be a useful way to engage patients in treatment decisions and in turn support adherence.

Below is a case study of a patient who you believe has not been adhering to his medication. Think through how you might address this with Jon in this situation while referring to the PAPA model. What questions might you ask?

Name of Patient: Jon Monroe	Date of Birth: 03/07/1954
Case summary	Jon is a 65-year-old man who has hypertension (high blood pressure) and Type II diabetes. Jon takes medication for his diabetes and is here to pick up a refill for a prescription for his diabetes, although it is not well controlled, and he always comes in late for his prescription.
History of present illness/complaint	You are not aware when Jon was diagnosed with diabetes and hypertension although you know that he has been with the medical practice for over 10 years. His hypertension and diabetes you expect might relate to lifestyle factors; Jon is noticeably overweight, so you are not sure what his diet/activity levels are like. You are also concerned that Jon always comes in late for his tablets, in fact when you were doing his last prescription you realised that he is around 40 tablets down. You are not sure why but want to address this with him.

First, you could explore with Jon how **necessary** he feels his medication is. Questions you might ask could include: how important is the medication for your diabetes and your health? What would happen if you did not take your medication?

You could then explore any **concerns** Jon may have about his medication? Questions might include: does the medication disrupt your life? Do you worry about taking the medication for your diabetes? Does the diabetes medication prevent you from getting worse? How easy is it to take your medication?

Understanding these barriers would then help you tailor how to best support Jon to address any doubts about necessity and concerns about his diabetes medication, and to overcome any practical difficulties.

Improving adherence: considerations and future directions

The National Institute Clinical Excellence have published good practice guidelines relating to medication adherence. This report focuses on the importance of 1) involving patients in decisions about their medicine, 2) supporting adherence, 3) importance of reviewing medicines regularly and 4) improving communication between the patient and healthcare professionals.

Improving communication with healthcare professionals plays a very important role in improving adherence, with evidence suggesting that there is a 19 per cent higher risk of nonadherence among patients whose healthcare professional communicates poorly than among patients whose healthcare professional communicates well. Training healthcare professionals in communication skills results has been shown to substantially and significantly improve patient adherence such that with communication training, the odds of patient adherence are 1.62 times higher than when a healthcare professional receives no training [38].

The most common interventions used are behavioural alone, with combined behavioural and educational being the next most common. A meta-analysis of 66 RCT studies of interventions to improve medication adherence revealed that each of these approaches led to an increase in adherence of 4 to 11 per cent with no single strategy appearing to be the best [39]. Therefore, it appears we still have some way to go until we can confidently say what the most effective intervention is. Technology advances have enabled us to consider more creative ways to improve our efforts with the use of m-health, and mobile technologies, including the use of interactive SMS reminders [40].

Impact of hospitalisation and stressful procedures

What is a hospital?

The earliest documented institutions which aimed to provide cures were seen in ancient Egyptian temples. This soon took precedent across many other countries, China, India and across Europe, although often referred to as healing institutions and delivered by the religious community. In fact, the first secular hospital was not seen until the fifteenth century, when, in response to a petition of the people of London, the church abruptly ceased to be the supporter of hospitals. The word hospital only became part of English language around the fifteenth century, which then meant 'a home for the infirm or the down-and-out'. It is now defined as 'a place where people who are ill or hurt have medical treatment' (*Longmans Dictionary of English*, p.506) or 'a healthcare facility providing inpatient beds, continuous nursing services and an organised medical staff, diagnosis and treatment for a variety of diseases and disorders at both medical and surgical level' ([41], p. 346).

What have your experiences been of hospitals? Take a few minutes to think back to an occasion when you found yourself in hospital either as a patient or visitor. Write down a brief account of your experience(s): what was important to you? Did you (or the visitor) receive the care you expected? See if you can identify themes that describe your experience.

Attending hospital can be a daunting process. We are expected (whilst feeling unwell) to enter an unfamiliar environment, with new people and are naturally nervous about what might happen. We are then expected to register and perhaps answer lots of administrative questions, we might then be ushered into a room with strange equipment and in some cases stripped of own clothes and property, but, perhaps most importantly, asked to entrust ourselves to complete strangers. As put by Wilson [42] the patient comes **unbidden** to a large organisation which **awes** and **irritates** him even as it also **nurtures** and **cares**. As he strips off his clothing, so he **strips off**, too, his favourite **costume** of **social roles**, his **favoured style**, his customary **identity** in the world. He becomes **subject** to a **time schedule** and a pattern of activity **not** of his **own making**.

(p.70)

There are also unwritten expectations on us, the patients. We are expected to be cooperative, friendly and trusting, conform to medical schedules and procedures, ask the right amount of questions at the right time and in the right manner, demand attention at appropriate times, from the appropriate people and for appropriate reasons and tolerate fragmented care and not feel patronised by the often 'empty' niceties of the several staff you will meet throughout your stay. It is perhaps then not surprising for some that hospitalisation can be one of the most distressing events that they have experienced in their lifetime. Not only does the individual suffer the stress of their health worries, they also suffer the stress of hospitalisation itself [43]. The hospital has also been found to be a very noisy environment which can lead to increased sensitivity to pain, poorer sleep and an increase in painkillers [44].

The patients' role

When a patient enters a hospital, they are an outsider in the health professional's place of work. Like any other workers, doctors and nurses try to arrange for their work to be conveniently and easily performed. Therefore, patients are involved in becoming part of the institution and living up to its expectations, a process usually associated with (in)voluntary loss of control and depersonalisation. Depersonalisation is often used by hospital staff to protect and distance themselves from emotional involvement and concentrate on the task in hand [45], which can contribute to slowing the recovery process [46] (Figure 7.6).

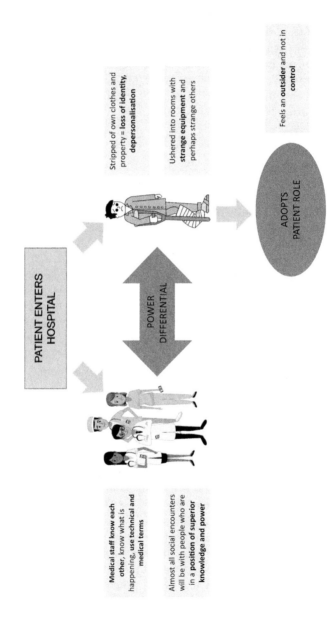

Figure 7.7 A visual representation of the patients' journey into hospital

The good versus bad patient

It has been found that patients do generally agree that they should conform to expectations and try to not 'cause trouble'. However, there has been a wide variation as to how much patients are prepared to conform. There is an ambiguous source of conflict between patients and medical staff in regards to complaints of pain and discomfort, whereby patients who complain more about discomfort are more regarded as 'deviant' patients [47].

The Gomer "Grand Old Man of the Emergency Room" Phenomenon was a term used by young physicians to describe patients. A Gomer is depicted as an older man, debilitated, and in many cases, a chronic alcoholic on public assistance. He would have a history of multiple hospitalisations and prefers life inside the hospital to life outside. He would be less able to return to his usual adult role, less able to return to own home and would normally remain longer in hospital [48]. Gomers were no more ill than control patients. However, their problems were more frustrating, engendered disagreem4ent, and aroused uncertainty in the house-staff caring for them. Nonetheless, Gomers represented the failure of medicine to eliminate illness and to heal the aging as well as the failure of society to provide humane care for the socially isolated patient whose illness is not tidily resolved by either cure or death [48].

Factors affecting adjustment to hospital

The importance of adequate information should not be understated. A systematic review found that about 52 per cent of patients for all conditions rated information given as inadequate [49]. Furthermore, a study of hospitalised women found that 40 per cent of women felt increased stress due to staff disregarding their needs for information on care [50]. Therefore, whilst providing information is important it is imperative that the information given is matched to the patient's preferences; i.e. the more information received by patients matched their preferences, the better their adjustment to treatment [51].

Coping styles are also shown to play an important role in adjustment to hospital. **Active coping** strategies i.e. information gathering, seeking social support and reframing our perceptions of the stress, have been shown to be beneficial if the hospital environment provides such opportunities (McIntosh, Stern, & Ferguson, 2004). **Avoidant coping** strategies i.e. denial, withdrawal and helplessness, and no information-gathering have conversely been shown to be less effective. However, interestingly for some people, e.g. dental surgery patients, research has shown active coping is linked to better psychological outcomes [52].

Children in hospital

Hospitalisation for children can be particularly traumatic. For one, children are less physically and psychologically mature, and may have a very different understanding of the experience compared to adults. A child being admitted into hospital, particularly long term, can have a huge disruption on the parent/caregiver-child relationship and have a negative effect on the family as a whole.

During the twentieth century accounts of being in hospital were more focused on disease eradication rather than psychological support. During this time typical death rates in children included: diphtheria 20%, Scarlet fever 15–25%, whooping cough 1%, measles 0.3%, mumps 0.00002%. Below is an account of an adult recalling his time in a hospital during this time period.

The Second World War had a big impact on our views towards hospitalisation in children. Family life has been seriously disrupted, with many children who became homeless or orphaned, with many fathers away at war. Towards the end of the war, parents were increasingly reluctant to allow children's evacuation out of cities, with many families preferring to remain together in danger than to be separated and safe. The disruption of family life during the war highlighted possible long-term psychological damage to children as a result of separation from their parents. Consequently, children's psychological welfare became paramount in a way that had not previously happened. The war highlighted problems suffered by the separation of children from parents and there was a trend moving away from the Victorian

---

Box 7.3 Account of a hospitalisation as a young child during the twentieth century

I was born a very small sickly baby. I'm afraid my mother smoked heavily all through her pregnancy, we didn't realise that that was a bad thing to do at that time. Maybe it was because I'd had a bit of a bad start in life that I seemed to catch all kinds of illnesses as a child. When I was four, I had both diphtheria and whooping cough at the same time. I had to go to a sanatorium, my parents weren't allowed to visit me so as not to spread the infection. I don't know how long I was there, but I was told that it was such a long time that finally, when my parents came to take me home, I no longer recognised them.

Boy, 4-years-old

---

model of the family's role as child trainer in favour of the family as the context or giving love and affection.

The publication of *Child Care and the Growth of Love* by Dr John E. J. M. Bowlby (1953) was an immediate bestseller that fuelled the topical widespread debate at the time on the best way of caring for children in homes and in hospitals. Bowlby proposed the Theory of Maternal deprivation as he stated,

> What is believed to be essential for mental health is that an infant and young child should experience a warm, intimate and continuous relationship with his mother (or permanent mother-substitute – one person who steadily 'mothers' him) in which both find satisfaction and enjoyment.
>
> [53], p. 13

Based on Bowlby's clinical work with delinquent children, he 'unearthed the common factor of deprivation of maternal care caused by either being in institutions, or posted, like parcels, from one mother-figure to another' [54].

Whilst the Theory of Maternal Deprivation has now been extensively modified and largely abandoned, it had huge influence at the time. Many of the features that we now regard as standard in hospitals for children began to be introduced after this time, e.g. flexible visiting hours and overnight stays for parents. Policy issues have continued to be influenced by Bowlby's early work, and versions of the theory are regularly presented in the media to justify certain approaches to childcare.

In the 1970s there was an increased focus on maternal-infant 'bonding' with increased fears among mothers that babies separated from them soon after birth would suffer detrimental outcomes because of disruption to bonding. However, later, several studies actually exposed that hospitalised babies suffered less impact longer term. For example, Svejda, Campos and Emde [55] conducted a controlled observation study, where they put mothers giving birth into one of two conditions. There was an experimental condition whereby the mother had close contact with their baby after delivery, and extended contact at feeding, and a control condition, which meant that the mothers had no contact at delivery, and only 30 minutes' contact for four-hourly feeds. The findings revealed that there were no differences between those babies hospitalised immediately after birth and non-hospitalised controls, and that parents 'caught up' with bonding later on in their babies' lives.

The hospital can still even today be a traumatising experience for children. A review conducted by Wright [56] revealed that there is a range of detrimental factors which influence the experience for children:

- child's age and temperament;
- the extent to which the child feels in control of the situation, the more in control the less traumatising the experience;
- being in hospital longer than two weeks;
- painful injuries and illnesses;
- inadequate preparation for routine admission;
- previous adverse admissions;
- absence of parents, and/or highly anxious parents.

There have also been a number of observational studies which have tried to understand how children adjust to being in hospital. For example, Runeson, Hallström, Elander and Hermerén [57] found that during threatening situations, children were observed to need control over the situation, feel nearby presence of parents, be familiar with surroundings, have support from staff and sometimes have the need to be alone. However, during non-threatening situations, children were observed to need activity, particularly play, new experiences, humour, information, praise and recognition. Children also managed hospital fear by expressing it and asking for help, accepting the fear, rejecting it, meeting friends and siblings, and by means of material objects that create pleasure.

How can we better support patients including children in hospital settings?

In hospital settings, the demand for psychological support often exceeds supply. The role of the health psychologist can go beyond direct work with patients to include education, training, research and consultancy with other multidisciplinary team members. A paediatric gastroenterology service, which often has various psychological aspects related to the care, commissioned a psychology consultancy to provide support to staff and patients. An evaluation of this additional service demonstrated that medical staff really appreciated being able to talk about 'difficult' cases, where more psychological factors were present and were appreciative of hearing alternative viewpoints, receiving advice and having additional support with difficult interactions. It was also found that it improved referrals to psychology services and was able to prevent unnecessary medical interventions [58].

Summary

Historically, the hospital was somewhere where the poor and sick were looked after and allowed to rest, rather than where they were 'cured'. Hospitalisation has since become dominated by technology and by the needs of the medical profession. Involvement of patients in decision-making is desirable, but not always easy and not all patients are willing or able to take part in decision-making. For some, hospitalisation can be traumatic, and people have different coping mechanisms (active coping, avoidant coping) to manage this.

There have been many changes over the twentieth century, especially after the Second World War. The importance of psychological care, particularly to children, was being increasingly recognised, a movement which led to the development of theories around infant-maternal attachment in a healthcare context. Nonetheless, parental anxiety and invasive procedures still remain traumatic. More recent interventions have explored possibilities for health psychologists to support siblings of children, which could provide a useful strategy in supporting families during periods of medical hospitalisation.

Final overview and summary

- Patient satisfaction has become an integral aspect of medical care, whereby poor levels of satisfaction, which can impact not only health indirectly through lack of knowledge and understanding, poorer coping, but also directly. Communication models and empirical literature have been useful to help us understand what influences this, but also and perhaps more importantly how we can improve expectations and outcomes for patients.
- The hospital can be a traumatic experience for children and adults alike. Psychological research and theory have influenced the provision of healthcare for children and adolescents and adults in hospitals over the last century. There is now an increased focus of improving support to families through the provision of psychological support.
- Health psychology can play an important role in all aspects of healthcare, from delivering communication training to healthcare professionals, to improving doctor-patient relationships, to improving adherence in those who do not take their medication as described, to supporting hospitals

and other institutions on improving psychological and eHealth outcomes of patients, particularly children.

References

[1] Pendleton, D., Schofield, T., Tate, P., & Havelock, P. (1984). *The Consultation: An Approach to Learning and Teaching*. Oxford University Press: Oxford.

[2] Chipidza, F. E., Wallwork, R. S., & Stern, T. A. (2015). Impact of the doctor-patient relationship. The *Primary Care Companion for CNS Disorders*, *17*(5), 10.4088/PCC.4015f01840. doi:10.4088/PCC.15f01840

[3] Szasz, T. S., Knoff, W. F., & Hollender, M. H. (1958). The doctor-patient relationship and its historical context. *American Journal of Psychiatry*, *115*, 522–528.

[4] Kaba, R., & Sooriakumaran, P. (2007). The evolution of the doctor-patient relationship. *International Journal of Surgery*, *5*(1), 57–65. doi:https://doi.org/10.1016/j.ijsu.2006.01.005

[5] Hellin, T. (2002). The physician–patient relationship: Recent developments and changes. *Haemophilia*, 8(3), 450–454.

[6] Hall, J. A., Roter, D. L., & Rand, C. S. (1981). Communication of affect between patient and physician. *J Health Soc Behav*, *22*(1), 18–30.

[7] Duffy, F. D., Gordon, G. H., Whelan, G., Cole-Kelly, K., & Frankel, R. (2004). Assessing competence in communication and interpersonal skills: the Kalamazoo II report. *Academic Medicine*, *79*(6), 495–507.

[8] Gordon, C., & Beresin, E. V. (2016). The doctorpatient relationship. In T. A. Stern, M. Fava, & T. E. Wilens (Eds.), Massachusetts General Hospital Comprehensive Clinical Psychiatry (2nd ed., pp. 1–7). Philadelphia, PA: Elsevier Health Sciences.

[9] Byrne, P., & Long, B. (1976). *Doctors Talking to Patients: A Study of the Verbal Behaviour of General Practitioners Consulting in Their Surgeries*. London: HMSO.

[10] Edelman, R. J. (2000). *Psychosocial Aspects of the Healthcare Process*. London: Pearson Education.

[11] Zachariae, R., Pedersen, C. G., Jensen, A. B., Ehrnrooth, E., Rossen, P. B., & Maase, H. v. d. (2003). Association of perceived physician communication style wituh patient satisfaction, distress, cancer-related self efficacy, and perceived control over the disease. *British Journal of Cancer*, *88*, 658–665.

[12] Hall, J. A., & Roter, D. L. (2002). Do patients talk differently to male and female physicians? A meta-analytic review. *Patient Education and Counseling, 48*, 217–224.

[13] Coulter, A., & Collins, A. (2011). *Making Shared Decision-Making a Reality.* London: King's Fund.

[14] Robinson, A., & Thomson, R. (2001). Variability in patient preferences for participating in medical decision making: implication for the use of decision support tools. *Quality in Health Care, 10*(1), 34–38.

[15] Ford, S., Schofield, T., & Hope, T. (2003). What are the ingredients for a successful evidence-based patient choice consultation? A qualitative study. *Social Science and Medicine, 56*, 589–602.

[16] Bridges, J. (2008). *Listening Makes Sense: Understanding the Experiences of Older People and Relatives Using Urgent Care Services in England.* City University London: London, UK.

[17] Office for National Statistics. (2013). One third of babies born in 2013 are expected to live to 100. Retrieved from https://webarchive.nationalarchives.gov.uk/20160105221229/http://www.ons.gov.uk/ons/rel/lifetables/historic-and-projected-data-from-the-period-and-cohort-life-tables/2012-based/sty-babies-living-to-100.html

[18] Department of Health. (2000). *Shaping the Future NHS: Long Term Planning for Hospitals and Related Services. Consultation document on the findings of the national beds inquiry.*

[19] Strull, W. M., Lo, B., & Charles, G. (1984). Do patients want to participate in medical decision making? *Jama, 252*(21), 2990–2994.

[20] MacLaughlin, E. J., Raehl, C. L., Treadway, A. K., Sterling, T. L., Zoller, D. P., & Bond, C. A. (2005). Assessing medication adherence in the elderly. *Drugs & Aging, 22*(3), 231–255.

[21] Fleisher, J. E., & Stern, M. B. (2013). Medication Non-adherence in Parkinson's Disease. *Current Neurology and Neuroscience Reports, 13*(10), 10.1007/s11910-11013-10382-z. doi:10.1007/s11910-013-0382-z

[22] Arlt, S., Lindner, R., Rosler, A., & RentelnKrus, W. V. (2008). Adherence to medication in patients with Dementia: Predictors and strategies for improvement. *Drugs & Aging, 25*(12), 1033–1047.

[23] Bergman, U., & Wiholm, B. E. (1981). Drug-related problems causing admission to a medical clinic. *European Journal Clinical Pharmacology, 20*, 193–200.

[24] Col, N., Fanale, J. E., & Kronholm, P. (1990). The role of medication noncompliance and adverse drug reactions in hospitalizations of the elderly. *Archives of Internal Medicine, 150*(4), 841–845.

[25] Kane, S., & Shaya, F. (2008). Medication non-adherence is associated with increased medical health care costs. *Dig Dis Sci, 53*(4), 1020–1024. doi:10.1007/s10620-007-9968-0

[26] Horwitz, R. I., Viscoli, C. M., Berkman, L., Donaldson, R. M., Horwitz, S. M., Murray, C. J., … Sindelar, J. (1990). Treatment adherence and risk of death after a myocardial infarction. *Lancet, 336*(8714), 542–545.

[27] Malhotra, S., Karan, R., Pandhi, P., & Jain, S. (2001). Drug related medical emergencies in the elderly: role of adverse drug reactions and non-compliance. *Postgraduate Medical Journal, 77*(913), 703–707. doi:10.1136/pmj.77.913.703

[28] Ley, P. (1988). *Communicating with Patients*. London: Croom Helm.

[29] Miller, L. G., Liu, H., Hays, R. D., Golin, C. E., Ye, Z., Beck, C. K., … Wenger, N. S. (2003). Knowledge of antiretroviral regimen dosing and adherence: A longitudinal study. *Clinical Infectious Diseases, 6*(4), 514–518.

[30] Ley, P. (1989). Improving patients' understanding, recall, satisfaction and compliance. In A. Broome (Ed.), *Health Psychology*. London: Chapman & Hall.

[31] Kaplan, S. H., Greenfield, S., & Ware, J. E. (1989). Assessing the effects of physician-patient interactions on the outcomes of chronic disease. *Medical Care, 27*(7), 679.

[32] Roberts, K. J. (2002). Physician-patient relationships, patient satisfaction, and Antiretroviral medication adherence among HIV-infected adults attending a public health clinic. *AIDS Patient Care and STDs, 16*(1), 43–50.

[33] Horne, R. (2001). Compliance, adherence and concordance. In K. Taylor & G. Harding (Eds.), *Pharmacy Practice*. London: Taylor and Francis.

[34] Horne, R., & Weinman, J. (2002). Self-regulation and self-management in asthma; exploring the role of illness perceptions and treatment beliefs in explaining non-adherence to preventer medication. *Psychology and Health, 17*(1), 17–32.

[35] Horne, R., & Weinman, J. (1999). Patients beliefs about prescribed medicines and their role in adherence to treatment in chronic physical illness. *Journal of Psychosomatic Research, 47*(6), 555–567.

[36] Horne, R., Cooper, V., & Gellaitry, G. (2007). Patients perceptions of highly active antiretroviral therapy in relation to treatment uptake and adherence: the utility of the necessity-concerns framework. *Journal of Acquired Immune Deficiency Syndromes, 45*(3), 334–341.

[37]   Neame, R., & Hammond, A. (2005). Beliefs about medications: a questionnaire survey of people with rheumatoid arthritis. *Rheumatology*, *44*, 762–767.

[38]   Zolnierek, K. B. H., & DiMatteo, M. R. (2009). Physician communication and patient adherence to treatment: a meta-analysis. *Medical Care*, *47*(8), 826.

[39]   Peterson, A., Takiya, L., & Finley, R. (2003). Meta-analysis of trials of interventions to improve medication adherence. *American Journal of Health-System Pharmacy*, *60*(7), 657–665. Retrieved from www.ajhp.org/content/60/7/657.abstract

[40]   Free, C., Phillips, G., Watson, L., Galli, L., Felix, L., Edwards, P., … Haines, A. (2013). The effectiveness of mobile-health technologies to improve health care service delivery processes: a systematic review and meta-analysis. *PLoS Medicine*, *10*(1), e1001363.

[41]   Mosby. (2016). *Mosby's Medical Dictionary*. USA: Elseiver.

[42]   Wilson, R. N. (1963). The social structure of a general hospital. *The ANNALS of the American Academy of Political and Social Science*, *346*(1), 67–76. doi:10.1177/000271626334600107

[43]   Rokach, A., & Parvini, M. (2011). Experience of adults and children in hospitals. *Early Child Development and Care*, *181*(5), 707–715.

[44]   Holmberg, S. K., & Coon, S. (1999). Ambient sound levels in a state psychiatric hospital. *Archives of Psychiatric Nursing*, *13*(3), 117–126.

[45]   Mackintosh, C. (2007). Protecting the self: A descriptive qualitative exploration of how registered nurses cope with working in surgical areas. *International Journal of Nursing Studies*, *44*(6), 982–990.

[46]   Hughes, B. M. (2001). Psychology, hospitalization and some thoughts on medical training. *European Journal of Psychotherapy, Counselling & Health*, *4*(1), 7–26.

[47]   Lorber, J. (1975). Women and medical sociology: Invisible professionals and ubiquitous patients. *Sociological Inquiry*, *45*(2-3), 75–105. doi:10.1111/j.1475-682X.1975.tb00332.x

[48]   Leiderman, D. B., & Grisso, J.-A. (1985). The Gomer Phenomenon. *Journal of Health and Social Behavior*, *26*(3), 222–232. doi:10.2307/2136754

[49]   Kiesler, D. J., & Auerbach, S. M. (2006). Optimal matches of patient preferences for information, decision-making and interpersonal behavior: Evidence, models and interventions. *Patient Education and Counseling*, *61*(3), 319–341.

[50] Yap, J. N.-K. (1988). A critical review of pediatric preoperative preparation procedures: Processes, outcomes, and future directions. *Journal of Applied Developmental Psychology, 9*(4), 359–389.

[51] McIntosh, B. J., Stern, M., & Ferguson, K. S. (2004). Optimism, coping, and psychological distress: Maternal reactions to NICU hospitalization. *Children's Health Care, 33*(1), 59–76.

[52] Kiyak, H. A., Vitaliano, P. P., & Crinean, J. (1988). Patients' expectations as predictors of orthognathic surgery outcomes. *Health Psychology, 7*(3), 251.

[53] Bowlby, E. J. M. (1953). *Child Care and the Growth of Love: Based by Permission of the World Health Organization on the Report 'Maternal Care and Mental Health'*. Harmondsworth: Penguin.

[54] Bowlby, J. (1944). Forty-four juvenile thieves: Their characters and home-life. *International Journal of Psycho-Analysis, 25*, 19–53.

[55] Svejda, M. J., Campos, J. J., & Emde, R. N. (1980). Mother–infant" bonding": Failure to generalize. *Child Development*, 775–779.

[56] Wright, M. (1995). Behavioural effects of hospitalization in children. *Journal of Paediatrics and Child Health, 31*(3), 165–167.

[57] Runeson, I., Hallström, I., Elander, G., & Hermerén, G. (2002). Children's participation in the decision-making process during hospitalization: an observational study. *Nursing Ethics, 9*(6), 583–598.

[58] Douglas, J. L., & Benson, S. (2015). Psychological consultation in a paediatric setting: A qualitative analysis of staff experiences of a psychosocial forum. *Clinical Child Psychology and Psychiatry, 20*(3), 472–485.

Glossary

Addiction   Commonly associated with drugs, alcohol and nicotine, it reflects the compulsive engagement of seeking out an activity for rewarding effects despite adverse consequences.

Aetiology   The cause of a disease or condition.

Affective   Relates to mood, emotions and feelings.

Appraisals   Refers to an individual's interpretation of a situations, event or behaviour.

Autoimmune condition   A condition where your immune system mistakenly attacks its own body, unable to tell the difference between own cells and foreign cells. Common autoimmune conditions include: Type 1 diabetes, multiple sclerosis, inflammatory bowel disease and rheumatoid arthritis.

Avoidant coping   A coping style characterised by engaging in behaviours that distract from the problem directly and distancing oneself from the problem itself.

Behavioural pathogen   A behaviour or type of lifestyle thought to be damaging to health.

Bio-psycho-social   A view that diseases and symptoms can be explained by a combination of physical, social, cultural and psychological factors (cf. Engel, 1977).

Body mass index   A measurement derived from the mass (weight) and height of a person. It is calculated as the weight in kilograms divided by height in metres (squared) expressed in units of kg/m^2. The result can be used as an index of weight (underweight, healthy weight, overweight, obese).

British Psychological Society A registered charity which is the leading learned society and professional body in the UK for psychologists.

Causal attribution The beliefs regarding the causes of an event or people's behaviour.

Cervical smear Smear of cells taken from the cervix to examine for the presence of cell changes indicating risk of cervical cancer.

Classical conditioning Also referred to as Pavlovian conditioning, it refers to an automatic learning procedure where a neutral stimulus (can be anything, e.g. bell) is paired with an unconditioned stimulus (e.g. food) to produce a conditioned response (salivate) to the stimulus (e.g. when you hear the bell you salivate even if was not followed by food).

Condition Experimental studies often involve allocating participants to different conditions: for example, information versus no information, relaxation versus no relaxation, active drug versus placebo.

Coping self-efficacy The belief that one can carry out a particular coping behaviour when dealing with challenges and threats.

Coronary heart disease A narrowing of the blood vessels that supply blood and oxygen to the heart. It results from a build-up of fatty material and plaque (atherosclerosis) and can result in angina or myocardial infarction.

Cortisol A stress hormone that regulates metabolism and the immune response.

Cross-sectional design A study that analyses data at one specific point in time.

Decisional balance Where the cons of behaviour are weighed up against the pros of that behaviour.

Denial response Taking a view that denies any negative implications of an event or stimulus. If subconscious, it is considered a defence mechanism.

Dependence When the body relies on or needs a substance to bring it back to its 'normal' state, avoiding an unpleasant state.

Dependent variable A variable measured that changes as a result of the independent variable, often referred to as the outcome variable: for example, a relaxation technique (the independent variable) causes a change in perceived stress (the dependent variable).

Diabetes (Type I and II) A lifelong disease marked by high levels of sugar in the blood and a failure to transfer this to organs that need it. It can be caused by too little insulin (Type I), resistance to insulin (Type II), or both.

Dual Process model Fear-arousing messages point to two sets of cognitive processing: danger and fear control (cf. Leventhal, 1984).

Dualism The idea that the mind and body are separate entities (cf. Descartes).

Emotional expression The disclosure of emotional experiences through verbal and non-verbal behaviour as a means of reducing stress.

Endocrine glands Glands of the endocrine system that produce and secrete hormones into the blood or lymph systems.

Endorphins Naturally occurring hormones released in the brain and nervous system to relieve stress and pain.

Environmental re-evaluation Realising the negative impact of an old behaviour or the positive impact of a behaviour change on the individual's social and physical environment.

Epidemiology A branch of medicine which is interested in incidence, distribution and control of diseases and other factors relating to health.

Experimental design A controlled study to test or refute a hypothesis, often used to establish cause and effect. Variables are manipulated in order specifically to examine the relationship between the independent variable (the cause) and the dependent variable (the effect). Experiments typically have controls to minimise the effects of variables other than the independent variable.

General Adaptation Syndrome A sequence of physiological responses to prolonged stress, from the alarm stage through the resistance stage to exhaustion.

Health Action Process Approach (HAPA) A psychological theory of health behaviour change, which suggests that the adoption, initiation and maintenance of behaviour is centred around two stages: a motivation phase and a volition (action) phase (cf. Schwarzer, 1992).

Health Behaviour An action to maintain, attain or regain good health.

Health Belief Model (HBM) A social psychological model proposed by Rosenstock (1966) and further developed by Becker, Haefner and Maiman (1977), which has been used to explain and predict health related behaviour. The HBM suggests that behaviour is a result of an individual's beliefs regarding their susceptibility, severity, benefits and barriers to action, cues to action and health motivation.

Health locus of control Individual beliefs based on past experiences, which reflect the extent that someone feels that their health is: under personal control (internal locus of control) or is controlled by powerful others or external factors such as fate or luck.

Health value The value which an individual place on their health, often self-reported.

Heart failure A condition where the heart is not able to pump enough blood around the body to meet the demands of the body.

Holistic Concerned with the belief that treatment should consider the whole person, e.g. take account of the psychological and social factors rather than addressing the purely physical or observable.

Human Papillomavirus (HPV) A family of over 100 viruses, of which 30 types can cause genital warts and be transmitted by sexual contact. Some HPV infections may markedly elevate the risk for cancer of the cervix.

Humoural theory Relates to the theory of the four humours. This theory suggests that when someone becomes ill it is due to an imbalance of four fluids (blood, black bile, yellow bile and phlegm) (cf. Hippocrates).

Hypertension A condition in which blood pressure is significantly raised, which, left untreated, can increase an individual's risk of serious problems such as heart attacks.

Hypothalamus The small but important region of the brain, located at the base, responsible for releasing hormones, regulating body temperature, controlling appetite, managing sexual arousal and regulating emotional responses.

Illness behaviour Actions or reactions of an individual who is unwell and who seeks a remedy.

Illness cognition The cognitive processes involved in a person's perception or interpretation and understanding of symptoms or illness and their treatment.

Illness representations Beliefs and expectations about an illness or symptom, which are central to Leventhal's Self-Regulation Theory

Implementation–intentions A goal-setting theory based on the form of 'if–then' planning, relating to the anticipated situation and the response (cf. Gollwitzer & Sheeran, 2006).

Incidence The occurrence or frequency of a disease.

Independent variable The variable which causes a change in the dependent variable: for example, exercise (the independent variable) causes weight loss (the dependent variable).

Individual differences Demographic and psychological factors that distinguish us from each other (e.g. age, personality, intelligence).

Individualistic A cultural philosophy and ideology which emphasises the importance of the individual rather than the wider community.

Inflammatory bowel disease Used to describe two conditions: ulcerative colitis and Crohn's disease. Both conditions are long term and involve inflammation of the gut.

Intention A conscious decision reflecting a person's determination to act in a certain way.

Life events Occurrences in a person's life, which disrupt an individual's usual activities. Examples include: marriage, having a child, losing a job. Can be viewed negatively or positively.

Locus of control The degree to which an individual believes they have the internal control over the outcome as opposed to external factors beyond their control.

Longitudinal (design) A research design which involves repeated observations of the same variable or cohort over a period of time.

Lymphocyte White blood cells which play an important role in the immune system. Found in bone marrow, blood and in lymph tissue these cells make antibodies to help fight infection and disease.

Mediate/mediator A statistical term which seeks to explain the relationship and mechanisms between an independent variable and dependent variable.

Message framing The way in which messages are presented to influence positive health behaviours.

Meta-analysis A statistical approach which systematically assesses the results of pre-existing quantitative datasets, typically based on randomised controlled trials, which combines the analysis so as to provide large samples and high statistical power (over individual studies) from which to draw reliable conclusions about specific effects and resolve uncertainty.

Monism Greek: μόνος. meaning oneness or singleness, refers to the theological view that the mind and the body are part of the same system.

Morbidity Refers to having a disease, outside of normal wellbeing.

Mortality Refers to death, often used as a statistical measure to determine the number of deaths in a particular population (mortality rate).

Motivation A desire, something we want to do (a goal or something we aspire to) or avoid (want to go away). Influences the type, strength and persistence of our actions.

Multiple regression A statistical test that can tell us how much of the variance in the outcome variable (i.e. dependent variable) can be explained by the value of two or more variables.

Multiple Sclerosis A disorder of the brain and spinal cord caused by progressive damage to the myelin sheath covering of nerve cells. Can cause a wide range of symptoms including: fatigue, difficulty walking, numbness, muscle stiffness and vision problems.

Myocardial infarction   Also referred to as a heart attack, it is caused by decreased blood flow, which can stop part of a heart, causing damage to the heart muscle.

Natural killer (NK) cells   Cells of the immune system that can move in the blood and attack cancer cells and virus-infected body cells.

Negative affectivity   Refers to a variety of negative emotions such as fear, sadness, anger and poor self-concept.

Neurotransmitter   A body chemical messenger which transmits signals between neurons, nerve cells and other types of cell.

Noradrenaline   Also referred to as norepinephrine. A substance which is released from the sympathetic nervous system to get the body ready for action.

Objective   Based on real facts, unbiased, visible or systematically measurable.

Observational learning   Learning that occurs through watching and modelling behaviour of significant others; commonly associated with the Bandura Bobo doll studies.

Operant conditioning   Attributed to Skinner, this theory is based on the assumption that behaviour is learnt through rewards and punishment of behaviour.

Optimistic bias   The difference between an individual's expectation versus the outcome that follows. Also known as unrealistic optimism.

Outcome expectancies   What we expect to happen as a result of our behaviour.

Parasympathetic nervous system (PSNS)   One of three divisions with the autonomic nervous system. Sometimes referred to as the rest and digest system it helps us conserve energy by slowing the heart rate and regulates digestion.

Pathogen   A bacteria, virus or other microorganism that can cause disease.

Perceived behavioural control   An individual's belief in personal control over a certain specific action or behaviour. See Theory of Planned Behaviour.

Phagocyte   Greek phagein, "to eat" or "devour", and "-cyte". Refers to a type of cell that has the ability to ingest and sometimes digest foreign particles such as bacteria, dust or dye.

Placebo An intervention designed to have no therapeutic benefit, but given to encourage the patient to think they are getting the real treatment (i.e. a sugar pill).

Prevalence A statistical term, which refers to the number of established cases of a disease in a population at a given time.

Primary prevention Concerned with preventing disease before it ever occurs.

Problem-focused coping A coping style that is focused on resolving the stressful situation or altering the source of stress.

Prognosis Greek: πρόγνωσις "fore-knowing, foreseeing", a medical term to refer to the expected development of a disease "the doctor said I had a poor prognosis of recovery".

Prospective design Refers to a study design which follows subjects over a period of time (sometimes called longitudinal or cohort design) and often watches for outcomes, e.g. the development of a disease during a study period.

Protection Motivation Theory (PMT) A model to describe how individuals are motivated to react in relation to a health threat. This model assumes that threat appraisal and coping appraisal can explain how fear-arousing communications are processed and acted upon (cf. Rogers, 1975).

Prototype Willingness Model (PWM) This model suggests that prototypes (social images of what people who engage in the behaviour are like) play an important role in influencing our willingness to engage (or not) in a behaviour in a given situation. Willingness is said to be influenced by our attitudes, subjective norms, prior experience with behaviour and prototypes (cf. Gibbons & Gerrard, 1995).

PsychoNeuroImmunology (PNI) The study of the interaction between psychological processes and the nervous and immune systems of the human body.

Psycho-social Takes account of the inter relation of psychological (thoughts and behaviour) and social (e.g. where someone lives, social class).

Qualitative study A method of research which is subjective, concerned with understanding human behaviour from the individual's perspective. Assumes reality is dynamic and negotiated. Qualitative data is textual, often reported and described in terms of themes and categories.

Quantitative study   A method of research which is objective, concerned with numbers and quantities and assumes reality is fixed and measurable. Quantitative data is reported and analysed through statistical means.

Randomly allocated   Participants are allocated to different conditions by chance in order to minimise the effects of any individual differences. So, for a controlled study with two conditions (intervention/control) you would have a 50 per cent chance of being in the intervention group and a 50 per cent chance of being in the control group of a study.

Reinforcement management   Rewarding positive behaviour change and reducing any reward for the unwanted behaviour.

Reinforcers   Refers to something that increases the likelihood of a specific behaviour. There are different types of reinforcers which include: rewarding the behaviour (positive reinforcers); or removing and/or avoiding an undesired state or response (negative reinforcers).

Relapse prevention   These are coping skills essential to achieving long-term behavioural change which prepare them to resist temptation and to minimise the impact of any relapse should it occur. These often form an important role in alcohol or drug addiction recovery.

Repeated-measures design   Refers to a research design which involves taking multiple measures of the same variables on the same subjects in more than one time period or under different conditions.

Rheumatoid arthritis   A long-term autoimmune disease characterised by warm, swollen and painful joints.

Self-attribution   The extent to which people determine the causes and consequences of their behaviour, attributing to internal or external causes. The self-serving bias is an error of this, which suggest that we attribute positive outcomes to internal causes but negative outcomes to external causes. For example, I received an A could be because 'I am clever' (internal) or if you received a D you could argue that 'I received a low grade as the teacher did not explain the topic very well in class' (external).

Self-concept Self-constructed beliefs about yourself that allow you to feel you are distinct from others and that you exist as a separate person.

Self-efficacy The belief in one's capacity that they can perform a particular action in a given set of circumstances to produce specific performance attainment.

Self-liberation Making a firm commitment to change.

Self-re-evaluation A realisation that behaviour change is part of an individual's self-identity.

Self-regulation The process by which individuals control their own behaviour, emotions and thoughts.

Social cognition A model of social knowledge and behaviour that highlights the explanatory role of cognitive factors (e.g. beliefs and attitudes) and how people process, store and apply this information within social situations.

Social Cognitive Theory (SCT) Begun as the Social Learning Theory (SLT) developed by Bandura and provides a framework to understand how we are shaped by the environment around us. Observational learning and reproducing these behaviours are core to this theory as are beliefs in confidence to whether an individual can reproduce an observed behaviour (cf. Bandura).

Social comparison The process by which a person or group of people determine their own worth based on how they compare themselves to others.

Social desirability bias The tendency to answer questions about oneself or one's behaviour in a way that is thought likely to be viewed favourably by others.

Social identity A person's sense of who they are in a group, rather than at a personal, individual level.

Social Learning Theory (SLT) A theory that suggests that behaviour is learnt from the environment through the process of observational learning. Reinforcement, internal or external is thought to be an important predictor of future behaviour.

Socio economic status   Refers to the social standing of an individual, often measured as a combination of education, income and occupation. Higher social standing is associated with better health outcomes.

Stages of change model   See TTM

Stem cell   Cells that do not have any specific purpose or role in the body, but do have the ability to develop into many different cells for various tissues in the body, including blood, heart muscle, brain and liver tissue. Stem cells are found in the bone marrow.

Stimulus control   A term used in operant conditioning to describe a situation where a behaviour is triggered by the presence or absence of a stimulus e.g. when always eating when watching TV you associate TV with eating. Removing these cues to the unhealthy behaviour and adding reminders can support behaviour change.

Stress reactivity   The physiological arousal, such as increased heart rate or blood pressure, experienced during a potentially stressful encounter.

Stroke   A medical condition caused by poor blood flow, which prevents oxygen and other nutrients reaching parts of the brain.

Subjective   Personal beliefs or feelings, i.e. what a person thinks and feels as opposed to what is objective and measurable.

Subjective norm   A person's beliefs regarding whether important others (i.e. family, friends) will approve and support a particular behaviour. It is an index of social pressure, weighted generally by the individual's motivation to comply with the wishes of others (see Theory of Planned Behaviour).

Sympathetic nervous system   The part of the autonomic nervous system that directs the body's involuntary response to dangerous or stressful situations.

T cell   A cell that recognises antigens on the surface of a virus-infected cell, binds to that cell and destroys it.

Theory   A general belief or a reasonable explanation for an event or a phenomenon, which may or may not be supported by evidence.

Theory of Planned Behaviour (TPB) A value expectancy model which suggests that attitudes, subjective norms and perceived behavioural control shape an individual's intention to perform or engage in a health behaviour (cf Azjen, 1985).

Theory of Reasoned Action (TRA) A value expectancy model which suggests that attitudes and subjective norms shape an individual's intention to perform or engage in a healthy behaviour (cf Fishbein & Azjen, 1980).

Transtheoretical Model of change (TTM) A stage theory which posits that a person moves through six stages of change: pre-contemplation, contemplation, preparation, action, maintenance and termination, with the option of relapse between these stages (cf. Prochaska & DiClemente, 1983).

Unrealistic optimism Also known as "optimistic bias", whereby a person has an unrealistically positive prediction of outcome compared to the likelihood that it will happen.

Vaccinations The administration of a vaccine which contains a virus in a weakened state or a microorganism virus into a body to prevent infectious disease.

Within-subjects design This is a type of experimental design, whereby all participants are exposed to all treatment conditions.

Index

Printed in Great Britain
by Amazon